i-Ready Classroom

Mathematics

Grade K • Volume 2

NOT FOR RESALE

978-1-7280-4663-1

North Billerica, MA 01862

Printed by RRD in Dongguan, China, in October 2022.
2 3 4 5 6 7 8 9 10 11 12 13 14 15 24 23 22

Curriculum Associates

805507

Digital Resources

In addition to the instruction and practice provided in this Student Worktext, you have access to digital resources.

Log into **i-ReadyConnect.com** to explore the digital resources available on the Student Dashboard.

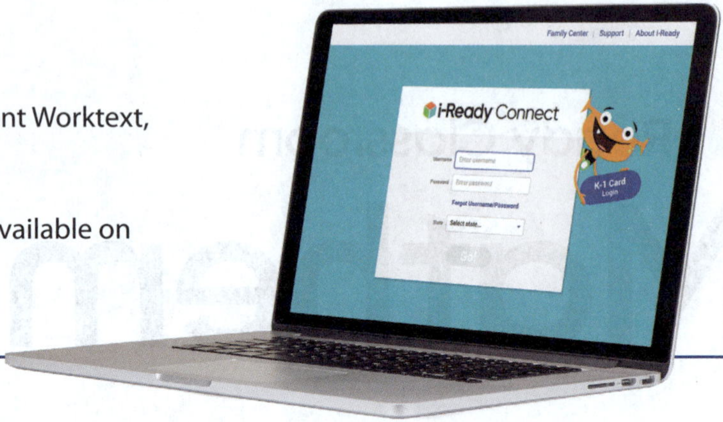

To Do

See your digital assignments on your dashboard. *English/Spanish*

Personalized Instruction lessons (when available) can help increase your understanding of math concepts.

Interactive Practice helps you reinforce skills and concepts while providing you helpful feedback.

My Path (when available) uses the Diagnostic to provide lessons customized to your math learning needs.

Comprehension Checks provide digital assessments on lesson and unit topics.

Student Bookshelf

Access your books, videos, and more!

- ✔ Online Student Worktext
  English/Spanish
- ✔ My Videos (Instructional Videos)
- ✔ Glossaries
  Multiple Languages
- ✔ Family Resources
  Multiple Languages
- ✔ Student Handbook
  English/Spanish
- ✔ Additional tools available, such as note-taking, text-to-speech, highlighting, and a calculator

Digital Math Tools

Explore mathematical concepts with digital tools.

English/Spanish

Counters and Connecting Cubes
Grades K–8

Base-Ten Blocks
Grades 1–8

Number Line
Grades 2–8

Perimeter and Area
Grades 2–8

Multiplication Models
Grades 2–8

Fraction Models
Grades 3–8

Learning Games

Play fun games to practice math facts and develop fluency.

English/Spanish

Hungry Guppy
Grades K–2

Hungry Fish
Grades K–8

Match
Grades K–8

Zoom
Grades K–8

Bounce
Grades K–8

Cupcake
Grades 2–8

Pizza
Grades 2–5

Cloud Machine
Grades 3–8

UNIT 1

Position, Length, Height, and Sorting

UNIT 2

Numbers to 5, Shapes, and Weight

UNIT 3

Addition and Subtraction Within 5 and Shapes

UNIT 4

Numbers to 10 and Shapes

UNIT 5

Numbers to 100

UNIT 6

Addition and Subtraction Within 10

UNIT 7

Teen Numbers and Shapes

Cumulative Practice by Unit

Let's get started!

UNIT 4

Numbers to 10 and Shapes

Show What You Know

Have children draw to show what they know about numbers to 10 and shapes. Tell children that after they have completed the unit, they will draw to show what they learned.

My Words

Mathematical
equal to
equation
greater
ten

Academic
after
part

Have children choose 2 to 4 words and show what they know about them using pictures, numbers, or words. Have children share their representations with peers.

To support children with word selection, ask:
- *Which words are new to you?*
- *Which words do you think are the most important? Why?*

Family Letters are also available in multiple languages.

LESSON 11

Count, Show, and Write Numbers 6 to 10

Dear Family,

Earlier in Kindergarten, your child counted groups of up to 5 objects. Now, your child is learning to count up to 10 objects and write the numbers 6 to 10.

More about the Math

To count, say the number names in order. The last number said tells how many.

A 10-frame is a tool you can use to organize up to 10 objects you are counting.

Your child can count in a variety of ways, including with fingers. Your child will recognize that they must use two hands to show numbers 6 to 10. As children build skills, they will begin to confidently form and use the numbers 6 to 10.

i-Ready Connect

Learning Games

Hungry Guppy

Match

Digital Math Tools

Counters and Connecting Cubes

Multilingual Glossary

six
seven
eight
nine
ten

ACTIVITY

Match My Count

Do this with activity with your child to explore counting groups of 6 to 10.

Materials: 20 small objects (such as pennies or pebbles)

- Divide the objects equally between you and your child.
- Choose a number of objects (e.g., 8 pennies) and place them in front of you.
- Say: *I picked some objects and made a set. Can you make a set with the same number?*
- Have your child count their objects and **SAY** how many there are in the set they made.
- Tell your child whether they correctly made a set with the same number.
- Have your child make a set for you to model.
- Demonstrate counting the objects out loud and saying how many. Ask your child if your set has the same number as their set.

SAY **1, 2, 3, 4, 5, 6, 7, 8. There are 8 pennies.**

Math on the GO!

Conversation Starter

Look for opportunities to count 6 to 10 items in real-world situations.

For example:

- When you are at the grocery store, ask your child to pick 6 apples.
- When you are washing dishes, ask your child how many clean glasses there are.

NAME:

LESSON 11

Number Sense

Project the scene. Ask children: *What do you notice? What do you wonder?*

Count up to 10 objects. Write or show a number to represent how many.

Investigate It

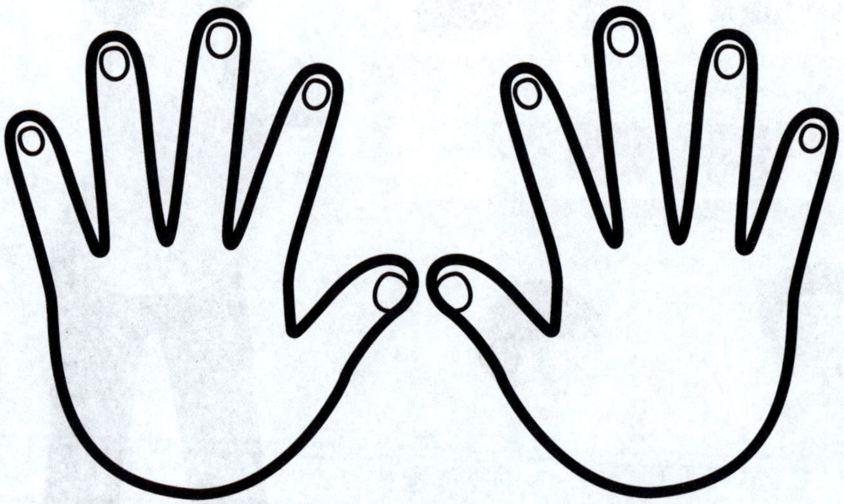

After doing the Discover It activity as a class, have children complete the Investigate It activity and record two ways to show the same number.

How do you know if both sets of hands show the same number?

NAME:

Try-Discuss-Connect

6

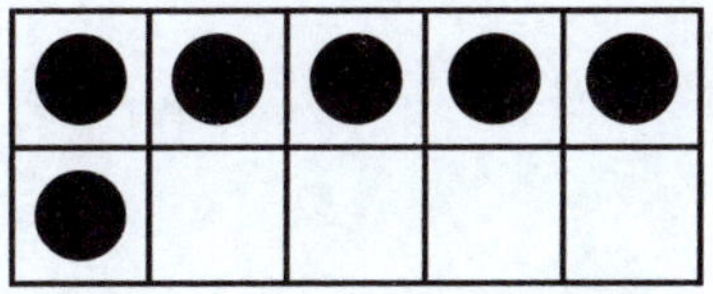

7

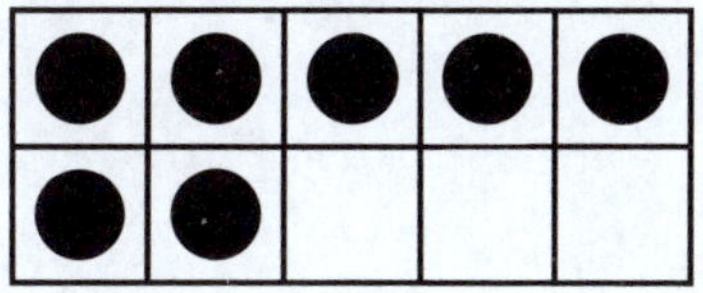

8

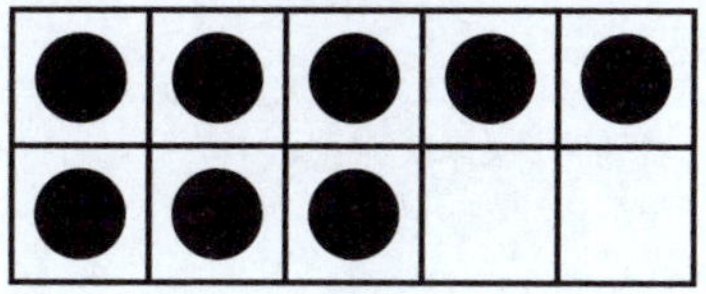

9

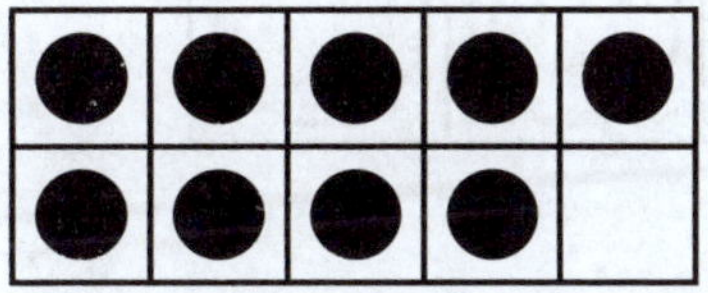

10

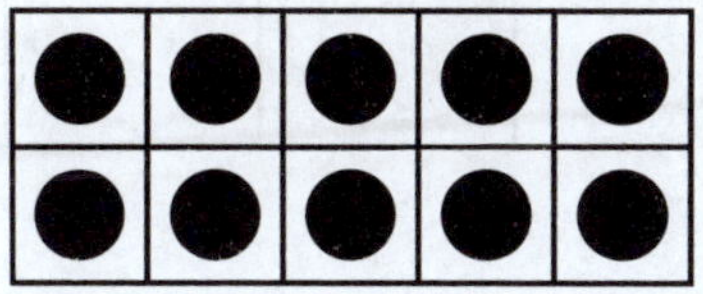

Make sense of the problem: *There are 6 tambourines in a music class. How can you tell which of the numbers is 6?* Have children circle the number that shows how many tambourines.

How does the tool on the page help you organize your counting?

Fill the Frames Activity

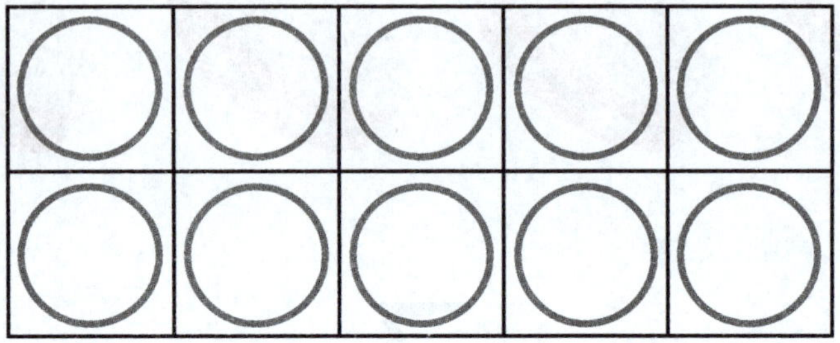

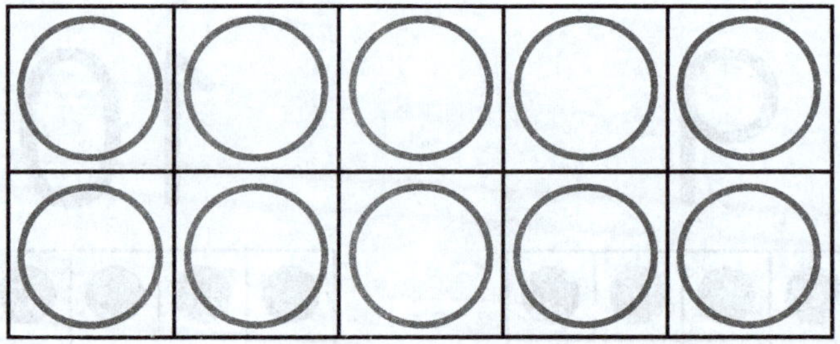

After children have completed the Fill the Frames Activity, have them record two turns by coloring circles in the 10-frames.

How is filling a 10-frame like filling a 5-frame?

NAME:

Practice

Color

Have children color one circle in the 10-frame for each instrument. Then have them count to tell how many.

Practice

Color

Have children color one circle in the 10-frame for each counter. Then have them count to tell how many.

NAME:

Try-Discuss-Connect

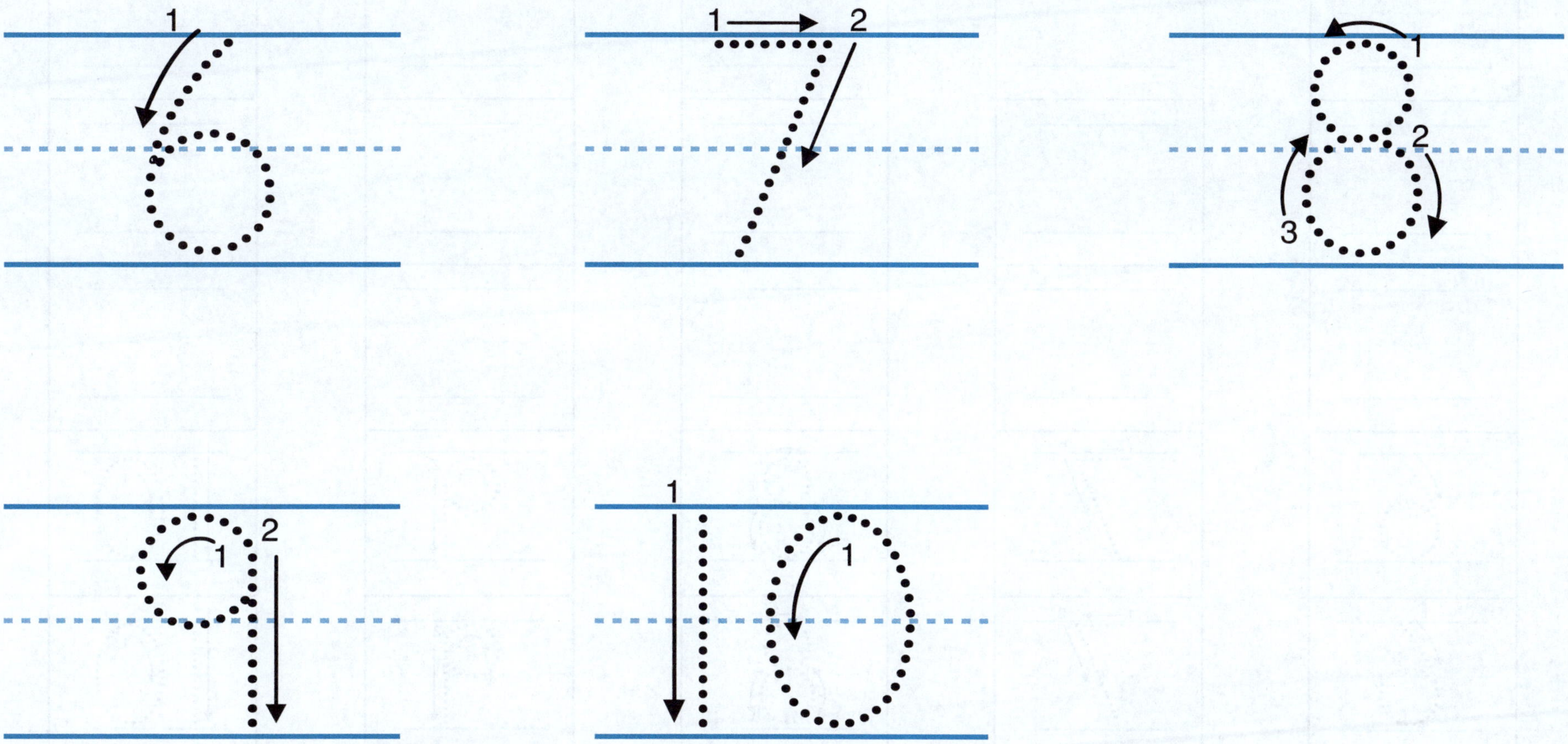

Make sense of the problem: *These are the numbers 6, 7, 8, 9, and 10. How can you describe the shape of each number?* Have children use their finger or a pencil to trace each number.

How would you describe writing each number?

Write to the Top Activity

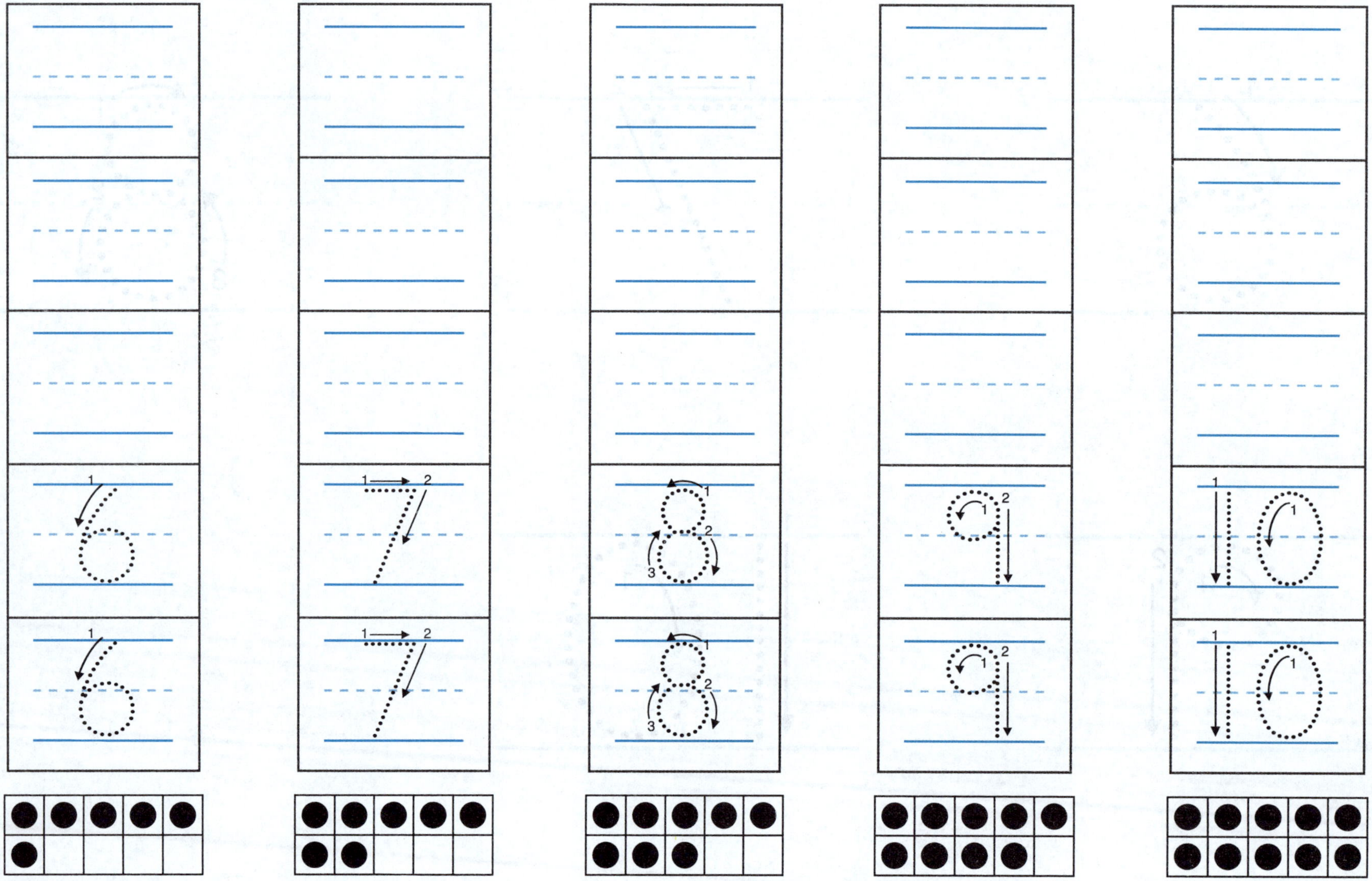

Have children select a 10-Frame Card and trace the number that matches the card. Starting at the bottom and working to the top, have children use this workmat as they complete the Write to the Top Activity.

How did you write each number?

NAME:

Practice

Write

Example

6 6

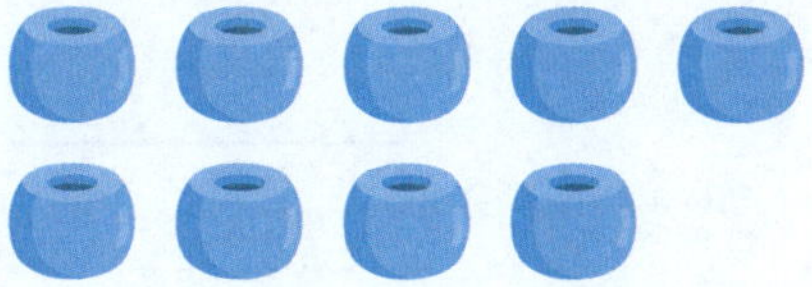

9

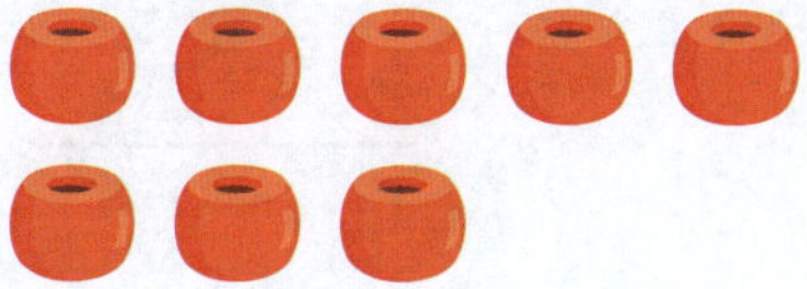

8

10

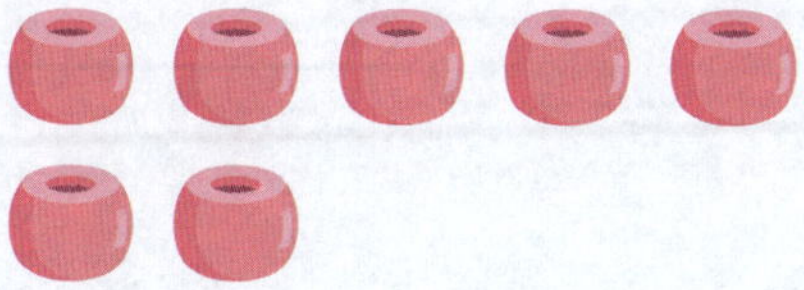

7

Ask children to count the beads. Then have them trace and write the number that shows how many.

Practice

Write

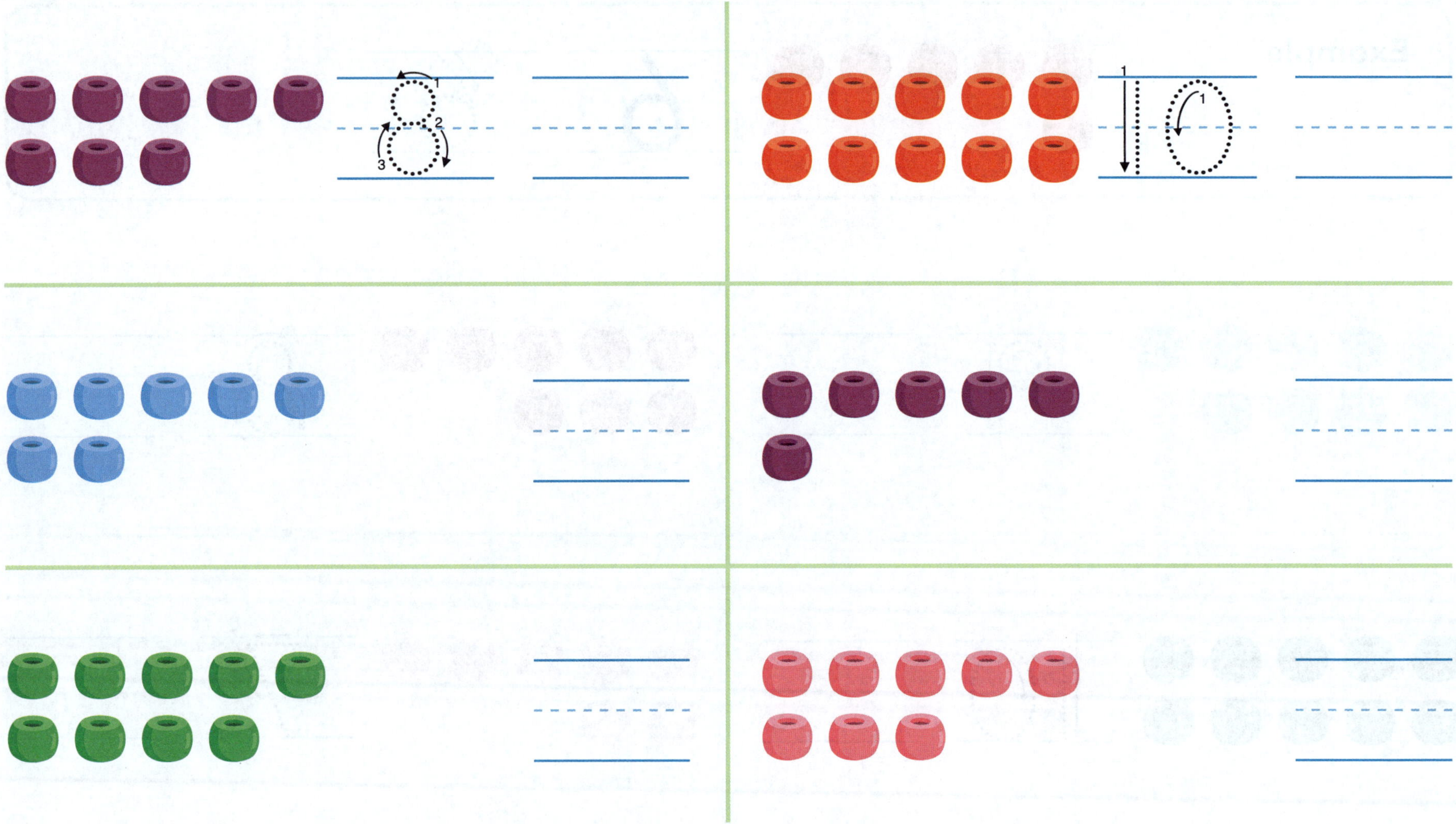

Ask children to count the beads. Then have them trace or write the number that shows how many.

NAME:

Make Connections

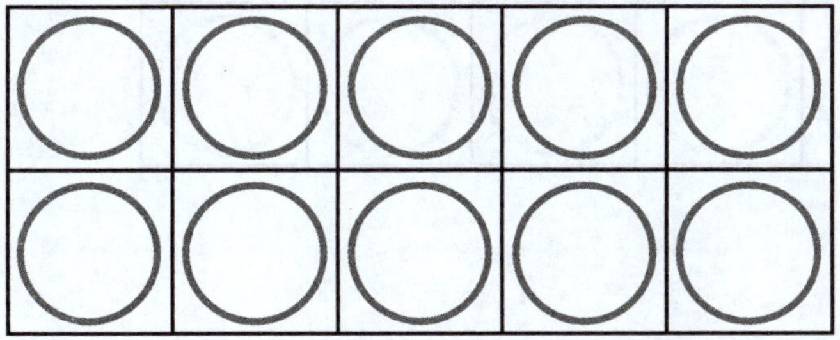

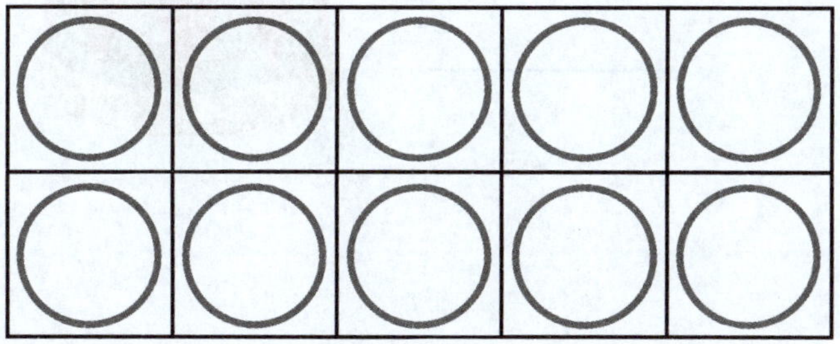

Ask children to count the tambourines. Then have them draw that many tambourines in the 10-frame. Tell children to write the number that shows how many tambourines.

Musical Items Activity

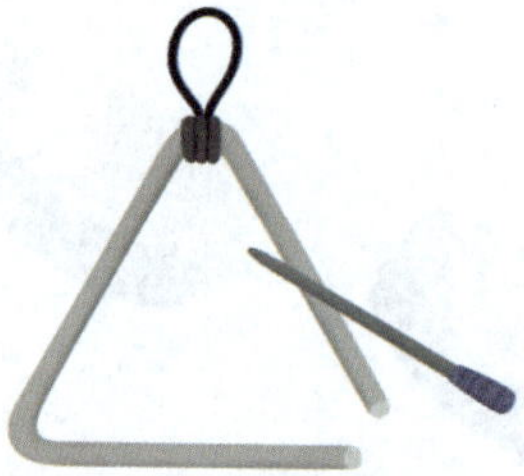

Ask children to write 6, 7, 8, 9, or 10 at the beginning of each row. Then have them color in the circles to show how many.

NAME:

Practice

Write Draw

Example

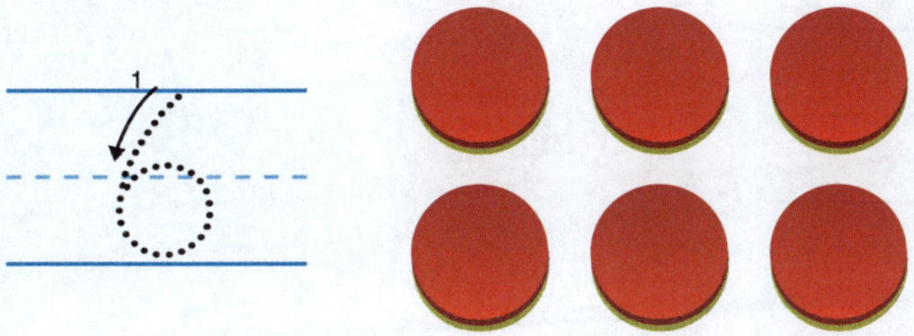

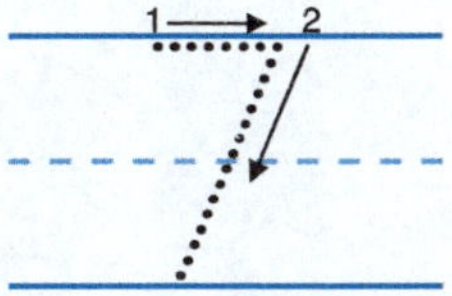

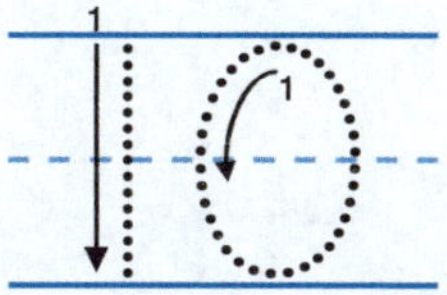

For each problem, ask children to trace the number. Then have them draw that many counters.

Practice

Write Draw

9

For each problem, ask children to trace or write a number from 6 to 10. Then have them draw that many counters.

NAME:

LESSON 11

Analyze It

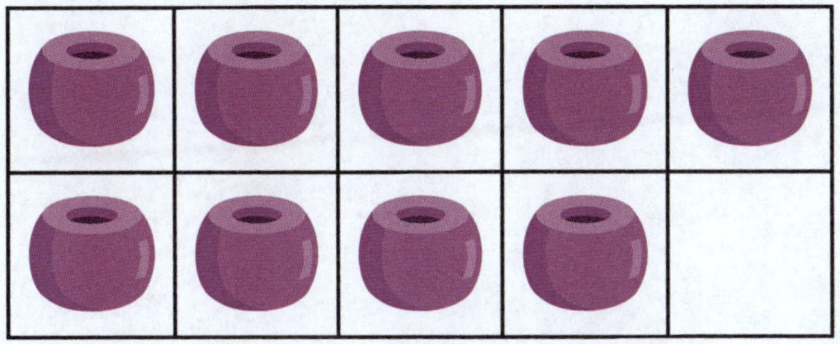

9

6

Read the problem: *The cat and dog both think they recorded the number of beads shown in the 10-frame. Do you agree with the cat, the dog, or both? Why?* Have children circle who they agree with.

Lesson Reflection

Have children use numbers, words, or drawings to show something they learned or did in this lesson to count, show, and write the numbers 6 to 10.

Practice

Write

Have children count the number of each sticker in the picture. Then have them write the number next to the sticker at the side of the page.

Practice

Write Color

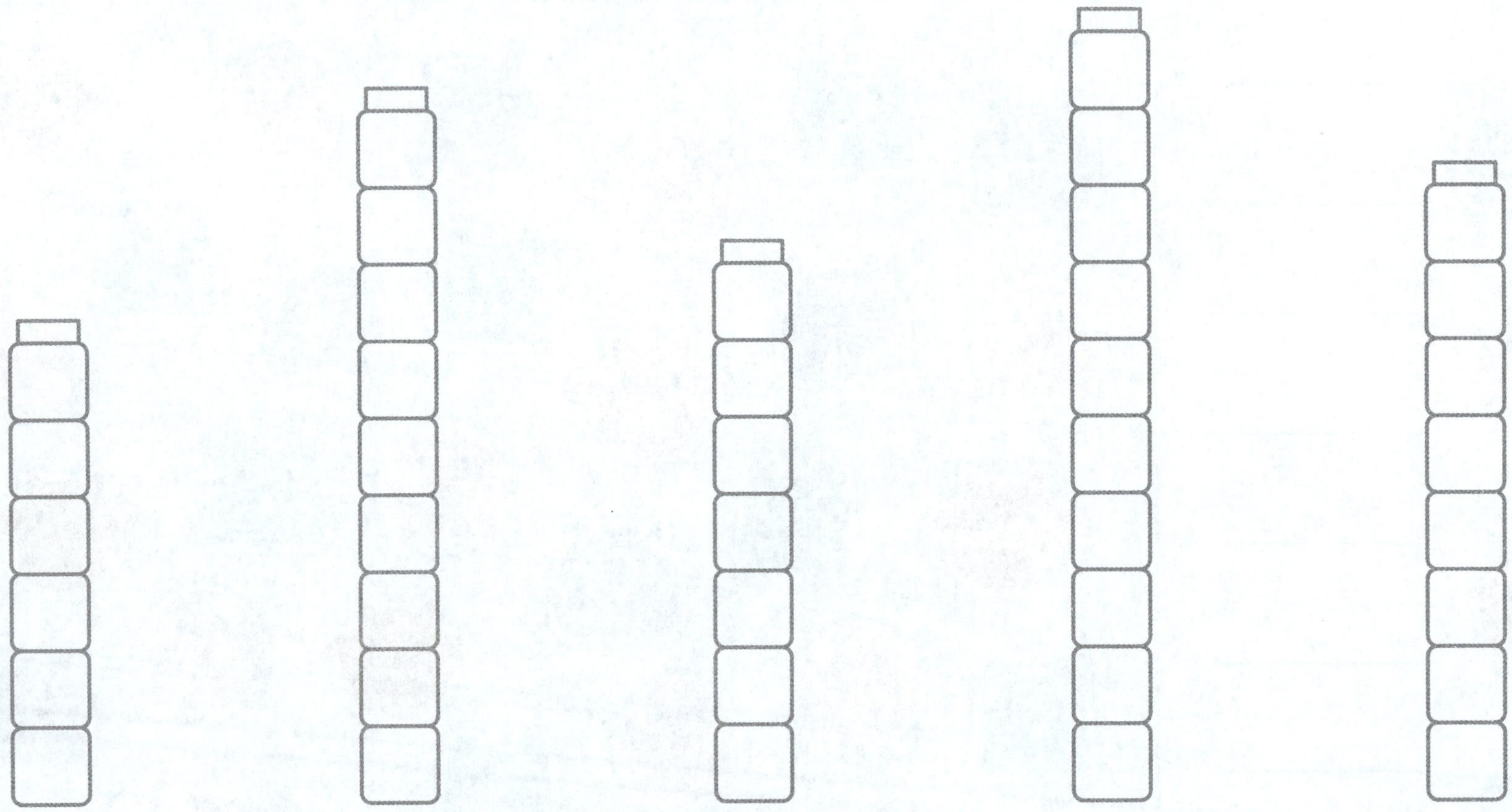

Have children count the cubes in each stack and write the number they counted. Then have them color the cubes in each stack.

Family Letters are also available in multiple languages.

Compare Numbers to 10

Dear Family,

Your child is comparing numbers up to 10. They compare the numbers of objects in two groups. They also compare two written numbers.

Your child will use the words **greater**, less, and **equal** to compare.

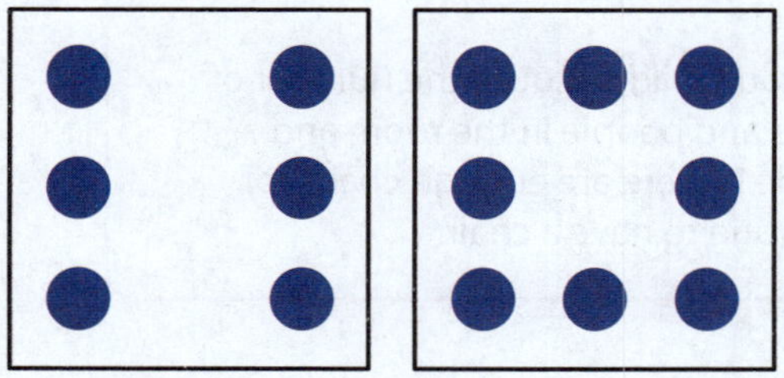

6 is less than 8.

8 is **greater than** 6.

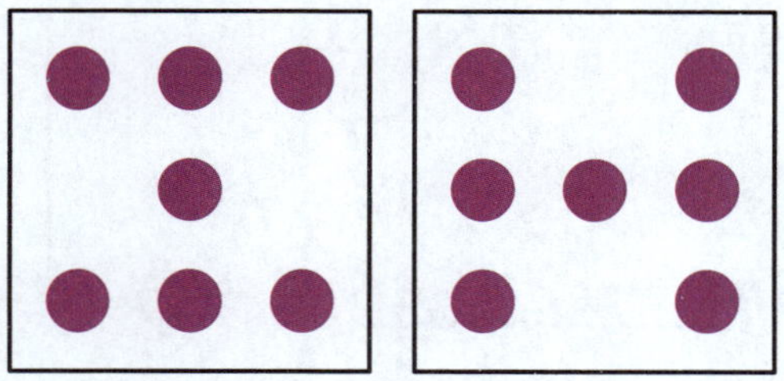

7 is **equal to** 7.

More about the Math

Your child will use a number path to compare numbers. They will see that on a number path, numbers that represent larger quantities come after numbers that represent smaller quantities.

1	2	3	4	5	6	7	8	9	10

As children build skills, they will begin to recognize connections between counting and comparing numbers. They will develop the understanding that a number that comes *before* when counting represents a quantity that is less than that of the numbers that come *after*.

i-Ready Connect

Learning Games

Bounce

Zoom

Digital Math Tools

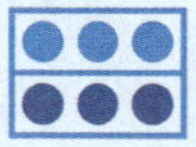

Counters and Connecting Cubes

Multilingual Glossary

equal
equal to
greater
greater than

ACTIVITY

Greater, Equal, or Less

Do this activity with your child to explore comparing groups up to 10.

Materials: 20 small objects (such as pebbles or pennies), 1 set of cards numbered 1 to 10

- You and your child each take 10 of the objects and place the set of number cards facedown between you.
- You each turn over a card and use the objects to make a group to represent the number.
- Ask your child whether the groups have an equal number of objects. Have your child count each group and compare the numbers. Encourage your child to **SAY** the comparison using numbers and words.
- Repeat the activity to have your child practice comparing additional numbers.

SAY 9 is greater than 6.

Math on the GO!

Conversation Starter

Look for opportunities to have your child compare numbers up to 10 in real-world situations. For example:

- If you have 4 books and your child has 8 books, who has a greater number of books?
- Ask your child to count the number of chairs and people in the room and decide if there are enough chairs for everyone to have a chair.

NAME:

LESSON 12

Number Sense

Project the scene. Ask children: *What do you notice? What do you wonder?*

Compare groups of up to 10 objects. Use the words *greater than, less than,* and *equal to.* Compare numbers from 1 to 10.

Investigate It

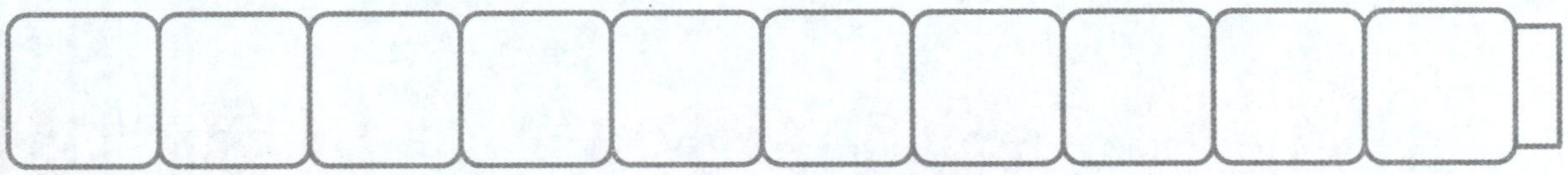

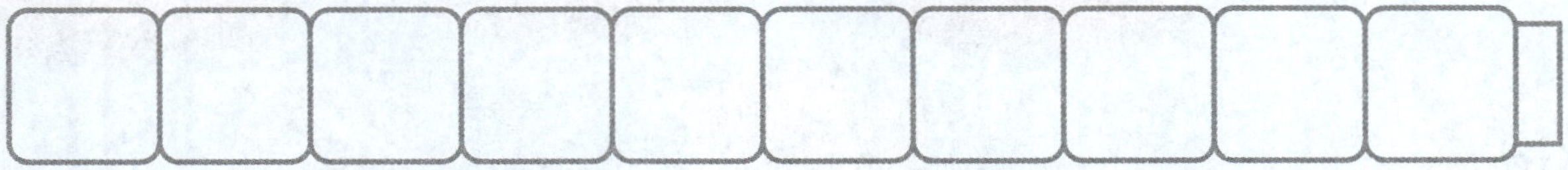

After doing the Discover It activity as a class, have children complete the Investigate It activity and record one of their comparisons by drawing dots on the cards and coloring to show the cube trains. Then have them circle the card and cube train that show more.

How did you decide how many cubes to use?

NAME:

Try-Discuss-Connect

1	2	3	4	5	6	7	8	9	10

Make sense of the problem: *Count the bears. How can you show how many bears there are?* Have children draw counters on each tool. Then have them explore what is the same and different about the two tools.

Which tools did you use? How did you use them?

Counter Spill Activity

1	2	3	4	5	6	7	8	9	10

1	2	3	4	5	6	7	8	9	10

1	2	3	4	5	6	7	8	9	10

1	2	3	4	5	6	7	8	9	10

After children have completed several rounds of the Counter Spill Activity, have them record two rounds of the game. Ask children to circle the greater number or to circle both numbers if they are equal.

How did the number path help you decide who had a greater number of counters?

NAME:

Practice

Color Circle

Example

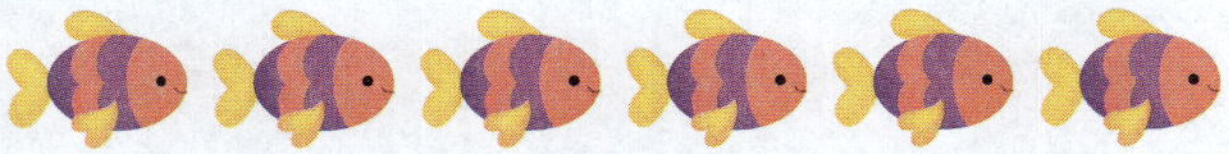

1	2	3	4	5	6	7	8	9	10

1	2	3	4	5	6	7	8	9	10

1	2	3	4	5	6	7	8	9	10

1	2	3	4	5	6	7	8	9	10

1	2	3	4	5	6	7	8	9	10

1	2	3	4	5	6	7	8	9	10

Have children color the number paths to represent the objects and then circle the group with the greater number of objects. If the numbers are equal, have them circle both groups.

Practice

Color Circle

1	2	3	4	5	6	7	8	9	10

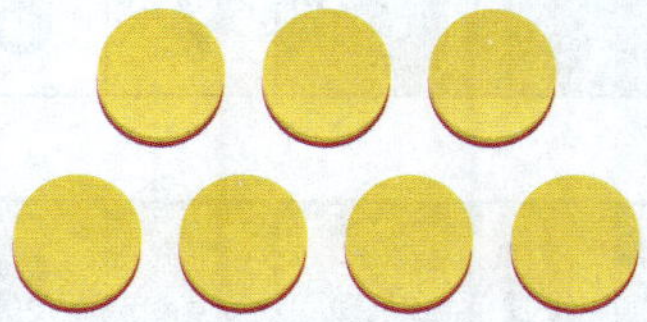

1	2	3	4	5	6	7	8	9	10

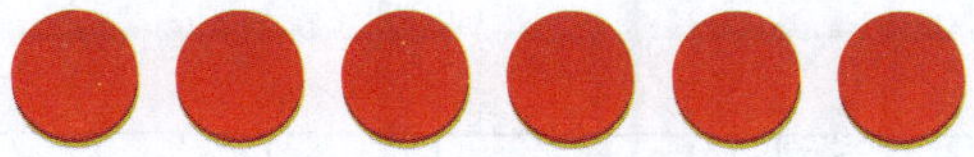

1	2	3	4	5	6	7	8	9	10

1	2	3	4	5	6	7	8	9	10

1	2	3	4	5	6	7	8	9	10

1	2	3	4	5	6	7	8	9	10

Have children color the number paths to represent the objects and then circle the group with the greater number of objects. If the numbers are equal, have them circle both groups.

NAME:

Try-Discuss-Connect

1	2	3	4	5	6	7	8	9	10

Make sense of the problem: *Find a cloud that has a number greater than the shaded number on the number path.* Have children use the number path to show how they solved the problem.

How did you find a number that is greater?

Compare and Cover Up Activity

1	2	3	4	5	6	7	8	9	10

Have children write a number from 1 to 10 in each space. As they complete the Compare and Cover Up Activity, have them use the page as their workmat.

How did you find a number on your workmat that was greater than the number on the card?

NAME:

Practice

Circle

Example

(7) 3	9 8	4 6
2 7	1 10	10 9

1	2	3	4	5	6	7	8	9	10

Have children use the number path to help them circle the greater number.

Practice

Write Circle

7	___
___	8
9	___
6	___
5	___
___	10

1	2	3	4	5	6	7	8	9	10

Have children write a number from 1 to 10 in each space. Then have them use the number path to help them circle the greater number.

Make Connections

Have children write numbers in each cloud. Tell them that for both rows, each number must be greater than the number before. Have children fill in the rows in two different ways.

Compare Clouds Activity

6

6

Have children write numbers in each cloud. Tell them that for both rows, each number must be greater than the number before.

NAME:

Practice

Draw Circle

Example

5	2	5	7

9	5	7	10

1	1	8	9

Have children compare the numbers in each row to the number on the flower. Have them draw a line under numbers that are less than the number on the flower and circle numbers that are greater than the number on the flower.

Practice

Draw Circle

9 4 1

2 10 7

9 3 8

Have children compare the numbers in each row to the number on the flower. Have them draw a line under numbers that are less than the number on the flower and circle numbers that are greater than the number on the flower.

Analyze It

Read the problem: *The cat and dog both think their number is greater than 7. Do you agree with the cat, the dog, or both? Why?* Have children circle who they agree with.

Lesson Reflection

1	2	3	4	5	6	7	8	9	10

2 1 3

Have children use numbers, words, or drawings to show something they learned or did in this lesson to compare groups or numbers up to 10.

NAME:

Practice

Color

1	2	3	4	5	6	7	8	9	10

Less than 5:

Equal to 5:

Greater than 5:

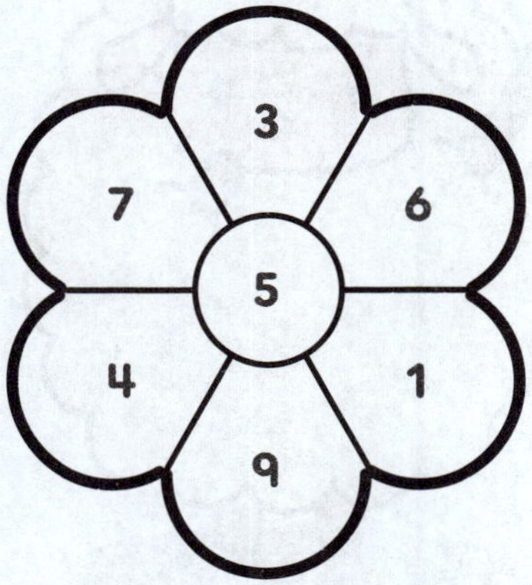

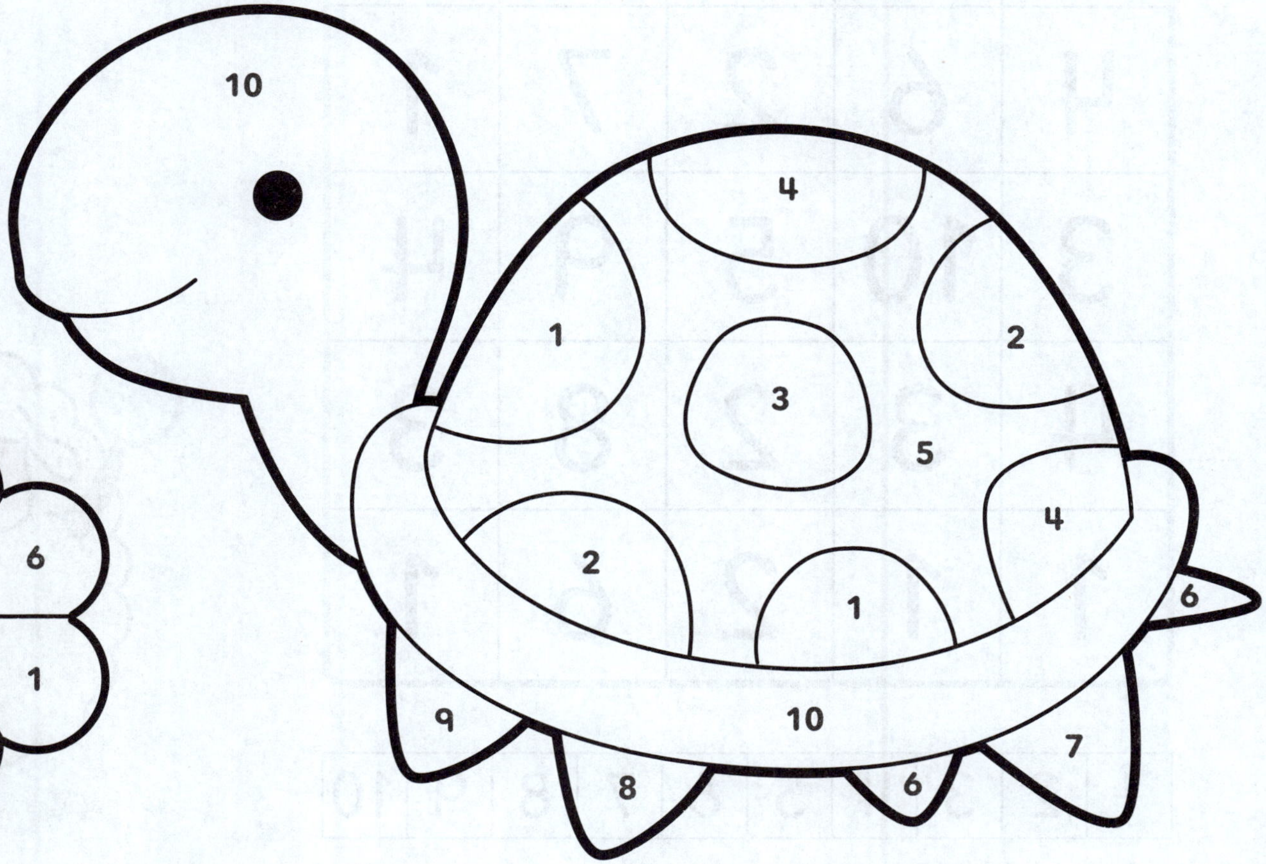

Ask children to color the spaces that show numbers less than 5 in one color, the spaces that show numbers equal to 5 another color, and the spaces that show numbers greater than 5 another color.

Practice

Color

2	8	4	10	3
4	6	2	7	1
3	10	5	9	4
4	3	2	8	3
1	1	2	6	1

1	2	3	4	5	6	7	8	9	10

Ask children to look at the number path. Have them color all the boxes with numbers that are greater than 4 on the number path. Then have them color in the boxes in the grid that show numbers greater than 4.

Family Letters are also available in multiple languages.

Compose Shapes

Dear Family,

Your child is learning to combine simple two-dimensional (flat) and three-dimensional (solid) shapes to **compose** (put together) larger shapes. The composite shapes may represent another shape or a real-world object.

Your child will describe the attributes of the composite shape (for example, number of sides/corners, number of faces/edges) and, when appropriate, will name the composite shape.

i-Ready Connect

Multilingual Glossary

compose

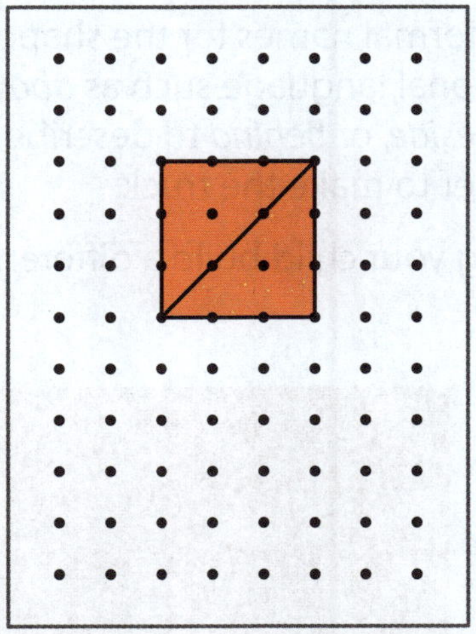

More about the Math

Your child could use pattern blocks, geometric solids, or dot paper to compose shapes. Learning to see how parts can make up a whole will help your child build a foundation for work in later grades with equal parts, fractions, area, and volume.

Build a Truck from Shapes

Do this activity with your child to explore composing shapes.

Materials: construction paper, scissors

- Cut out several squares, circles, triangles, and rectangles from construction paper. Make several of each shape and include at least two different sizes for each shape.
- Invite your child to use the flat shapes to build a truck. Ask: *What shape are the wheels of a truck? What shape is the trailer of a truck?*
- Have your child **SAY** the formal names for the shapes used in the truck and use positional language such as *above, below, next to, in front of, beside,* or *behind* to describe how the shapes are put together to make the truck.
- Repeat the process, having your child build a different truck this time.

Math on the GO!

Conversation Starter

Look for opportunities to find shapes in real-world situations. For example:

- What shapes do you see in a house?
- What shapes can you use to build a model train?

SAY The wheels are shaped like circles.

NAME:

Number Sense

Project the scene. Ask children: *What do you notice? What do you wonder?*

Use two or more shapes to compose a new shape. Name or describe shapes composed of two or more shapes.

Investigate It

3 4 5 6

After doing the Discover It activity as a class, have children complete the Investigate It activity. Then have children circle a number and record three shapes they drew that have that number of sides.

How can you compare the attributes of the shapes you draw with the shapes others draw?

NAME:

Try-Discuss-Connect

Make sense of the problem: *The mural designer is trying out different shapes for the center of the fish. What shapes could be put together to compose the hexagon?* Have children draw lines on both blank fish to show different ways to compose the hexagon from other shapes.

Which shapes did you use to compose your hexagons?

Compose Flat Shapes Activity

As children complete the Compose Flat Shapes Activity, have them circle the shape they composed and write the number of each type of pattern block they used to build the shape.

How do you know that you made the shape you circled?

NAME:

Practice

Draw Color

Example

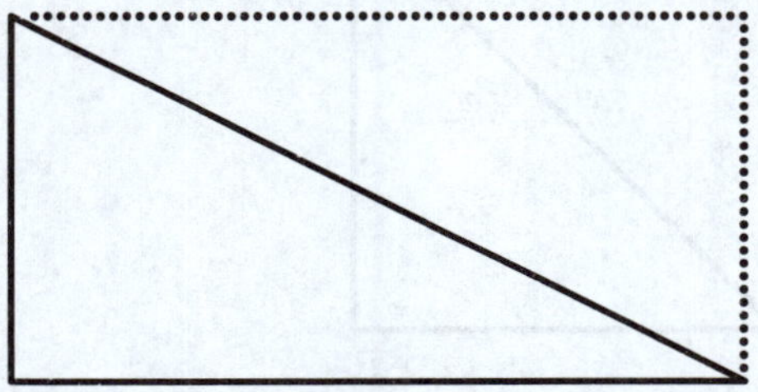

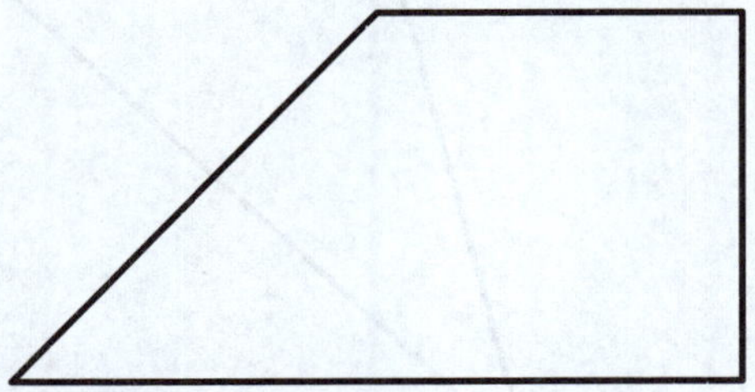

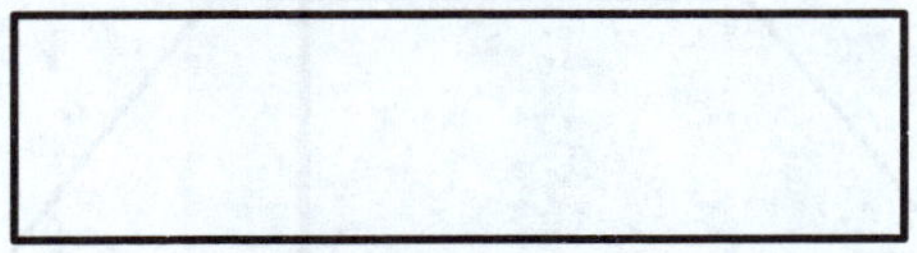

Have children add a shape to each existing shape to make a rectangle. Then have them color each rectangle.

Practice

Draw Color

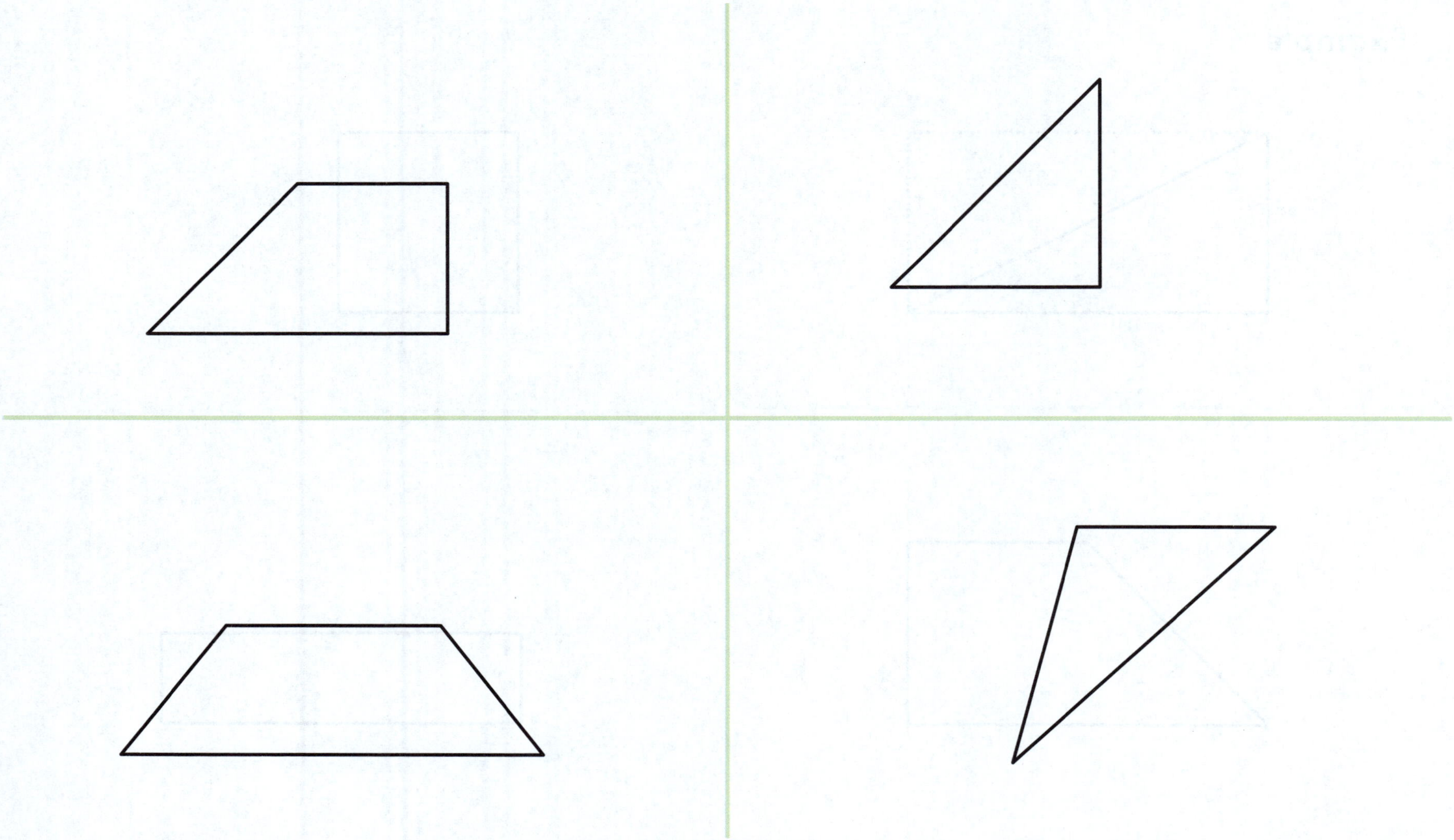

Have children add a shape to each existing shape to make a triangle. Then have them color each triangle.

NAME:

Try-Discuss-Connect

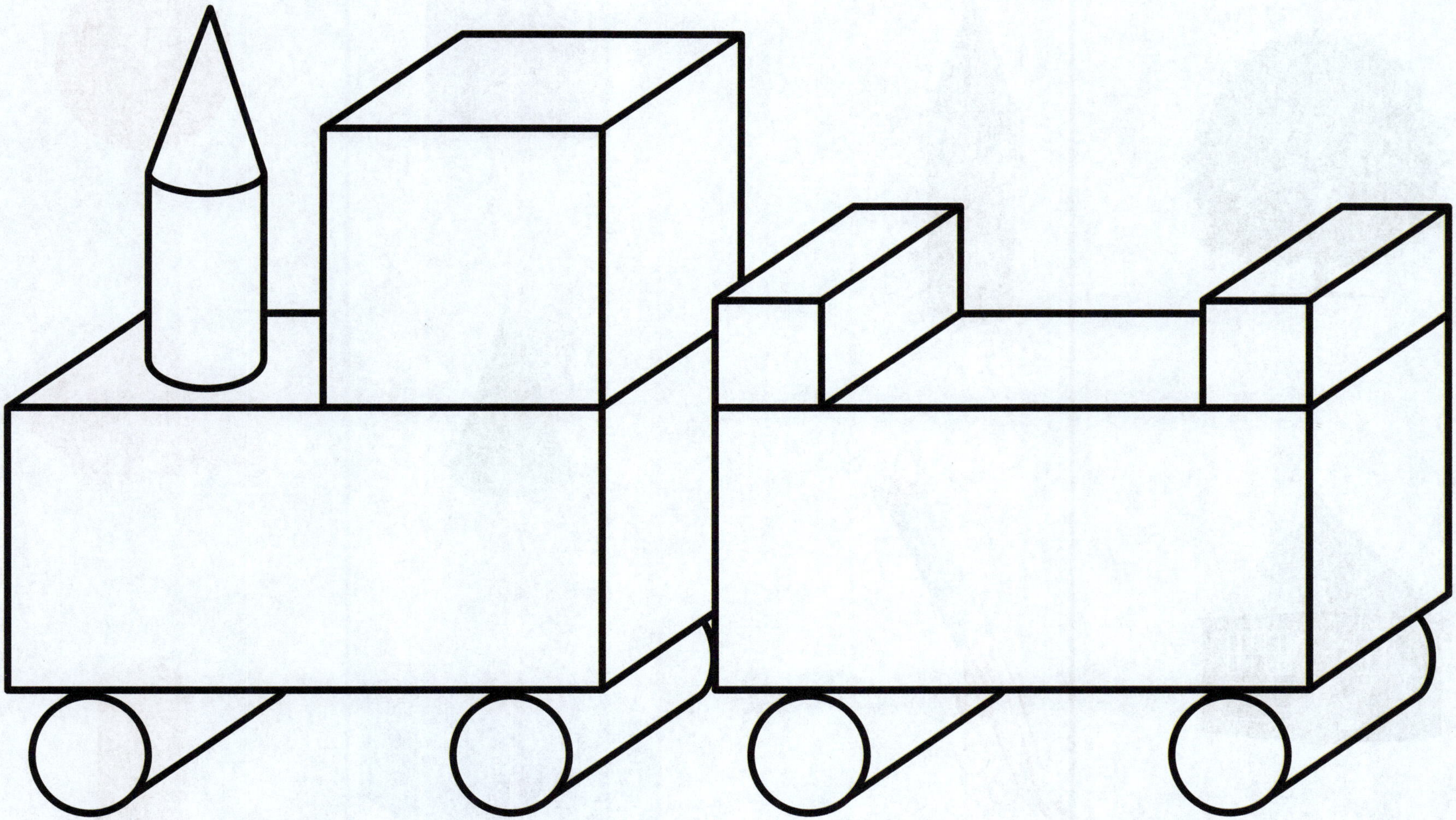

Make sense of the problem: *Your friend builds a train from wooden blocks. Color each type of shape a different color.* Have children identify and describe the shapes used to make the train. Then have them color each type of shape a different color.

How can you describe how many of each shape your friend uses and where they are?

Compose Solid Shapes Activity

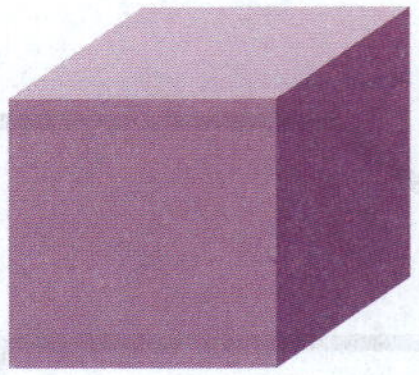

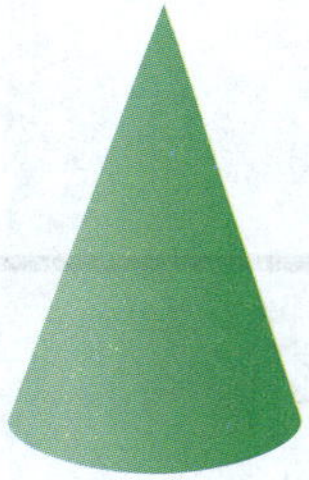
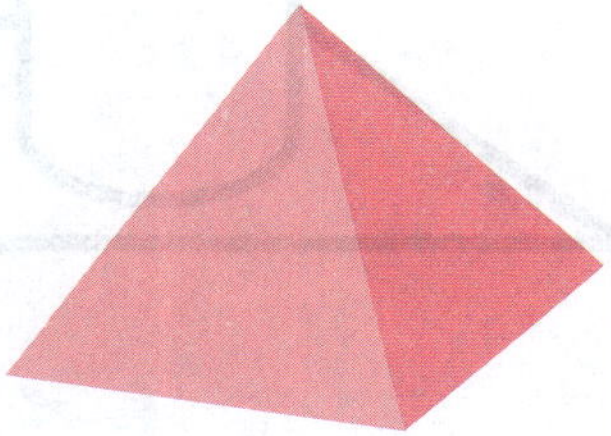

After children have completed several rounds of the Compose Solid Shapes Activity, have them record one of their compositions by circling an object on the left and then circling the solid shapes on the right they used to build the object.

How can you describe each composition for someone else to build it?

NAME:

Practice

Match

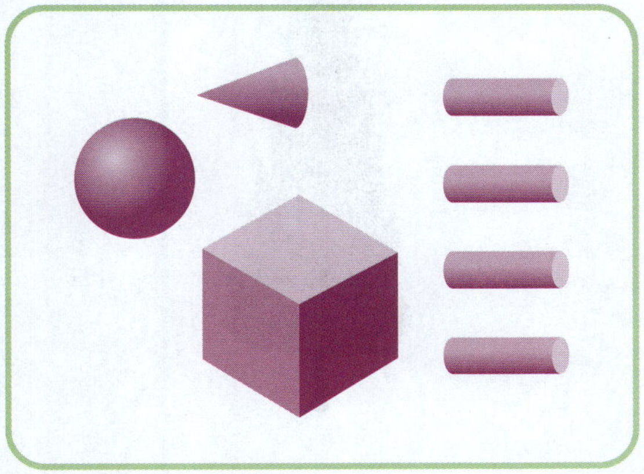

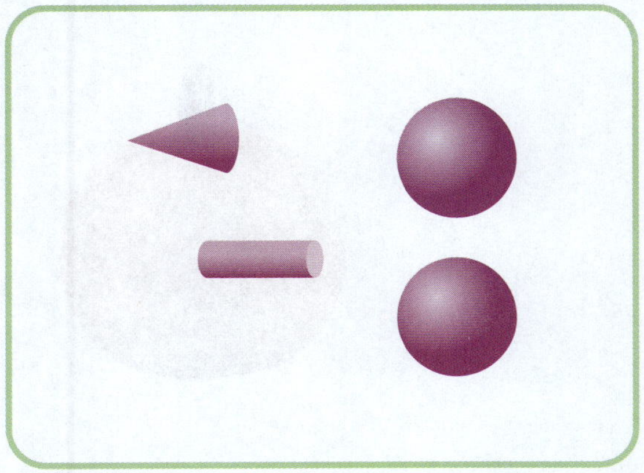

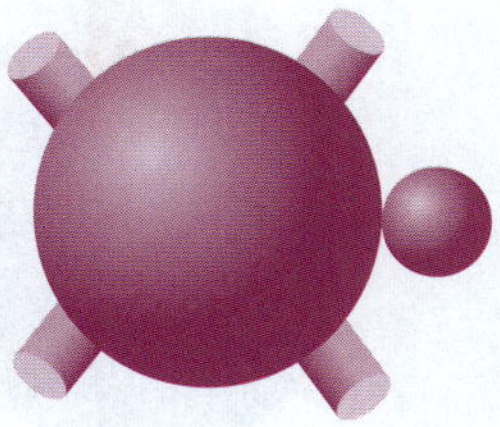

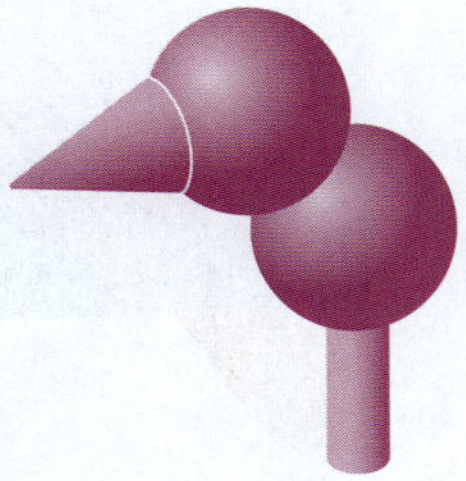

Have children match each set of solid shapes to the composite figure that the shapes can make. Allow children to use geometric solids as needed.

Practice

Match

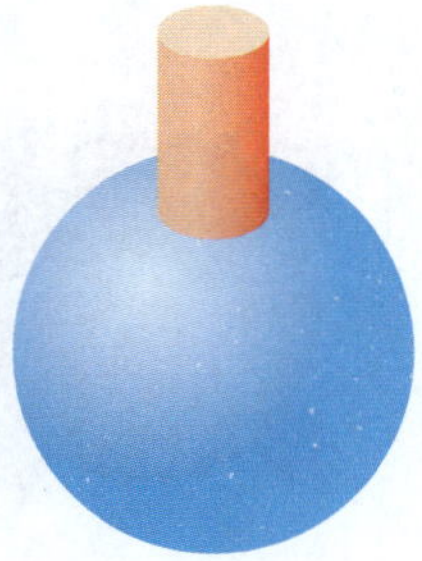

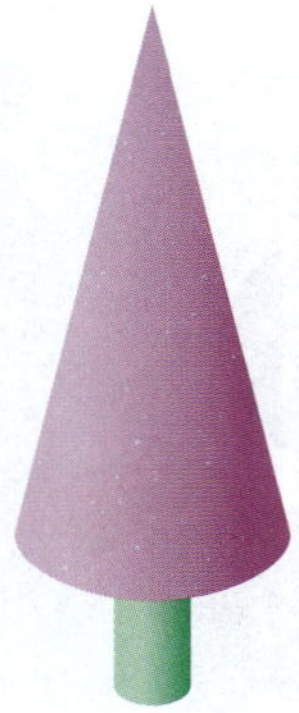

Have children match each real-world object to the composite shape it looks like. Allow children to use geometric solids as needed.

Make Connections

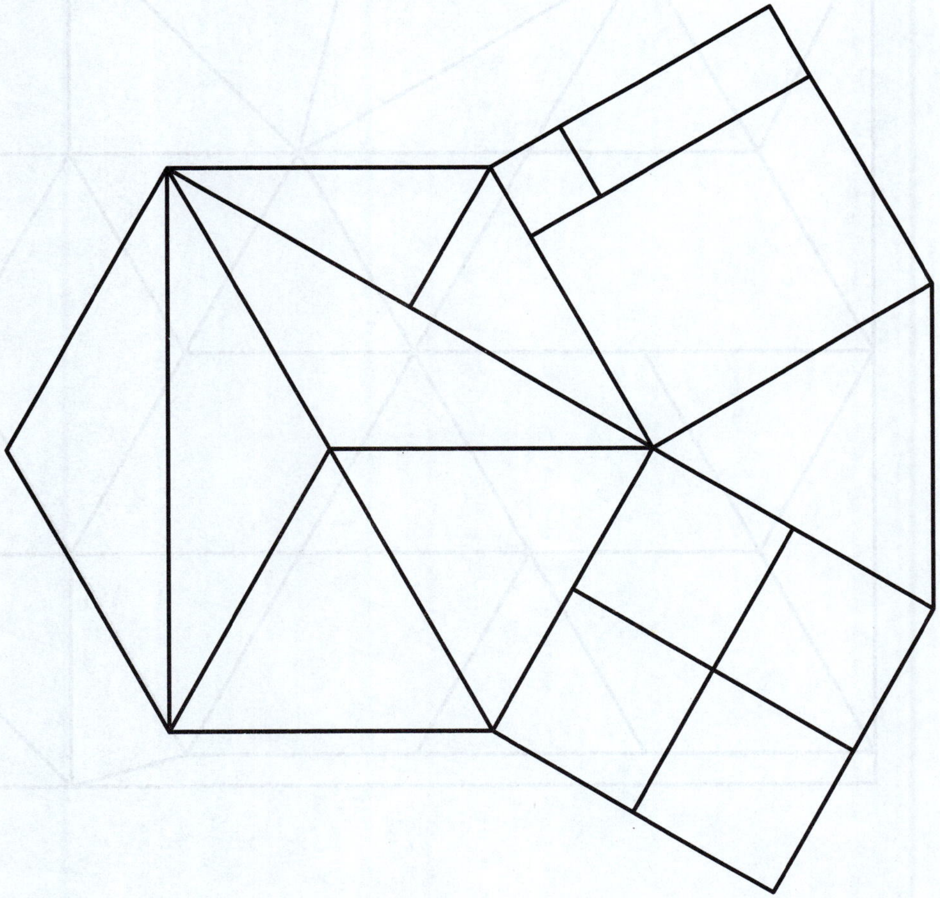

Have children color any two or more shapes to compose a rhombus. Tell them to color the swatch next to the rhombus the same color. Then have children repeat for the rectangle, using another color.

Color to Compose Shapes Activity

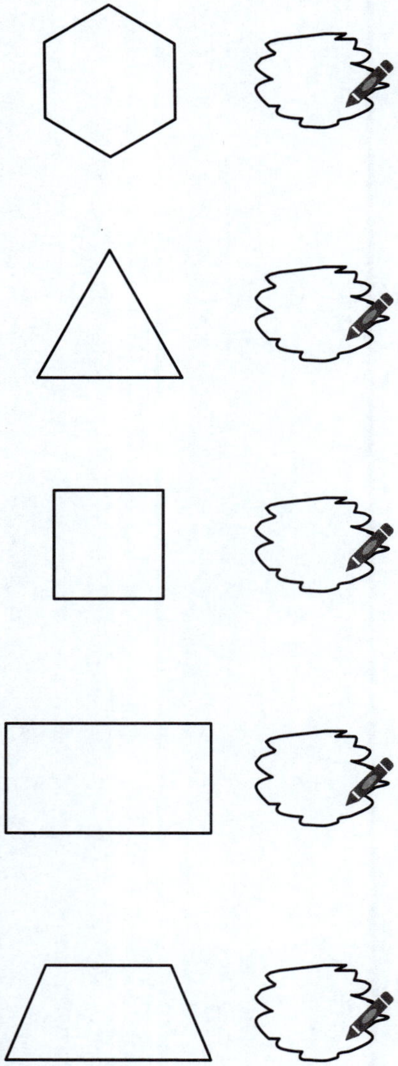

Have children color any two or more shapes to compose a hexagon. Tell them to color the swatch next to the hexagon the same color. Have children repeat for the remaining shapes, using a different color for each shape.

NAME:

Practice

Draw

Example

Ask children to draw lines to show how to compose each outlined shape from the given colored shapes. If needed, children may use pattern blocks to help compose the outlined shapes.

Practice

Draw

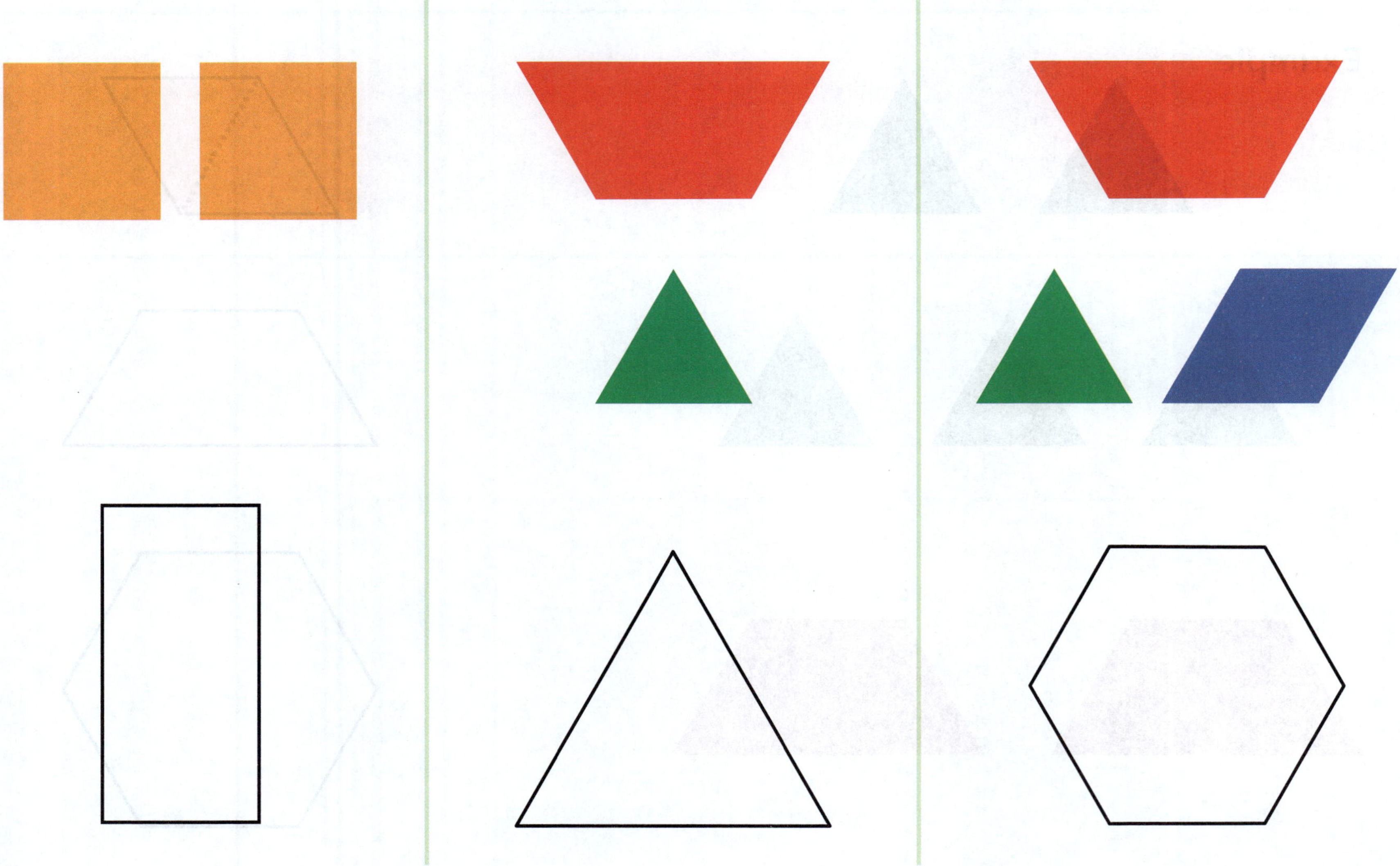

Ask children to draw lines to show how to compose each outlined shape from the given colored shapes. If needed, children may use pattern blocks to help make the outlined shapes.

Analyze It

Read the problem: *The cat and dog both use pattern blocks to compose a shape they think is a hexagon. Do you agree with the cat, the dog, or both? Why?* Have children circle who they agree with.

Lesson Reflection

Have children use numbers, words, or drawings to show something they learned or did in this lesson to compose shapes from smaller shapes.

Practice

Cut Glue

Have children cut out the solid shapes and put the shapes together to compose a building. Have them glue to record their work. Provide children with geometric solids to use as needed.

This page serves as the back of the cut and glue activity on the previous page.

Family Letters are also available in multiple languages.

Compose and Decompose 10

Dear Family,

In this lesson, your child will learn to **compose** (put together) two numbers to make 10. They will also learn to **decompose** (break apart) 10 into two numbers. The number 10 is very important in kindergarten. Children learn to count by 10s and learn that 10 is a two-digit number.

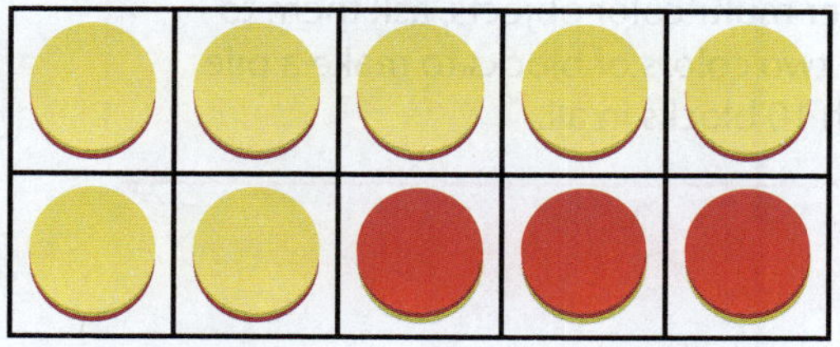

7 and 3 is 10
7 + 3

More about the Math

Your child will learn that numbers can broken into parts. Your child will use connecting cubes to explore ways that 10 can be broken into 2 or more parts. They will also use counters and 10-frames to find different combinations that make 10.

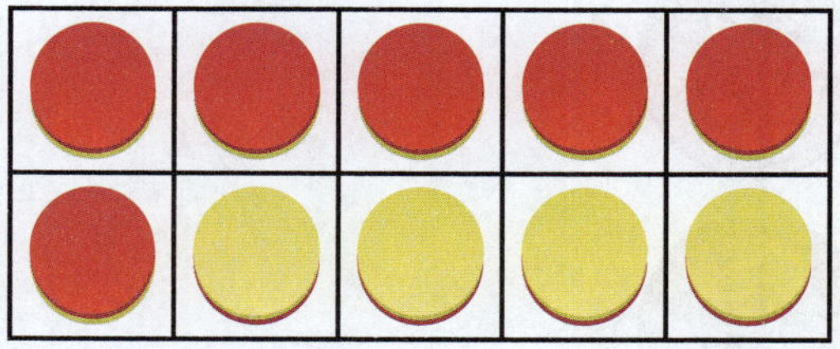

6 + 4

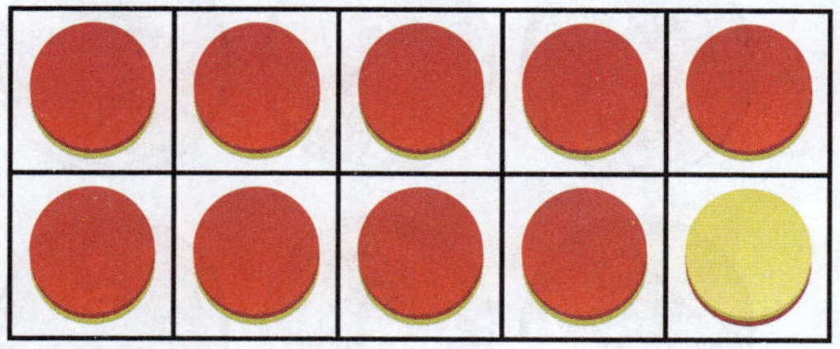

9 + 1

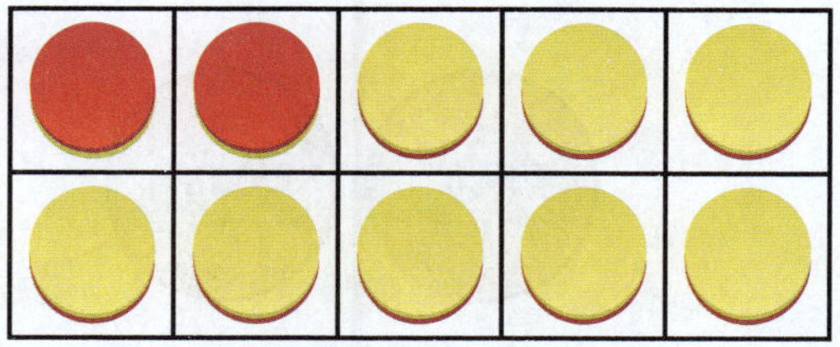

2 + 8

As children build this skill throughout this lesson and beyond, they will begin to recognize ways to make 10.

i-Ready Connect

Learning Games

- Hungry Fish
- Hungry Guppy

Digital Math Tools

- Counters and Connecting Cubes

Multilingual Glossary

compose
decompose

ACTIVITY

Make Number Partners for 10

Do this activity with your child to explore number partners for 10.

Materials: 10 coins

- Put the 10 coins in front of your child. Have your child count the coins to see that there is a total of 10.
- Have your child pick up the coins, shake them up, and spill them on a table. Instruct your child to put the coins that landed *heads up* in one group and the coins that landed *tails up* in another group. Then have your child count the number of objects in each group.
- Have your child **SAY** the number partners for 10.
- Repeat the activity several times.

SAY 2 and 8 make 10.

Math on the GO!

Conversation Starter

Look for opportunities to find number partners for 10 in real-world situations.

- Take a package of 10 granola bars. What are some ways the bars could be put into two piles?
- If your child has some building blocks or other multi-color objects, ask them to use two colors of blocks to make a pile with 10 blocks in all.

NAME:

Number Sense

Project the scene. Ask children: *What do you notice? What do you wonder?*

Break 10 into two parts in different ways. Show and record number partners for 10.

Investigate It

1

										10
										10
										10

2

										10
										10
										10

After doing the Discover It activity as a class, have children complete the Investigate It activity and record one full game with their partner by coloring squares to make rows of 10.

What ways did you make 10?

Try-Discuss-Connect

______ + ______

Make sense of the problem: *You need to put 10 milk cartons onto two tables. How many can you put on each table?* Have children choose a manipulative to find the answer. Then have them fill in the addition expression.

How did you decide how many milk cartons to put on each table?

10-Bead Bracelet Activity

____ + ____

____ + ____

____ + ____

____ + ____

After children have completed several rounds of the activity, have them record four number partners for 10 that they found using their bracelets.

How did you find the missing number of beads?

NAME:

Practice

Write

Example

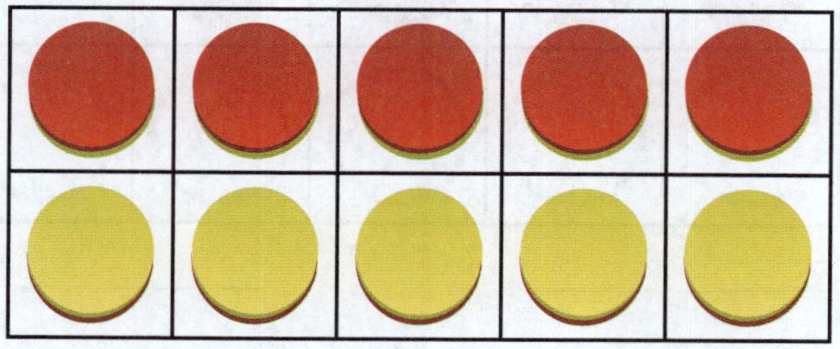

5 + 5

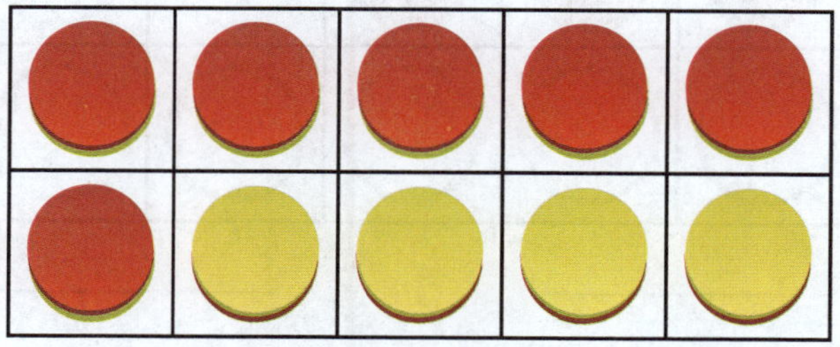

6 + ____

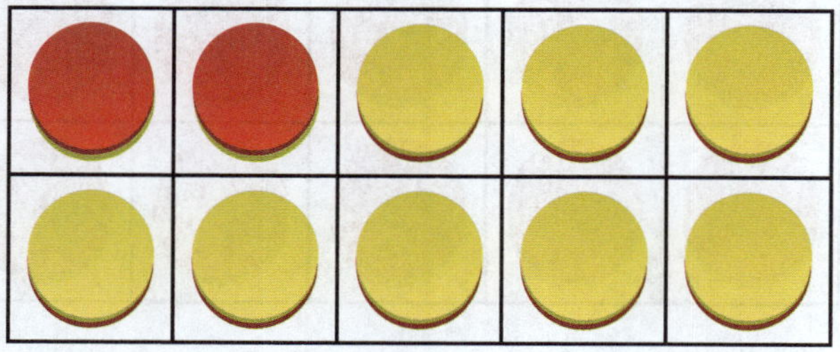

____ + ____

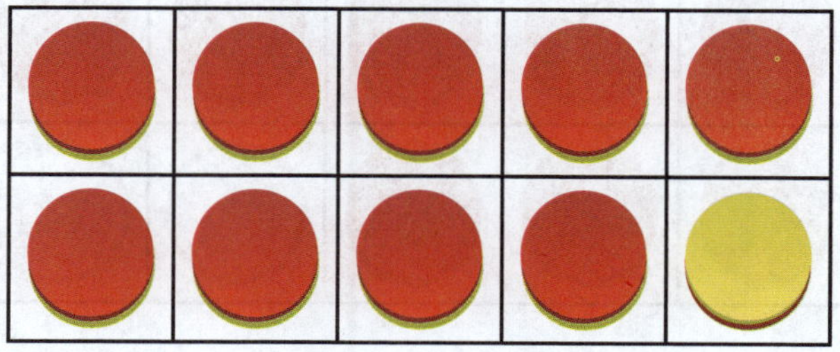

____ + ____

Have children write the number partners for 10 shown in each 10-frame.

Practice

Color Write

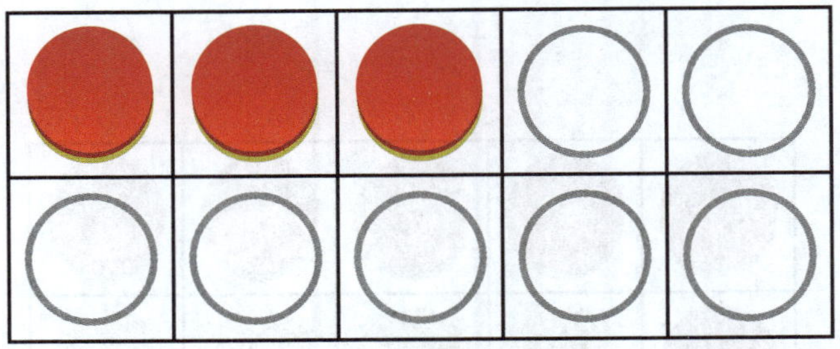

+

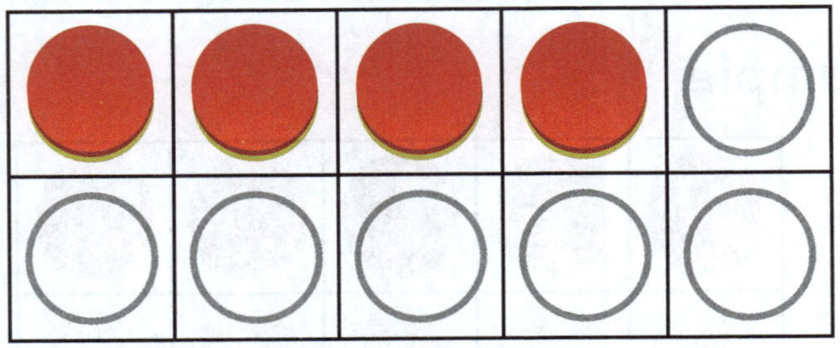

+

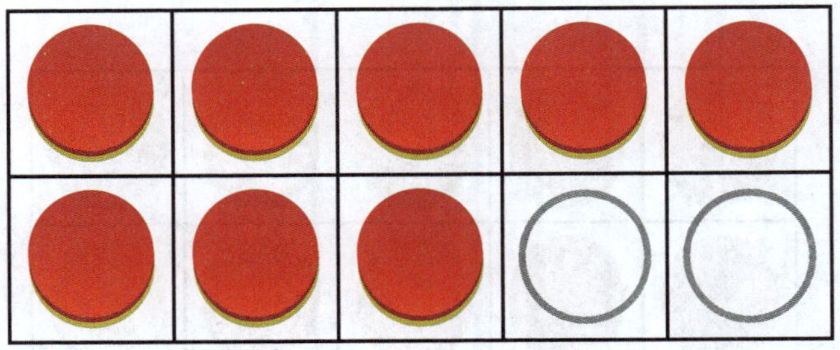

+

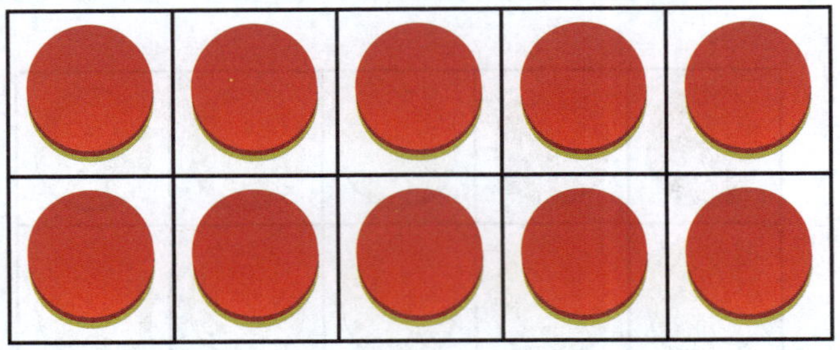

+

Have children finish coloring in the 10-frame, as needed. Then have them write the number partners for 10 shown in each 10-frame.

NAME:

Try-Discuss-Connect

_____ + _____

Make sense of the problem: *Ten children can sit at the lunch table. Some children are already at the table. How many more children can sit at the table to fill it?* Have children choose a manipulative to find the answer. Then have them fill in the expression.

How did you find how many more children could sit at the table to fill it?

10-Frame Fill Up Activity

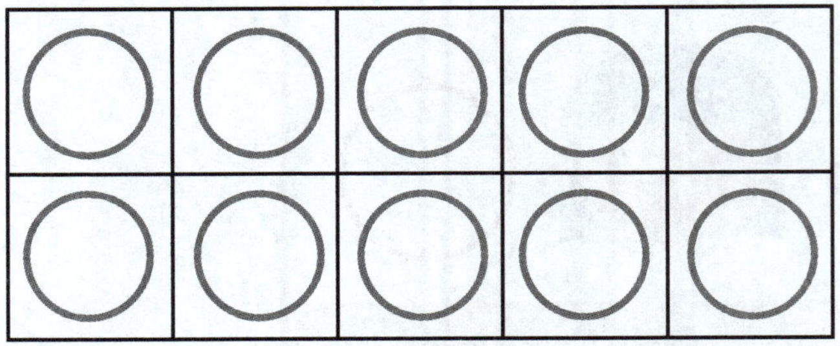

_____ + _____

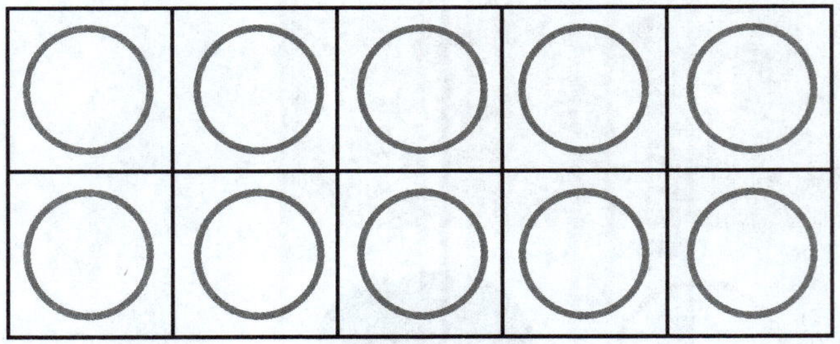

_____ + _____

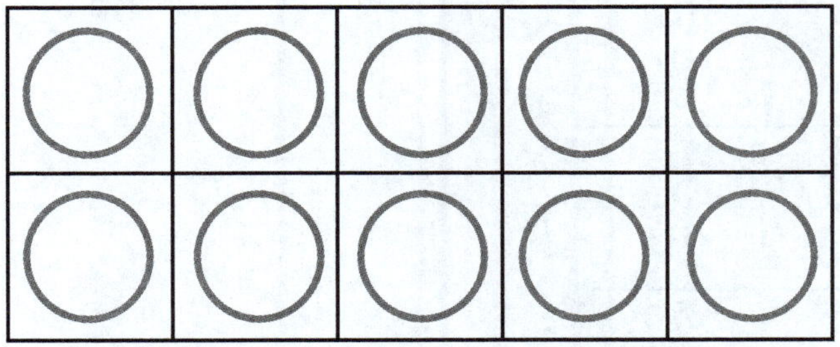

_____ + _____

Have children color counters in the 10-frames to record three rounds of the 10-Frame Fill Up Activity. Then have them write the corresponding number partners for 10.

How did you know what number should be on the second card?

NAME:

Practice

Match Write

____ + ____   ____ + ____   ____ + ____

Have children match each group of oranges to the group of pears that makes a total of 10.
Then have them write the corresponding number partners for 10.

Practice

Match Write

____ + ____ ____ + ____ ____ + ____

Have children match each group of red counters to the group of yellow counters that makes a total of 10. Then have them write the corresponding number partners for 10.

NAME:

Make Connections

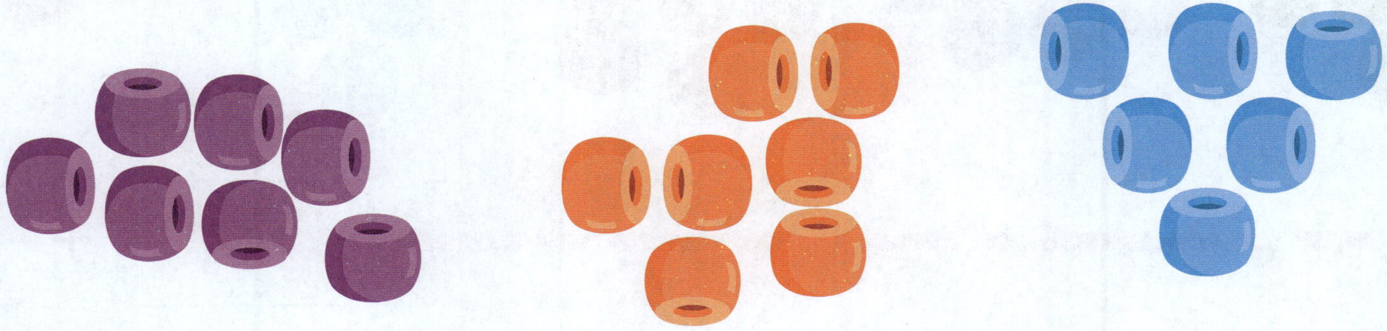

______ + ______

Have children draw and color to show 10 beads on the bracelet with no more than two different colors of beads. Then have them write the corresponding number partners for 10 shown by the bracelet.

Make 10 with Beads Activity

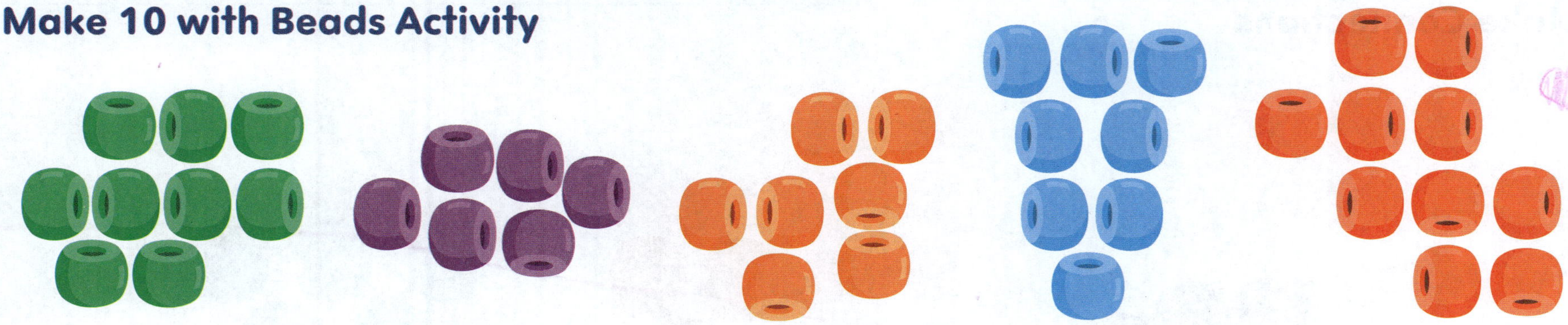

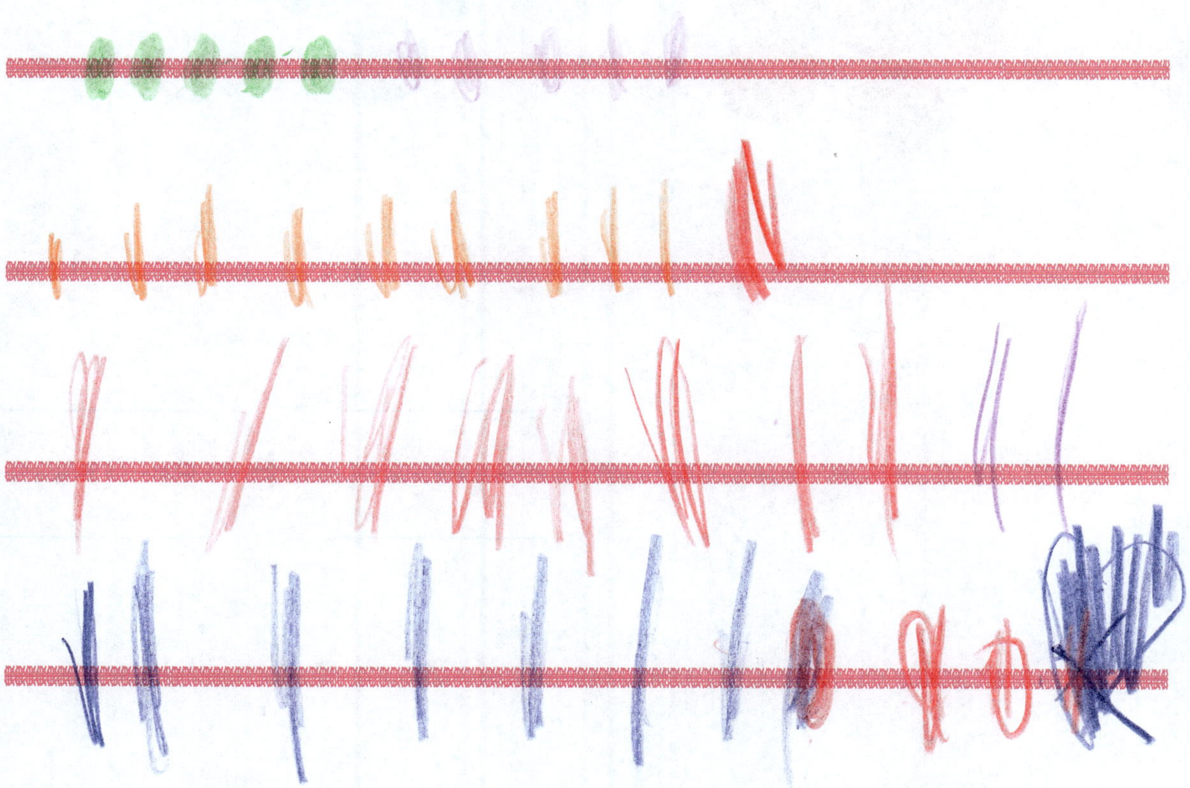

5 + 5

9 + 1

8 + 2

+ 7

Have children draw and color to show 10 beads on each bracelet so that each bracelet has no more than two different colors of beads. Then have them write the corresponding number partners for 10 shown by each bracelet.

NAME:

Practice

Color Write

Example

2 + 8

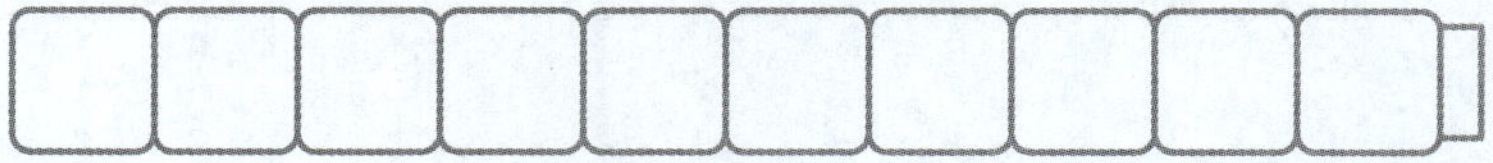

1 + 9

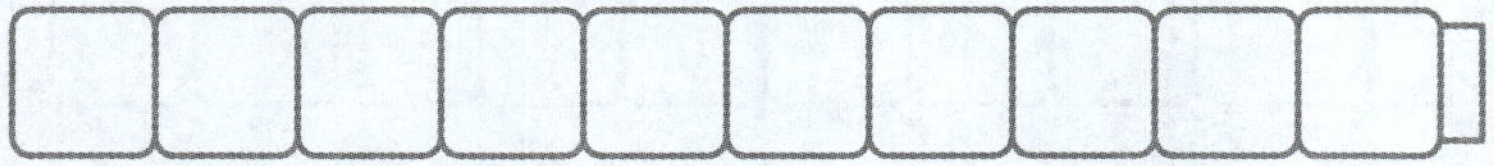

6 + ___

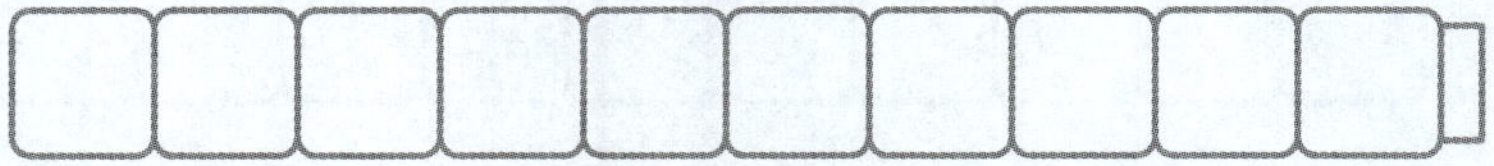

___ + 3

Ask children to color the connecting cubes to match the number or numbers given. Then have them write any missing numbers to show the corresponding number partners for 10.

Practice

Color Write

5 + ___

8 + ___

4 + ___

___ + 7

Ask children to color the connecting cubes to match the number given. Then have them write the missing numbers to show the corresponding number partners for 10.

Analyze It

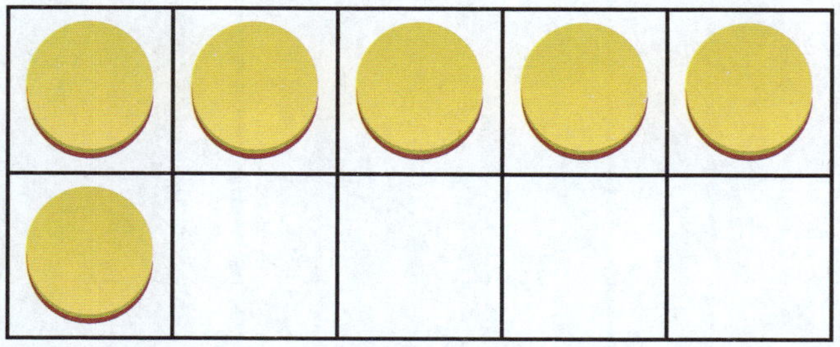

Read the problem: *The cat and dog both think they have counters that make 10 when added to the 10-frame. Do you agree with the cat, the dog, or both? Why?* Have children circle who they agree with.

Lesson Reflection

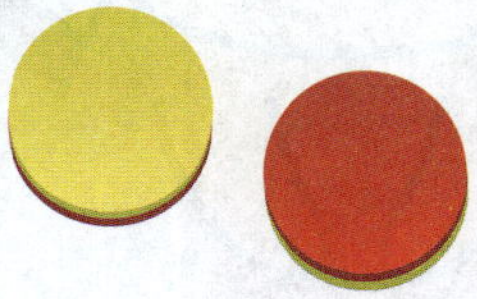

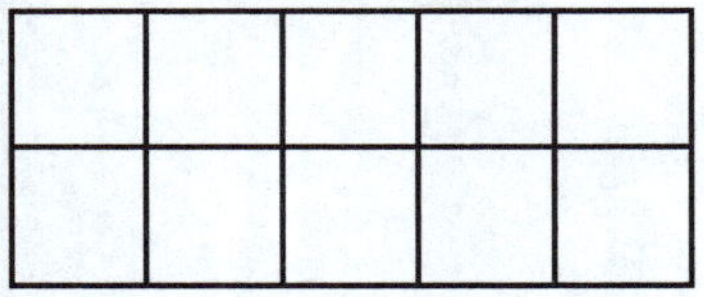

Have children use numbers, words, or drawings to show something they learned or did in this lesson to compose and decompose 10.

Practice

Match

Have children draw lines to match two groups of fruits to make a total of 10 pieces of fruit.

Practice

Write Draw

1 + ____

____ + 2

____ + ____

____ + ____

Have children write numbers in the expressions to match the top two lunch trays. Then have them draw their own number partners for 10 in the bottom two lunch trays and write expressions to match.

Family Letters are also available in multiple languages.

LESSON 15

Find Number Partners for 10

Dear Family,

In this lesson, your child is learning more about the meaning of the word *equal* and ways to show number pairs that equal 10. The pairs that equal 10 can be called number partners for 10.

The **equal sign (=)** is used to show that two groups have the same value. A number sentence using the equal sign is called an **equation**.

10 is the same as 4 and 6

or

10 = 4 + 6

More about the Math

10 is shown on the left and right of the equal sign to help your child understand that *equal* means "the same value as."

10 = 4 + 6

Ten has the same value as four plus six.

4 + 6 = 10

Four plus six has the same value as ten.

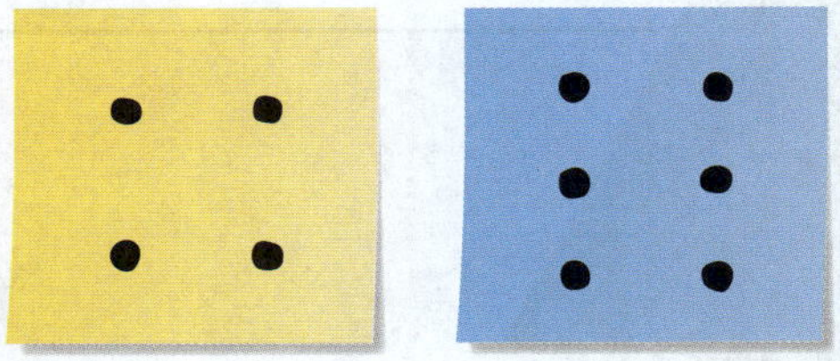

In this lesson, your child is finding different pairs of numbers that have the same value as 10.

Your child could use fingers, draw dots on paper, or count small objects to find number partners for 10. As children build this skill throughout the lesson and beyond, they will begin to recognize the number partners for 10.

i-Ready Connect

Learning Games

Hungry Guppy

Hungry Fish

Digital Math Tools

Counters and Connecting Cubes

Multilingual Glossary

equal sign (=)

equation

Hide and Think Game

Do this activity with your child to explore finding number partners for 10.

Materials: cup, 10 small objects (such as pennies or pebbles)

- While your child has their eyes closed, hide some of the objects under the cup and place the rest on the table.
- Tell your child to open their eyes.
- Have your child count the objects they see and determine the number of objects that are hidden.
- Lift the cup and count the number of objects to see if the number is correct.
- Encourage your child to SAY the equation that names the number partners for 10.
- Repeat with different numbers of objects under the cup.

SAY My number is correct!
$2 + 8 = 10$

Math on the GO!

Conversation Starter

Look for opportunities to find number partners for 10 in real-world situations. For example:

- If your child has selected two books at the library, how many more books can be checked out to equal 10?
- If you need 10 plates on the table and there are already 4 plates, how many do we need to make 10?

NAME:

Number Sense

Project the scene. Ask children: *What do you notice? What do you wonder?*

Break 10 into two parts and find how many more make 10 from a starting number. Show and record number partners for 10.

Investigate It

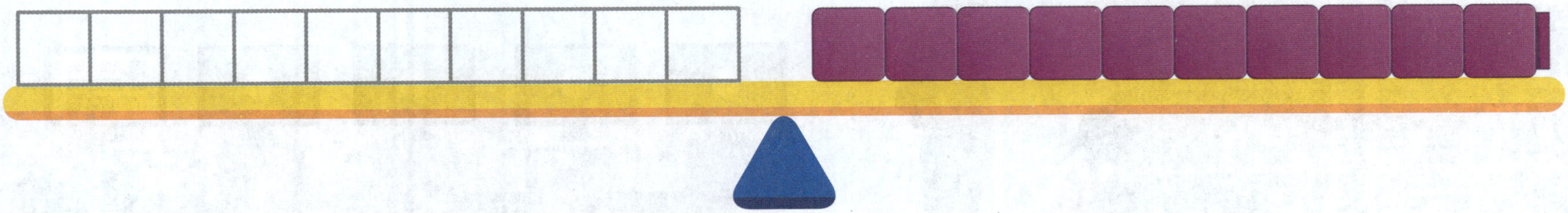

____ + ____ = 10

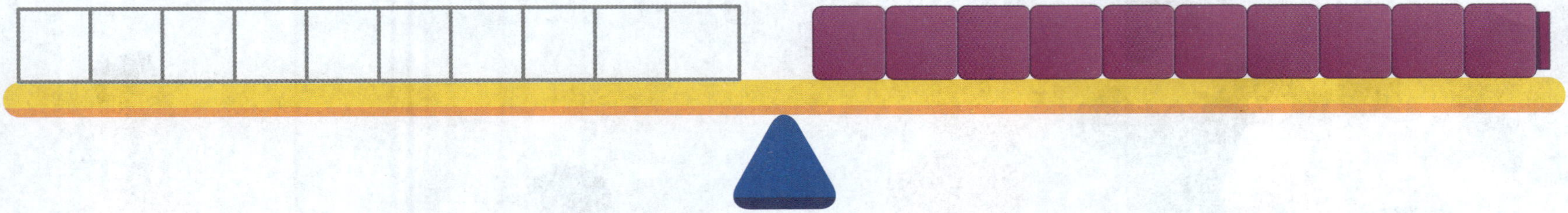

____ + ____ = 10

After doing the Discover It activity as a class, have children complete the Investigate It activity and record two of their results by coloring the cube trains and writing the number partners for 10.

What did you do to keep the sides equal?

NAME:

Try-Discuss-Connect

_____ + _____ = 10

Make sense of the problem: *There are 10 pillows on the rug. Some are round. Some are square. How many are round? How many are square?* Have children draw the round and square pillows and fill in the equation.

What can you say about the number of round and square pillows?

Pair It Up Activity

____ + ____ = 10

____ + ____ = 10

After children have completed several rounds of the Pair It Up Activity, have them record two pairs of number partners for 10. Have children draw dots and write the numbers on the cards. Then have them complete the equations.

How did you know the hidden number for each pair?

NAME: ____________

LESSON 15

Practice

Draw Write

Example

10 = 1 + 9

10 = ___ + ___

___ = ___ + ___

___ = ___ + ___

Have children draw to complete the 10-cube trains. Then have them write an equation for each 10-cube train.

Practice

Color Write

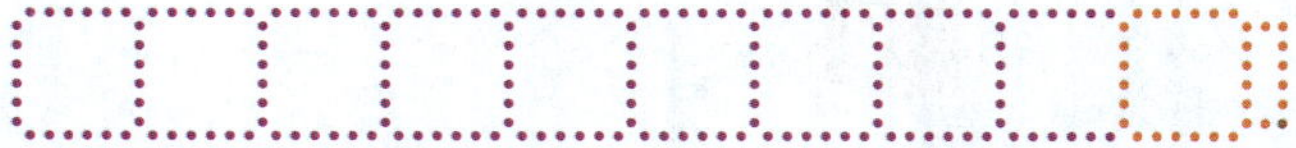

10 = 9 + 1

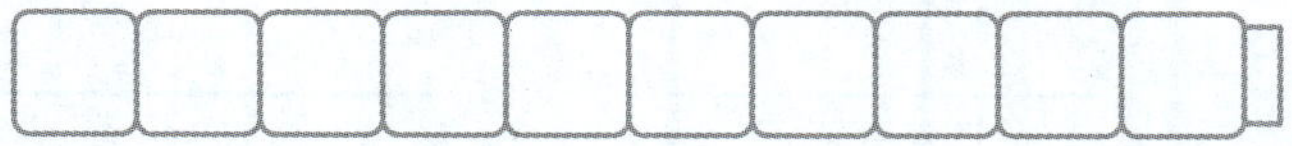

___ = ___ + ___

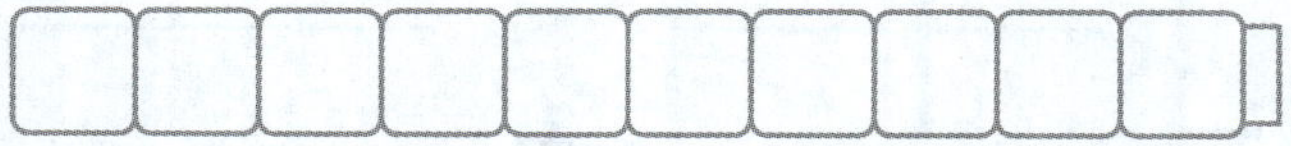

___ = ___ + ___

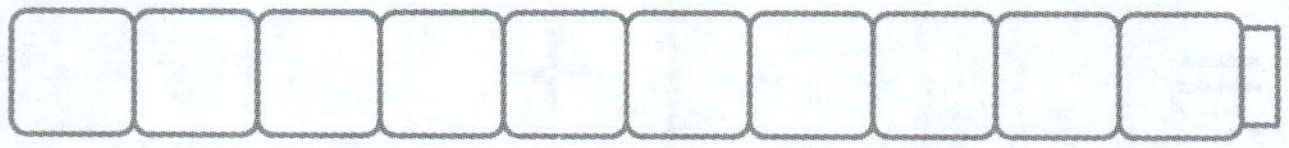

___ = ___ + ___

Have children color the cube trains two different colors to show number partners for 10.
Then have them write an equation for each cube train.

NAME:

Try-Discuss-Connect

3

10 = ___ + ___

Make sense of the problem: *You want to check out 10 books from the library. You already have a stack of 3 books. How many more books can you check out?* Have children write an equation for the books they can check out from the library.

How did you decide how many more books you can check out?

Fishing for 10 Activity

_____ + _____ = 10

_____ + _____ = 10

_____ + _____ = 10

_____ + _____ = 10

_____ + _____ = 10

_____ + _____ = 10

_____ + _____ = 10

_____ + _____ = 10

As children complete the Fishing for 10 Activity, have them record number partners for 10 by completing the equations.

What do you notice about number partners for 10?

Practice

Write

Example

7 + 3 = 10

___ + ___ = 10

___ + ___ = 10

___ + ___ = 10

___ + ___ = 10

___ + ___ = 10

Have children use number partners for 10 to fill in each equation.

Practice

Write

___ + ___ = 10

___ + ___ = 10

___ + ___ = 10

___ + ___ = 10

___ + ___ = 10

___ + ___ = 10

Have children use number partners for 10 to fill in each equation.

NAME:

Make Connections

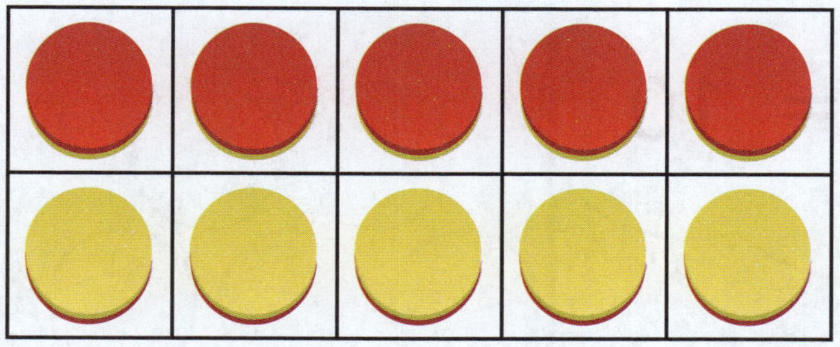

____ + ____ = ____

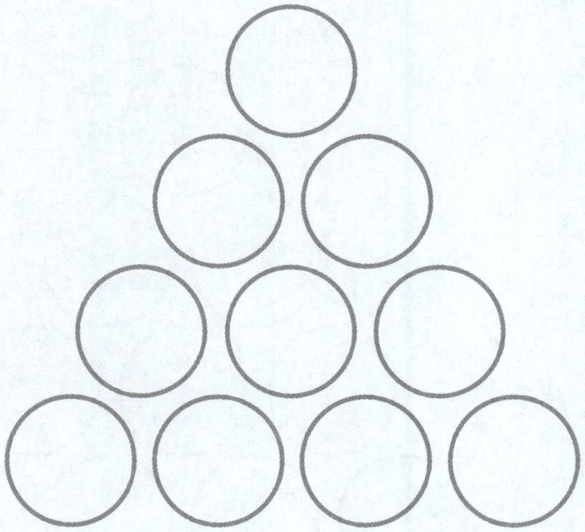

____ + ____ = ____

Have children fill in the equation next to the 10-frame. Next, ask children to look at the triangular model. Have them color the model so that it shows the same number partners for 10 as the 10-frame. Then have them fill in the equation next to the triangular model.

Model 10 in Triangles Activity

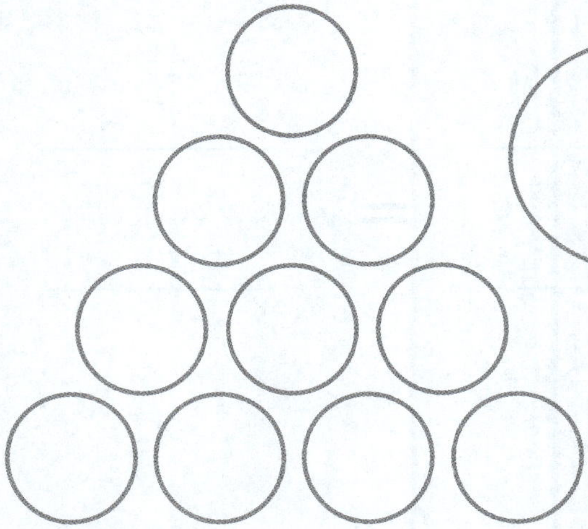

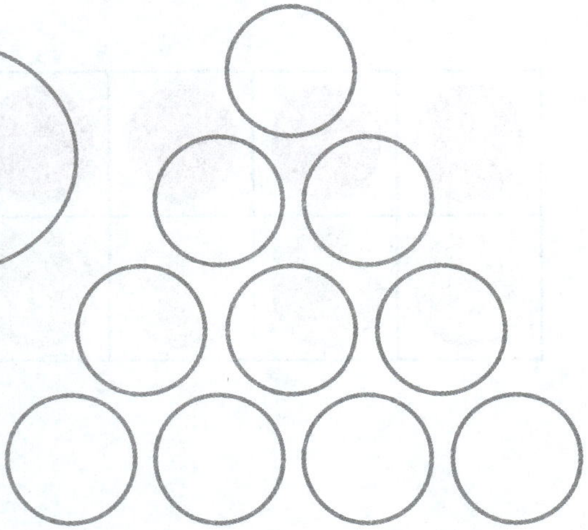

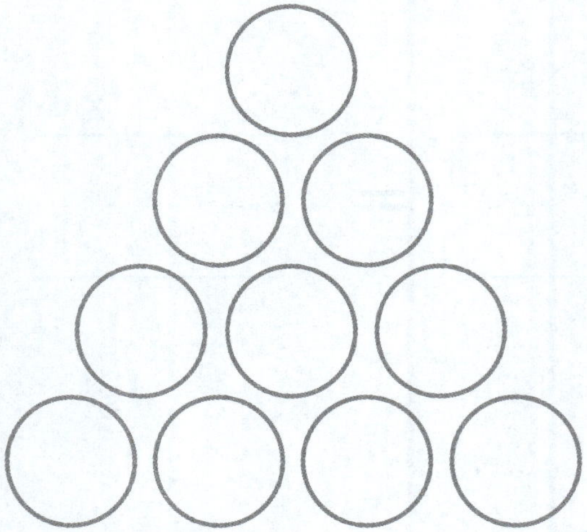

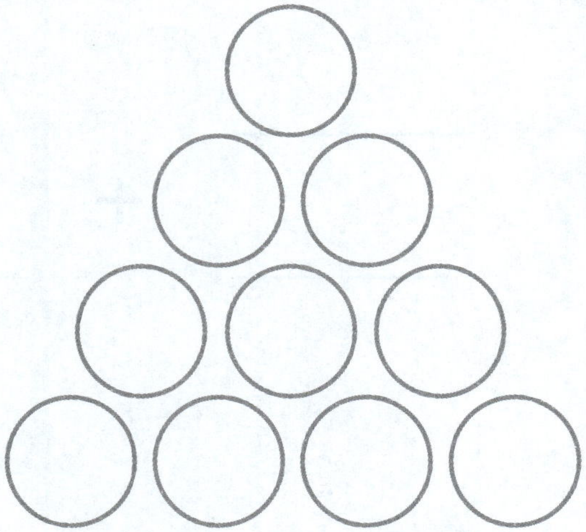

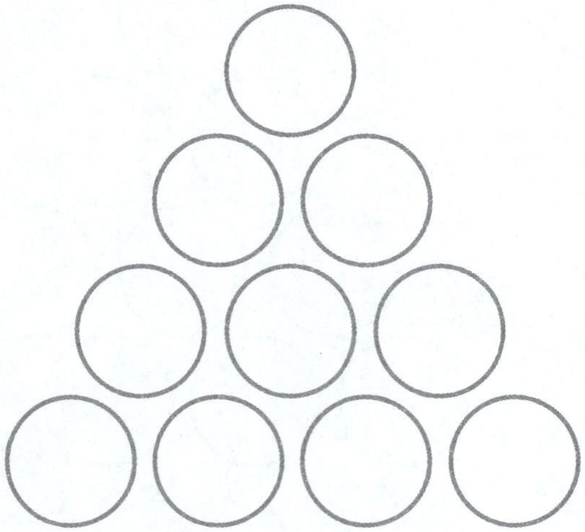

Have children choose their own number partners for 10 (other than 5 and 5) and write the number partners in the equation. Then have them color to show several different ways to show the number partners in the triangular models.

NAME:

Practice

Draw Write

Example

10 = 9 + 1

10 = ___ + ___

___ = ___ + ___

Ask children to draw different ways to show number partners for 10 with red and then yellow counters. Have them write the number of each color in the equations to show number partners for 10.

Practice

Draw Write

____ = ____ + ____

____ = ____ + ____

____ = ____ + ____

Ask children to use two colors to draw different ways to show number partners for 10 with different-color counters. Have them write the number of each color in the equations to show number partners for 10.

NAME:

Analyze It

Read the problem: *The cat and dog both think they have shown ways to make 10. Do you agree with the cat, the dog, or both? Why?* Have children circle who they agree with.

Lesson Reflection

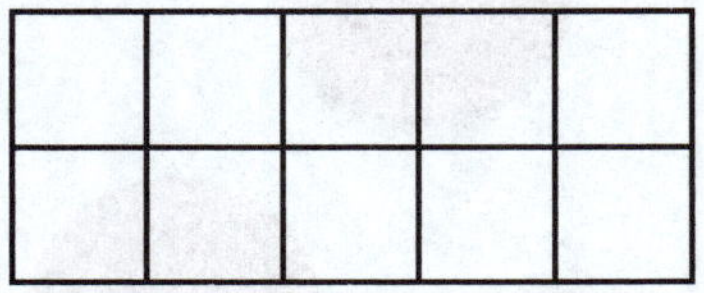

___ = ___ + ___

2 1 3

Have children use numbers, words, or drawings to show something they learned or did in this lesson to show number partners for 10.

Practice

Match

Have children draw lines to match each frog to a lily pad to show number partners for 10.

Practice

Circle

6	10	0	3	6	6
5	1	2	7	4	3
5	2	8	2	3	7
8	3	9	1	8	0
4	5	5	1	7	10

Have children circle as many number partners for 10 as they can find.

NAME:

Build a Playground

What do you want on the playground?

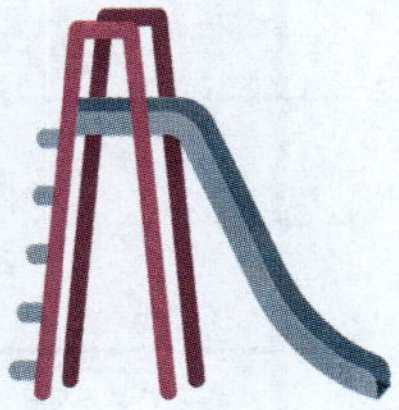

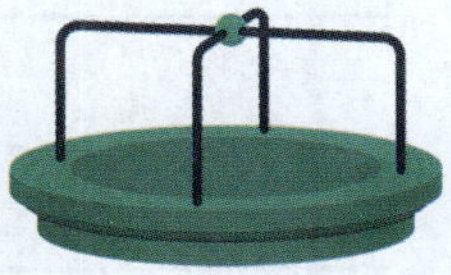

Have children use solid shapes or objects to build pieces for a playground.
Have them record the number of each piece they build.

Build a Playground with 10 Pieces

What do you want on the playground?

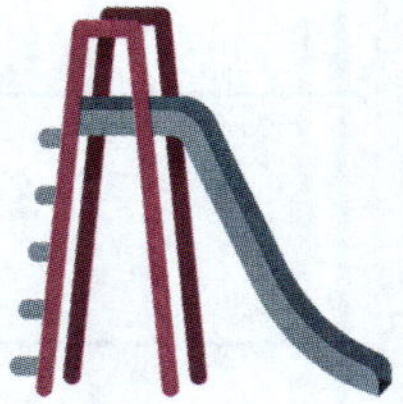

Have children use solid shapes or objects to build 10 pieces for a playground. Have them record the number of each piece they build.

How is your playground like your partner's playground? How is it different?

NAME:

My Playground Information

Have children circle a swing or a slide to show whether they want a playground with more swings or more slides. Then have them record the answers of four classmates the same way.

Look at your data. Do you think the class wants a playground with more swings or more slides? Why?

Reflection

What do you notice and wonder about the class data display?

I notice:

I wonder:

Have children notice and wonder about the class data display. Have them answer one of their questions using numbers, words, drawings, objects, and/or gestures.

NAME:

UNIT 4

Show What You Learned

Have children draw to show what they learned about numbers to 10 and shapes. Prompt children to reflect on their learning by posing questions such as: *What do you know how to do well? What math could you use in your everyday life? What is a question you still have?*

Draw

Color Circle

1	2	3	4	5	6	7	8	9	10

1	2	3	4	5	6	7	8	9	10

For the first problem, have children add a shape to the existing shape to make a triangle. Then have children color the triangle. For the next problem, have children color the number paths to count the objects, then circle the group with the greater number of objects.

NAME:

Circle

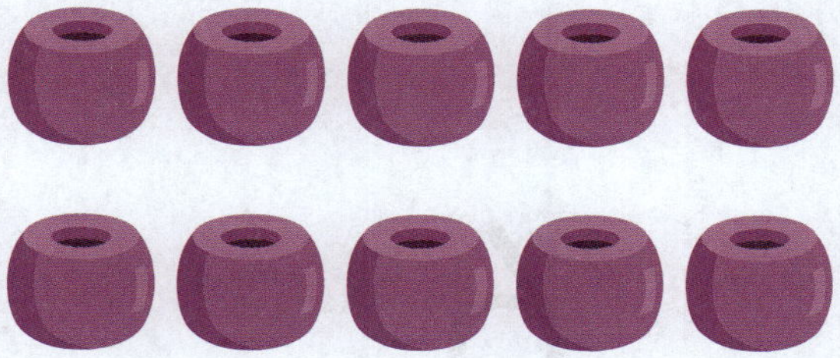

8   9   10

Write

$6 + \underline{\quad\quad} = 10$

Draw

8

For the first problem, ask children to count the beads and circle the number that shows how many. For the next problem, have children use number partners for 10 to fill in the equation. For the last problem, have children look at the number and draw that many counters.

Draw

7

8 4 6

Color Write

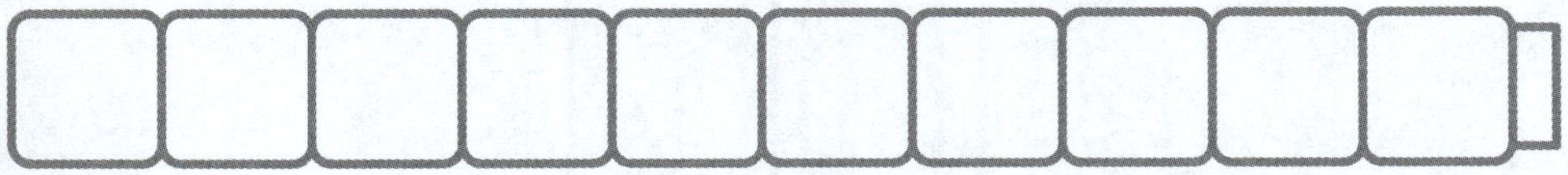

7 + ____

For the first problem, have children draw a line under numbers that are less than the number on the card. For the next problem, ask children to color the connecting cubes in two different colors to match the numbers given and write the missing number partner for 10.

UNIT 5

Numbers to 100

Show What You Know

Have children draw to show what they know about numbers from 1 to 100. Tell children that after they have completed the unit, they will draw to show what they learned.

My Words

Mathematical
count on
eleven
twelve
teen numbers

Academic
place
organize

Have children choose 2 to 4 words and show what they know about them using pictures, numbers, or words. Have children share their representations with peers.

To support children with word selection, ask:
- *Which words are new to you?*
- *Which words do you think are the most important? Why?*

Family Letters are also available in multiple languages.

LESSON 16

Count, Read, and Write Numbers 11 to 20

Dear Family,

In this lesson, your child is learning about numbers 11 to 20. Your child will count up to 20 objects and write the number that shows how many.

More about the Math

Earlier in Kindergarten, your child counted up to 10 objects. Now, your child will begin to explore patterns in **teen numbers**. Children will see that when they count beyond 10, the digit on the right starts at 1 again and goes up to 9.

1 2 3 4 5 …

11 12 13 14 15 …

Your child will count objects in different arrangements and use numbers to show how many are in a group.

i-Ready Connect

Learning Games

Hungry Guppy

Match

Digital Math Tools

Counters and Connecting Cubes

Multilingual Glossary

eleven, twelve,
thirteen, fourteen,
fifteen, sixteen,
seventeen, eighteen,
nineteen
teen numbers
twenty

Match My Count

Do this activity with your child to explore counting numbers up to 20.

Materials: 40 small household objects

- Divide the objects equally between you and your child.
- Choose a number of objects (e.g., 12 buttons) and place them in front of you.
- Say: *I picked some objects and made a set. Can you make a set with the same number?*
- Have your child count the objects out loud and **SAY** how many there are in the set they made.
- Tell your child whether they correctly made a set with the same number.
- Have your child make a set for you to model.
- Demonstrate counting the objects out loud and saying how many. Ask your child if your set has the same number as their set.

Math on the GO!

Conversation Starter

Look for opportunities to count 11 to 20 objects in real-world situations.
For example:

- When you are doing laundry, have your child count the number of socks or towels.
- When you are walking in your neighborhood, have your child count the number of poles on a fence or painted lines on a crosswalk.

SAY There are 12 buttons.

NAME:

LESSON 16

Number Sense

Project the scene. Ask children: *What do you notice? What do you wonder?*

Count a group of up to 20 objects. Read and write numbers up to 20.

Investigate It

10	11	12	13	14	15	16	17	18	19	20

After doing the Discover It activity as a class, have children complete the Investigate It activity and complete the part of the number path on their workmat by drawing objects and writing numbers to show one more and one less than 14.

How did you figure out where to place your objects on the number path?

NAME:

Try-Discuss-Connect

1 2  4 5 6 7 8 9 10

11 12 13 14 15 16 17  19 20

Make sense of the problem: *Which numbers are missing?* Have children fill in the missing numbers.

How could you find the missing number?

Write to the Top Activity

10	11	12	13	14	15	16	17	18	19	20

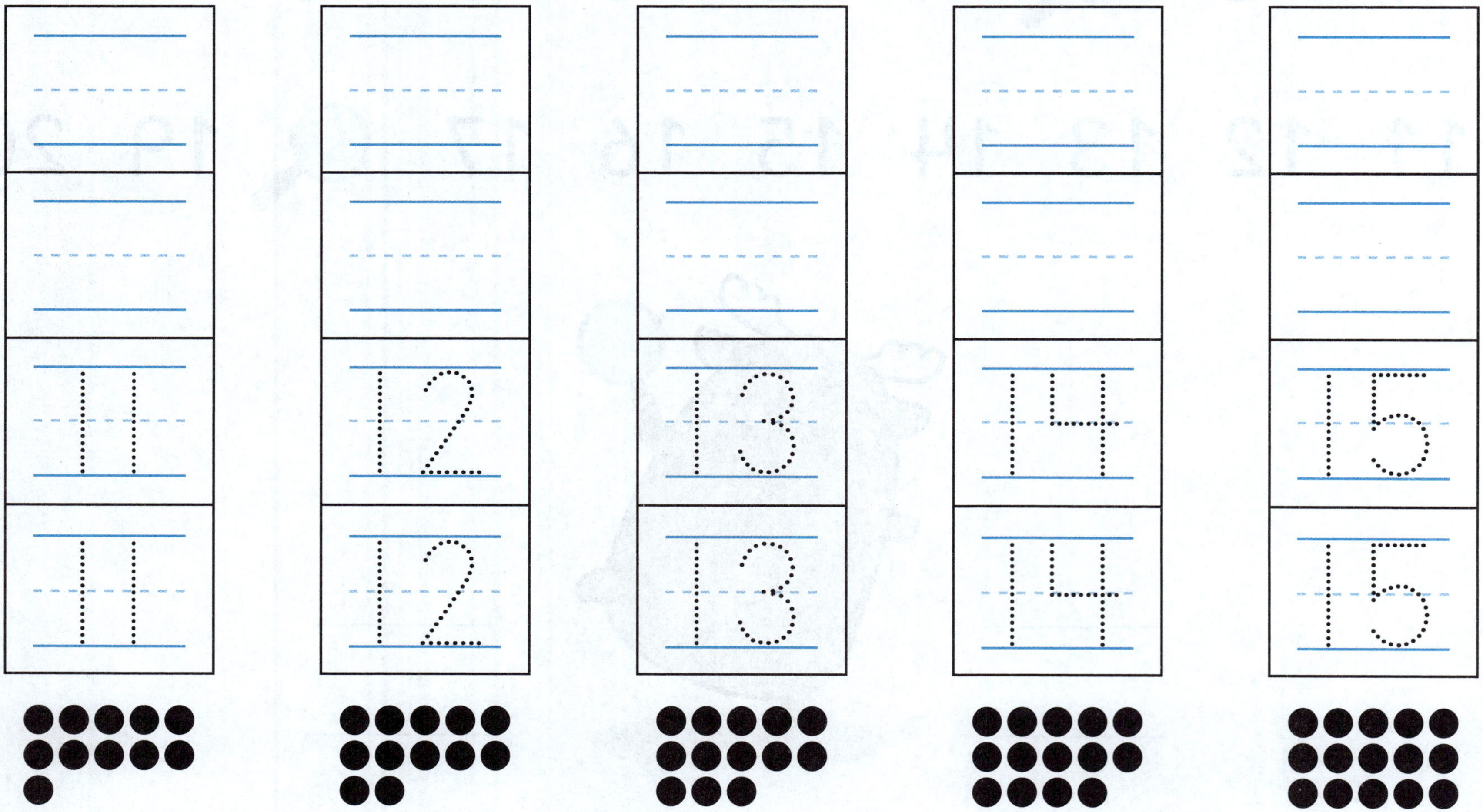

Have children choose two dot cards and count the total number of dots on both cards. Ask them to find the matching number of dots on this page. Have children trace or write the number above the dots.

Which numbers are easier to write? Which are harder?

NAME:

Practice

Match

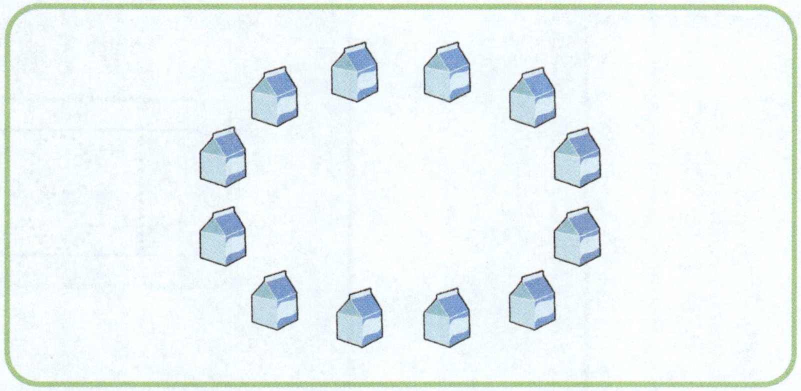

16

12

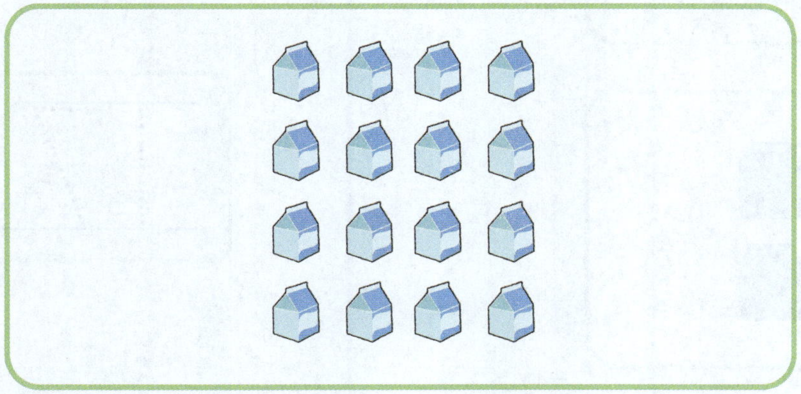

11

Have children match each group of objects to the number that shows how many.

Practice

Match

13

20

17

Have children trace each number. Then have them match each group of cubes to the number that shows how many.

NAME:

Try-Discuss-Connect

14
19
11

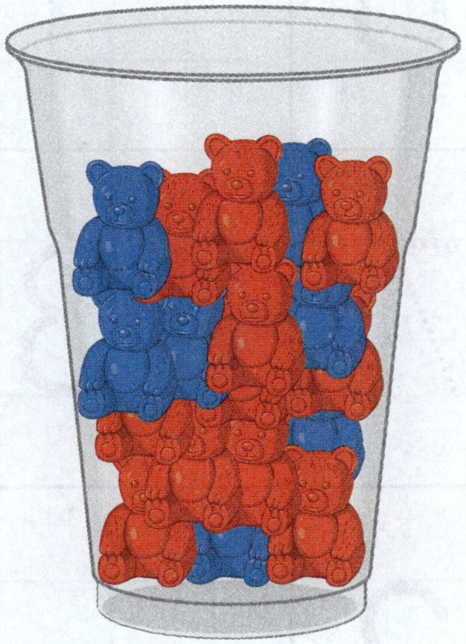

Make sense of the problem: *Each cup has a different number of counters. Which cup has 11 counters? 14 counters? 19 counters?* Have children write the correct number of counters below each cup.

How did you know which cup has 11 counters? 14 counters? 19 counters?

Count and Cover Up Activity

11	14	18	19
20		17	13
	16	12	
18			15

Have children trace the dotted numbers. Then have them fill in the empty spaces with any numbers from 11 to 20.

How did you keep track of the cubes as you counted?

NAME:

Practice

Write

Example

15 15

11

14

Have children count the counters and then trace and write the number that shows how many.

Practice

Write

13

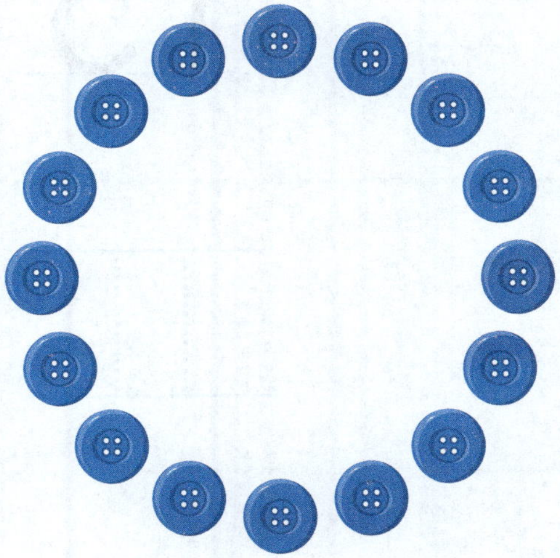

16

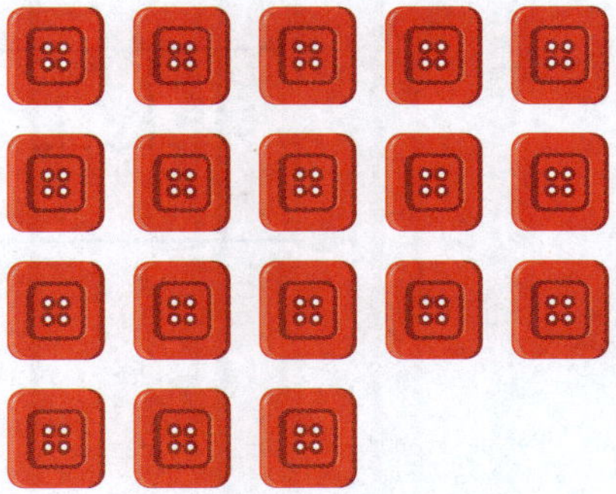

18

Have children count the buttons and then trace and write the number that shows how many.

NAME:

Make Connections

Have children write a number between 11 and 20 in the blank. Then have them pick a crayon and use it to color that many stars.

Color the Stars Activity

Have children write a number between 11 and 20 in one blank and choose a color for that number. Then have them color that many stars. Have them repeat with different numbers and colors to show different groups of stars.

Practice

Draw

Example

15

20

14

Have children draw the given number of objects.

Practice

Write Draw

Have children write a number. Then have them draw that number of objects.

Analyze It

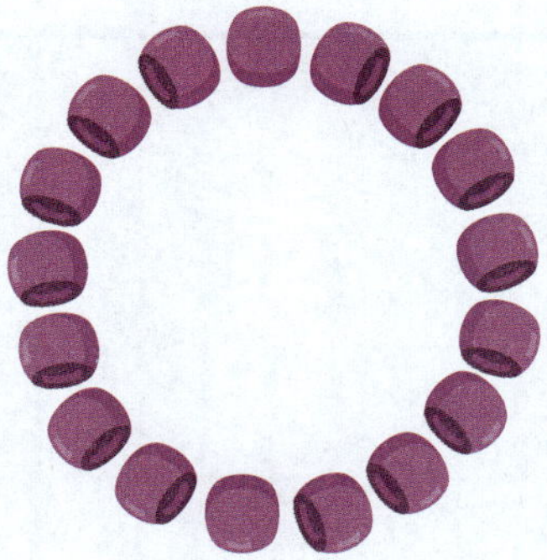

17

18

Read the problem: *The cat and dog counted the beads. They both think they wrote the number that shows how many. Do you agree with the cat, the dog, or both? Why?* Have children circle who they agree with.

Lesson Reflection

12

Have children use numbers, words, or drawings to show something they learned or did in this lesson to count, read, and write numbers from 11 to 20.

NAME:

Practice

Color Write

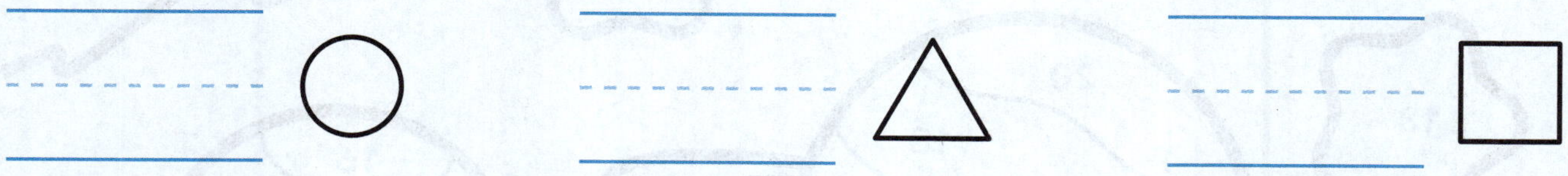

Have children choose a different color for each shape. Have them count as they color all the objects of one type and then write the number they counted using their chosen color.

Practice

Write Color

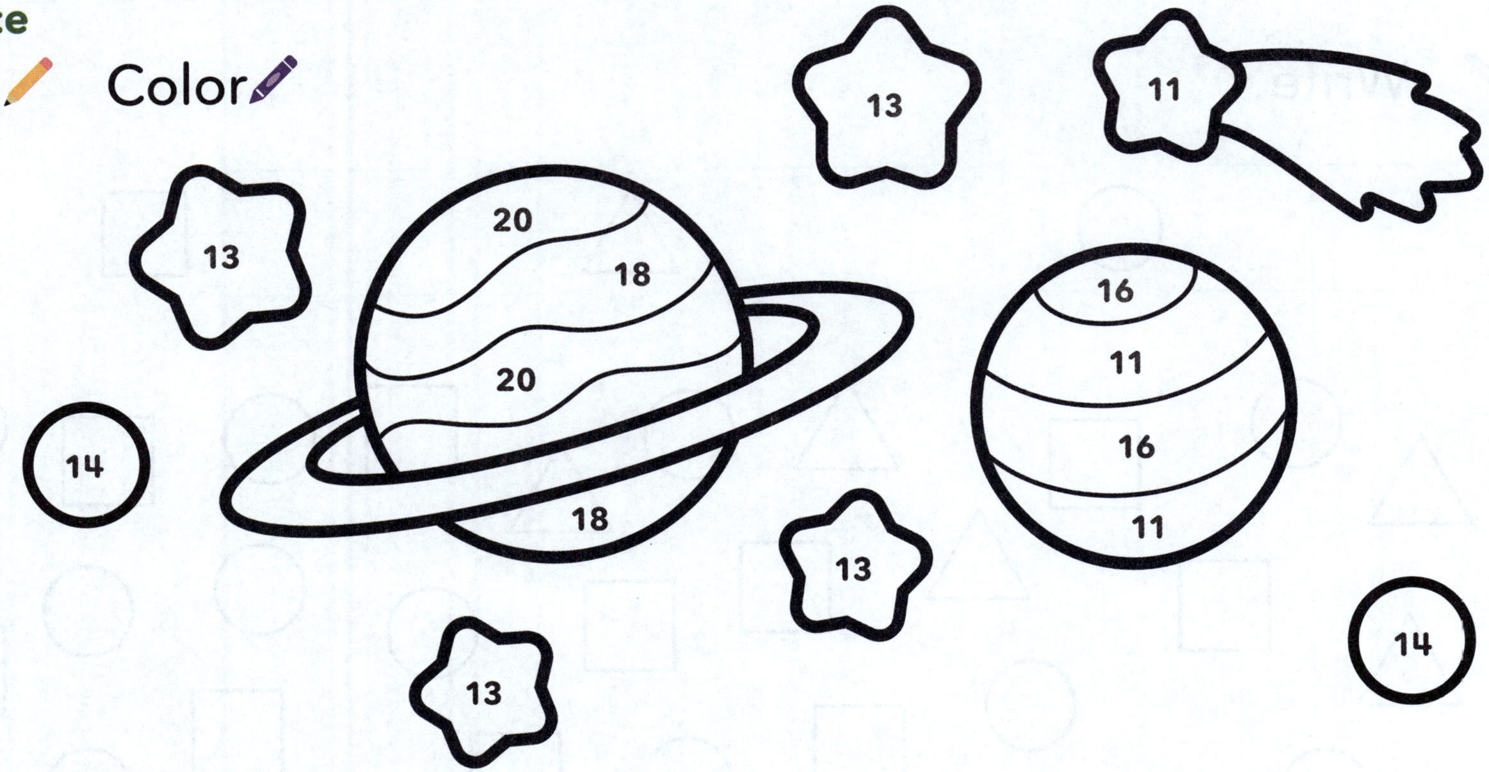

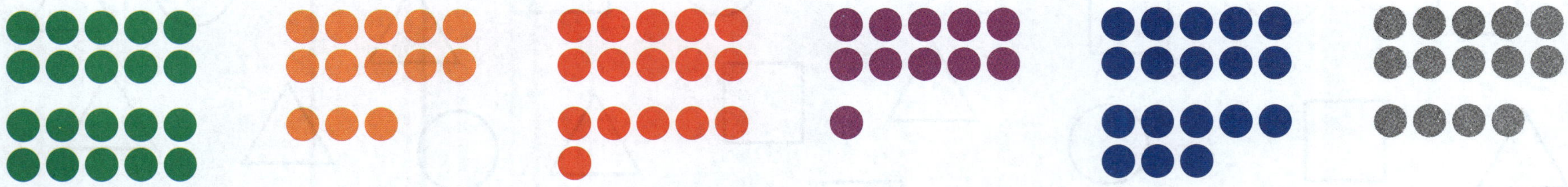

Have children count the colored dots and write the number. Tell children to use the dots as a key to color the picture. Have them find the number in the picture and then use that color for the sections that show the number they counted.

Family Letters are also available in multiple languages.

LESSON 17

Count Within 100

Dear Family,

Your child has been rote counting to 100 by 1s and 10s. In this lesson, your child is learning to connect the rote counting sequence to counting objects. They will count groups with up to 100 objects to tell how many objects there are.

More about the Math

Your child will also learn to **count on** by 1s, or start counting by 1s from any given number less than 100.

As children practice counting up to 100, they will develop strategies for keeping track of which objects they have counted and which objects they still need to count. They will also realize that they can check their counting by counting again and making sure they get the same number.

i-Ready Connect

Learning Games

- Hungry Guppy
- Match
- Zoom

Multilingual Glossary

count on

ACTIVITY

Count How Many

Do this activity with your child to explore counting within 100.

Materials: small objects (such as coins or pebbles), bag

- Place some of the objects in the bag.
- Have your child pour the objects out of the bag. Ask them to count the objects and **SAY** how many objects there are.
- Verify your child's count by counting the objects yourself. Discuss with your child whether you agree about how many objects there are. If not, count again to check.
- Put the objects back into the bag. Add or take away some objects to vary the amount. Then repeat.

SAY 1, 2, 3, 4, 5, 6, 7, 8, 9, 10, 11, 12. There are 12.

Math on the GO!

Conversation Starter

Look for opportunities to count up to 100 in real-world situations. For example:

- If you are cutting up apple slices, tell your child you have cut 12 slices already and ask them to count on from 12 by 1s.
- If you are shopping, point out boxes of 10 items. Ask your child to count the items in the boxes by 10s.

NAME:

LESSON 17

Number Sense

Project the scene. Ask children: *What do you notice? What do you wonder?*

Count to 100 by 1s and by 10s. Count on from any number less than 100.

Investigate It

After doing the Discover It activity as a class, have children complete the Investigate It activity. Have them draw more groups of 10 objects to show 100 objects.

How did your group decide how to organize the objects?

NAME:

Try-Discuss-Connect

Make sense of the problem: *Draw some buttons in the empty bin. How many objects are there in all of the bins?* Have children draw any number of buttons in the empty bin and then count all the objects.

How did you count all of the objects?

Cover and Count Activity

As children complete the Cover and Count Activity, have them use an index card to cover some of the buttons on the page. Then have them count the buttons they can see.

How did you count the buttons you saw?

NAME:

Practice

Draw

Tell children to draw more circles in each box so that both boxes have the same number of circles.

Practice

Draw

Tell children to draw more circles in each box so that all three boxes have the same number of circles.

NAME:

Try-Discuss-Connect

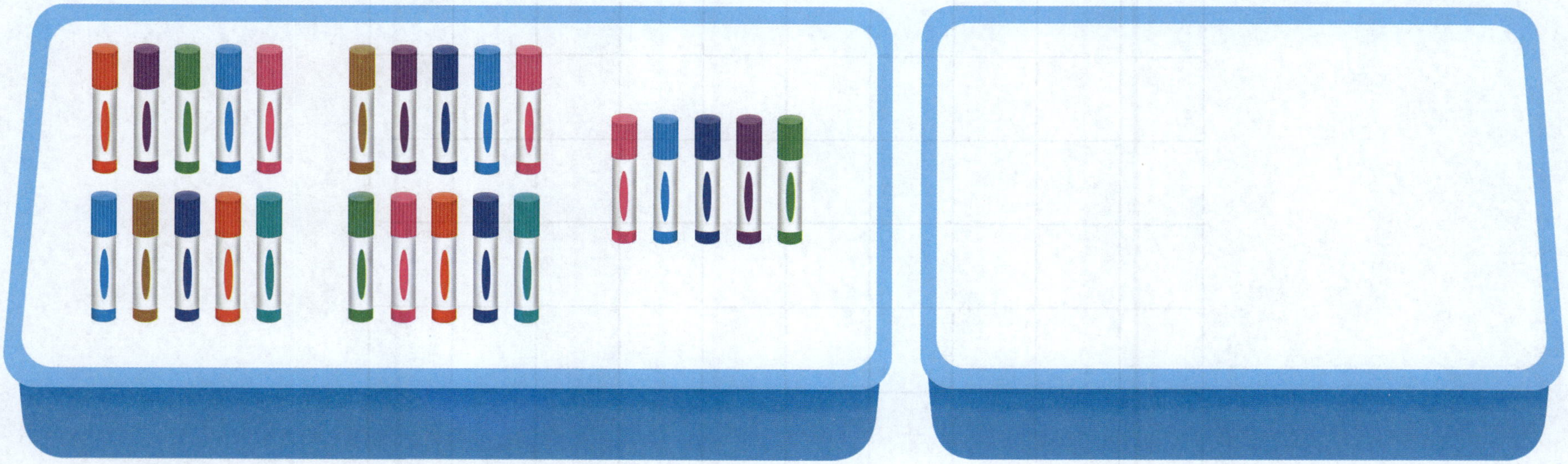

Make sense of the problem: *How many markers are there? Draw some more markers in the empty bin. How many markers are there now?* Have children count the markers already on the page, draw some more, and count how many in all.

How did you count all the markers?

Counting Handfuls Activity

Have children use the hundred grid to complete the activity in pairs. One child grabs a handful of objects and counts them aloud while their partner marks one space on the grid for each object counted. Children switch roles and then take turns until they count to 100.

How did you know what number to say next when counting on?

NAME:

Practice

Color

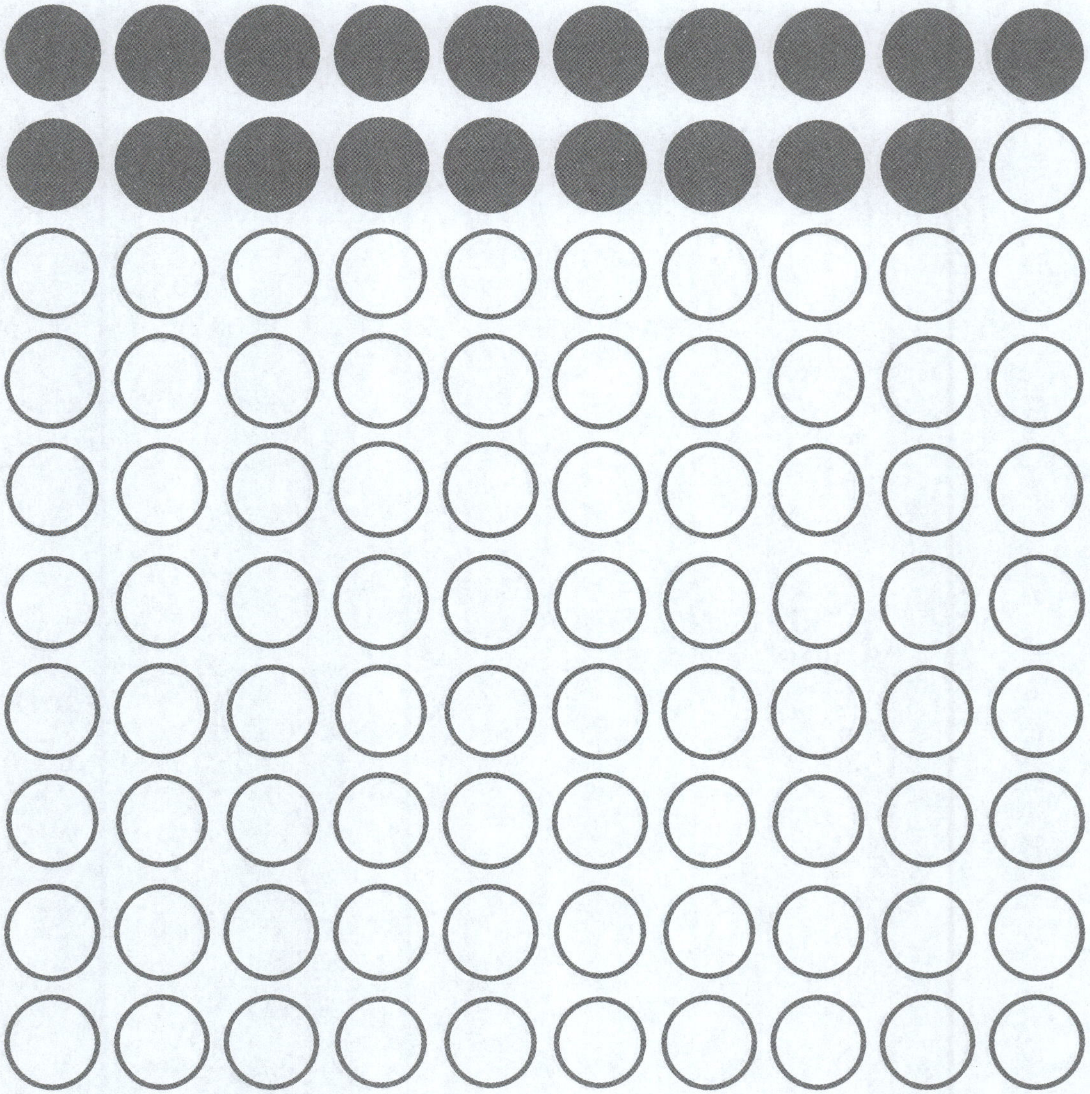

Have children count the shaded circles. Then have them count on, coloring more circles, until they count to 60.

Practice

Color

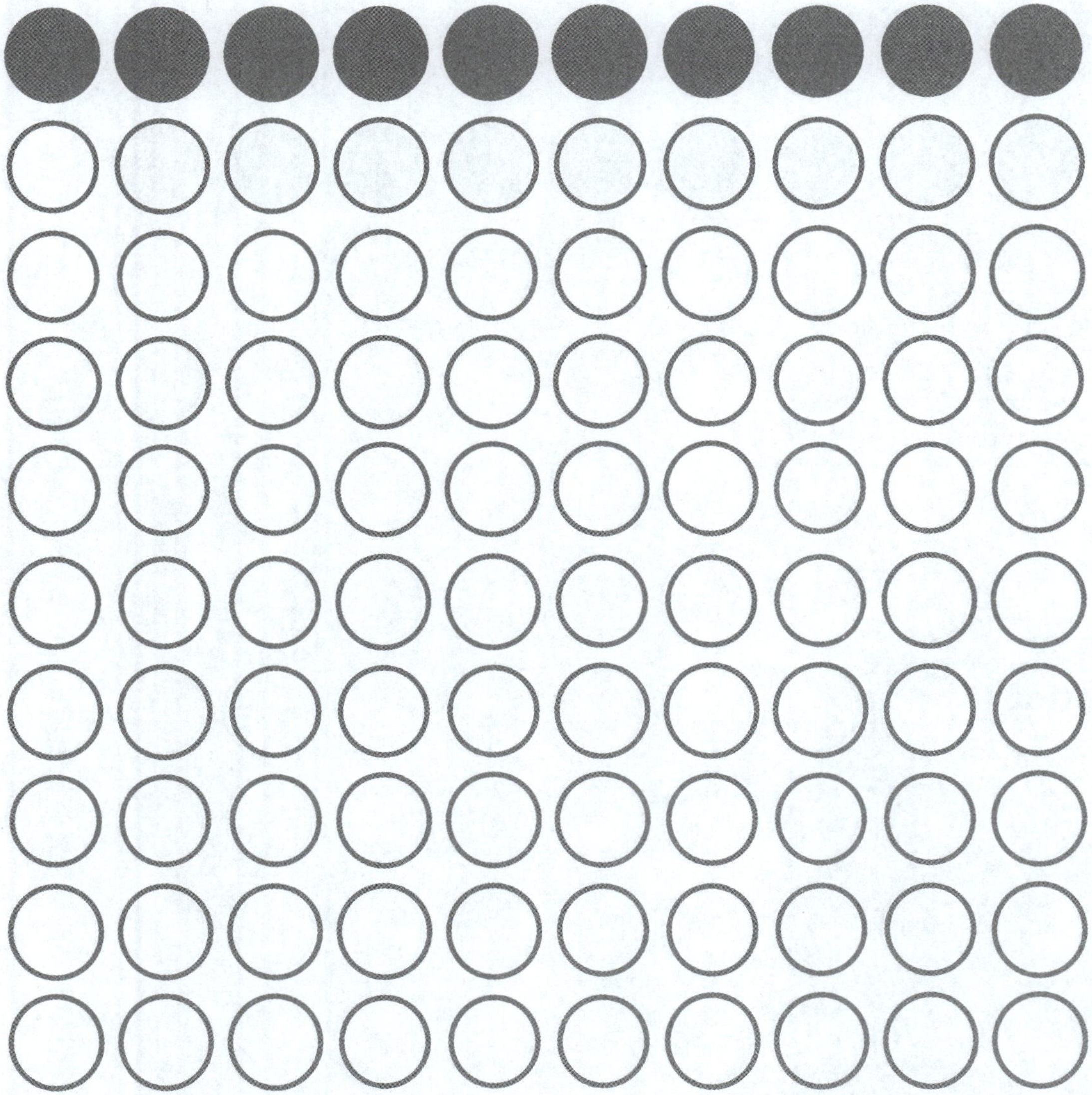

Have children count the shaded circles. Then have them count on, coloring more circles, until they count to 60.

NAME:

Make Connections

Have children circle any two groups of paper clips. Then have them count the number of paper clips they circled. Have children share their work with a partner to check their counting.

Circle and Count Activity

Have children circle any three groups of beads. Then have them count the number of beads they circled. Have children share their work with a partner to check their counting.

NAME:

Practice

Color

Have children color some bears. Then have them color the same number of cubes.

Practice

Color

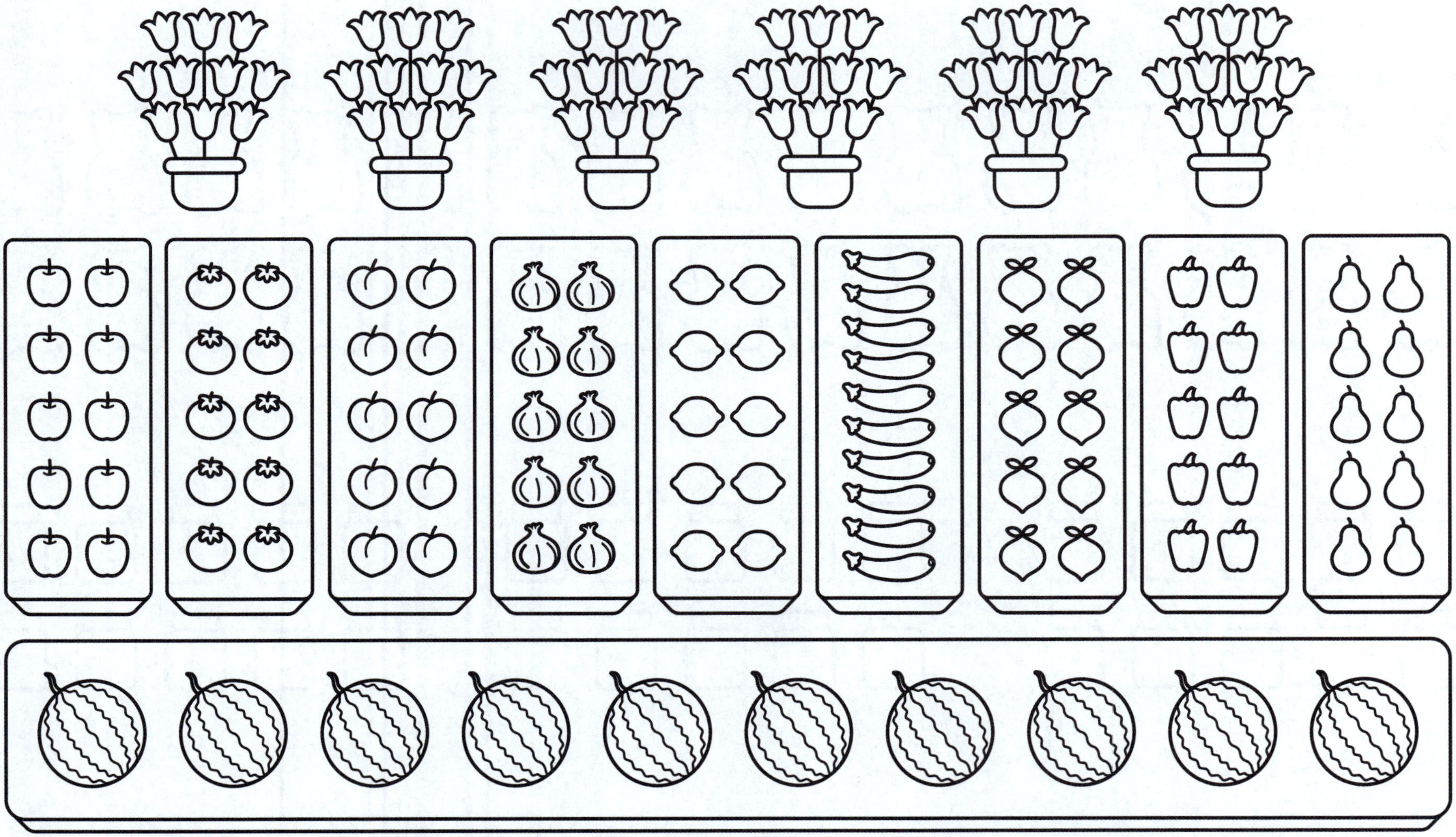

Have children color some flowers. Then have them color the same number of fruits and vegetables.

NAME:

Analyze It

Read the problem: *The cat and dog both think they have 30. Do you agree with the cat, the dog, or both? Why?* Have children circle who they agree with.

Lesson Reflection

Have children use numbers, words, or drawings to show something they learned or did in this lesson to count up to 100.

NAME:

Practice

Draw

Have children draw some stripes on the zebra. Then have them draw the same number of spots on the cheetah.

Practice

Color Draw

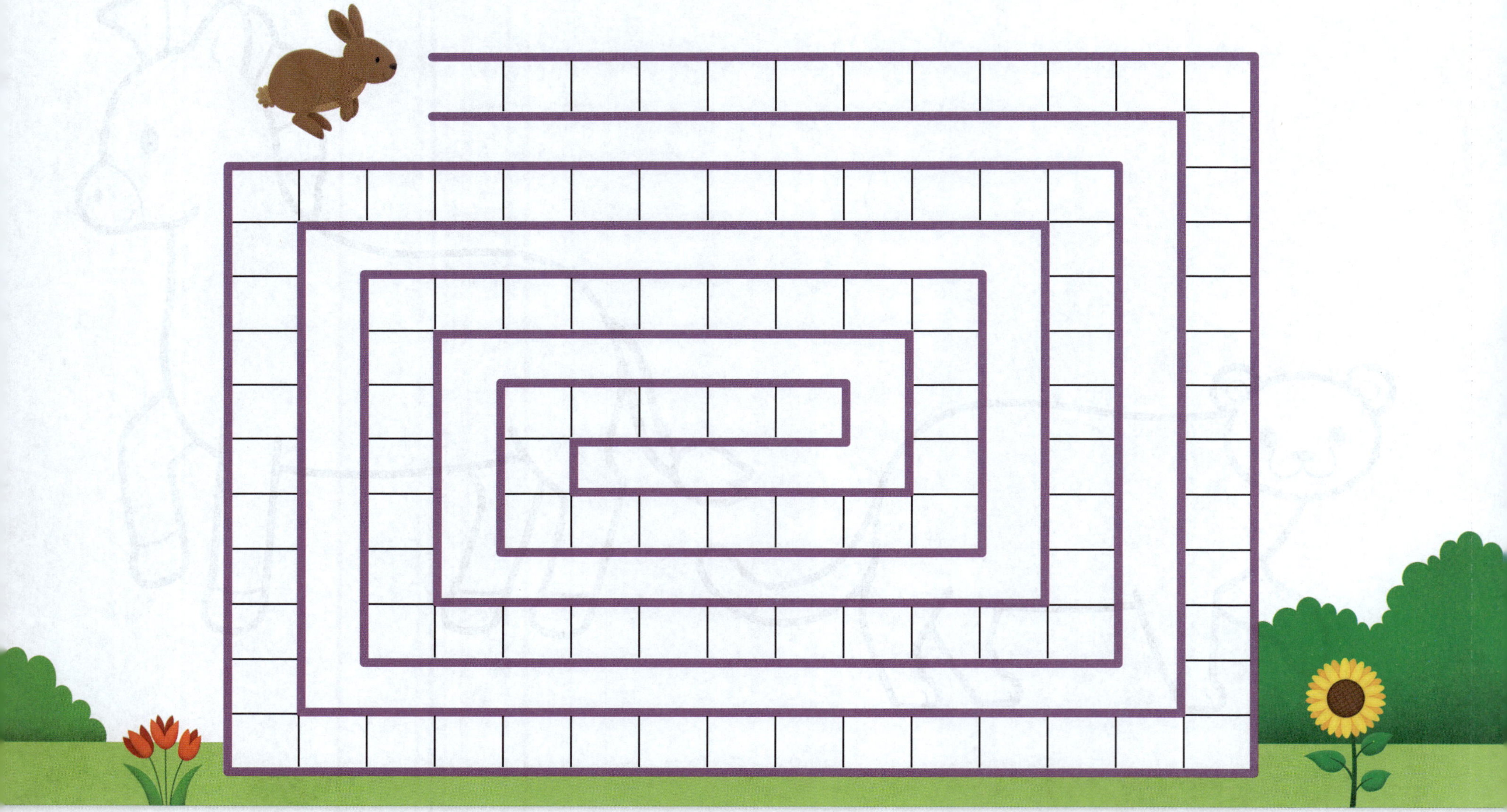

Tell children the bunny wants to hop 100 spaces along the path. Have children shade groups of 10 spaces as they move along the path. Have them use a different color for each group. Then have them circle where 100 is.

Family Letters are also available in multiple languages.

Compose and Decompose 6 and 7

Dear Family,

In this lesson, your child is learning to find number partners that make 6 and 7.

You can think of a number as being composed of lesser numbers. The number 6 can be made up of 3 and 3, 4 and 2, 5 and 1, or 6 and 0 with the numbers in either order.

More about the Math

Recognizing number partners will help your child prepare for adding and subtracting. For example, knowing that 2 and 4 make 6 lays the foundation for solving 2 + 4 = ? and 6 – 4 = ?.

In class, your child will show different ways to make 6 and 7 by placing counters in a 10-frame. Working with a 10-frame will help your child relate numbers to quantities. It also helps children develop an understanding of how numbers relate to 5 and 10.

i-Ready Connect

Learning Games

Hungry Guppy

Hungry Fish

Digital Math Tools

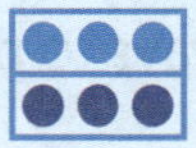
Counters and Connecting Cubes

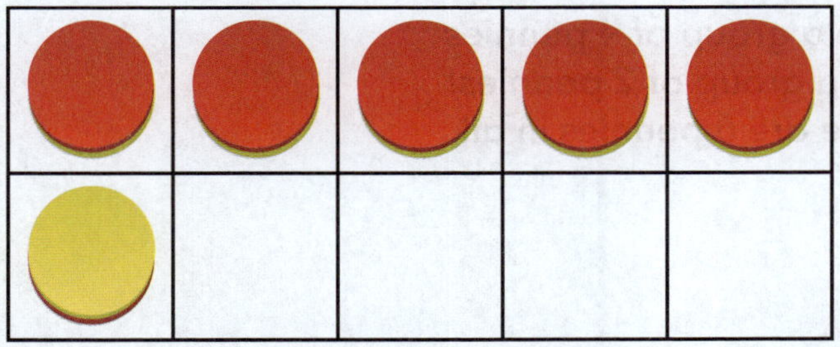

5 and 1 make 6

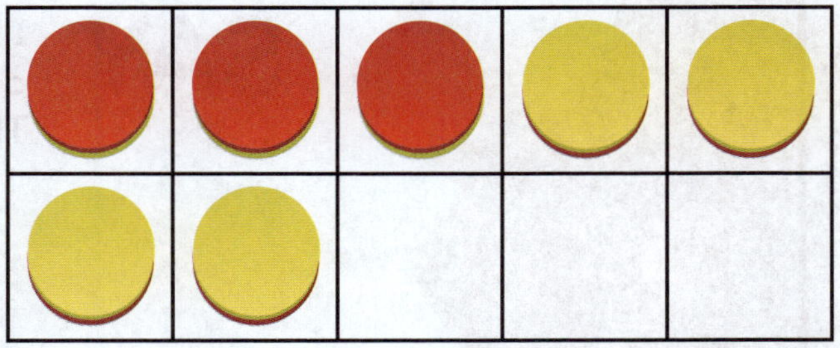

3 and 4 make 7

ACTIVITY

Make 6 and 7

Do this activity with your child to explore making 6 and 7.

Materials: 7 pennies (or other small objects), paper, 1 cup

- Use the base of a cup to trace a circle on a piece of paper. Then place 6 pennies in the cup.
- Put the paper with the circle on a table, and spill the pennies out onto the paper.
- Ask your child to group the pennies based on how many are inside the circle and how many are outside the circle. For example, your child may see a group of 4 pennies inside the circle and a group of 2 pennies outside the circle.
- Then have your child **SAY** the total number of pennies. Repeat until you have found several ways to make 6.
- Then repeat the activity with 7 pennies until your child has found several ways to make 7.

SAY **I see a group of 4 pennies and a group of 2 pennies! There are 6 pennies in all.**

Math on the GO!

Conversation Starter

Look for situations to find number partners for 6 and 7 in real-world situations. For example:

- If your child selects 2 toys from the shelf, how many more toys can they take to have 6?
- Suppose you need to walk 7 blocks to get to a friend's house and you already walked 5 blocks. How many more blocks do you need to walk?

NAME:

Number Sense

Project the scene. Ask children: *What do you notice? What do you wonder?*

Decompose 6 and 7 into all number partners. Show number partners for 6 and 7 with equations. Begin to see patterns and relationships between number partners for 6 and 7.

Investigate It

6

7

After doing the Discover It activity as a class, have children complete the Investigate It activity and record their design for 6 and their design for 7. Ask them to write a number next to each shape they used to record how many of the shape are in their design.

How do you know the design you recorded at the top has 6 pattern blocks?

Try-Discuss-Connect

6 = 2 + 4

6 = _____ + _____

6 = _____ + _____

Make sense of the problem: *The game mah-jongg has tiles with numbers and colorful designs. This tile breaks 6 apart into 2 and 4. How else could you break 6 into two parts?* Have children show two ways to break apart 6 by drawing on the tiles and filling in the equations.

How did you decide how to break 6 into two parts?

Break and Slide Activity

______ = ______ + ______

After children have completed several rounds of the Break and Slide Activity, have them draw cubes and write numbers to record one set of number partners for 6 or 7.

What is another equation you could write that uses the same numbers?

NAME:

Practice

Match

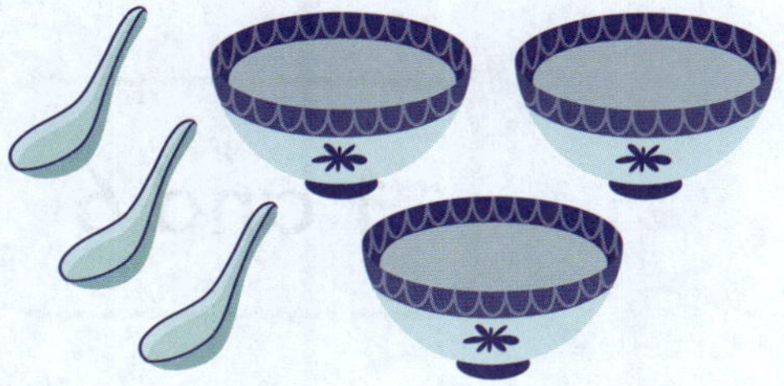

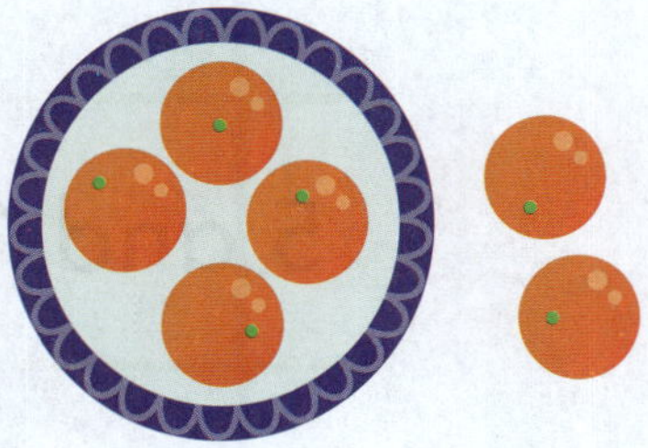

2 and 5

3 and 3

4 and 2

Have children identify the number of objects in each group. Then have them draw lines to match each group to the number partners that describe the group.

Practice

Match

1 and 6

4 and 3

5 and 1

Have children identify the number of objects in each group. Then have them draw lines to match each group to the number partners that describe the group.

NAME:

Try-Discuss-Connect

7 = ______ + ______

Make sense of the problem: *Look at the number cards. Find two cards that are number partners for 7.* Have children circle two number cards to show number partners for 7. Then have them fill in the equation.

How did you decide which cards to circle?

Domino Dots Activity

6: 7:

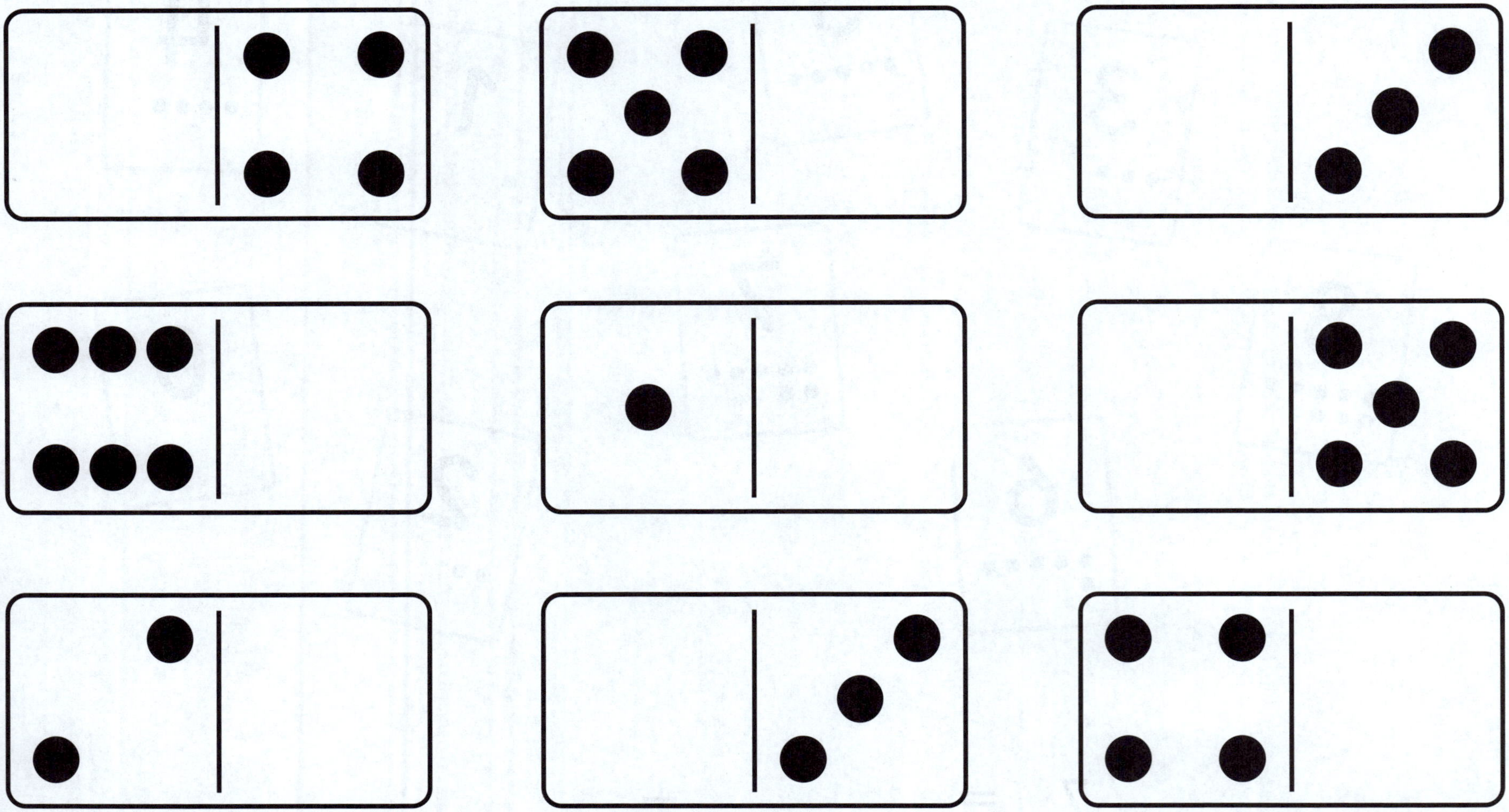

Have children use the dominoes to complete the activity. One child spins the spinner, draws dots on a domino to make the target number, and colors the domino to match the target number color. Group members take turns until they fill the workmat.

How did you know how many dots to draw on a domino?

NAME:

Practice

Draw Write

Example

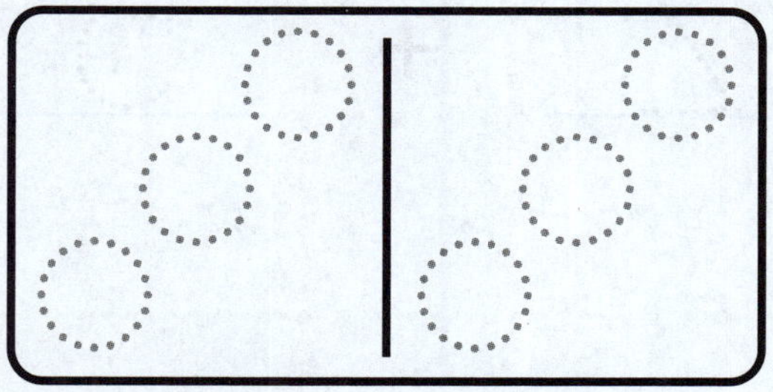

6 = 3 + 3

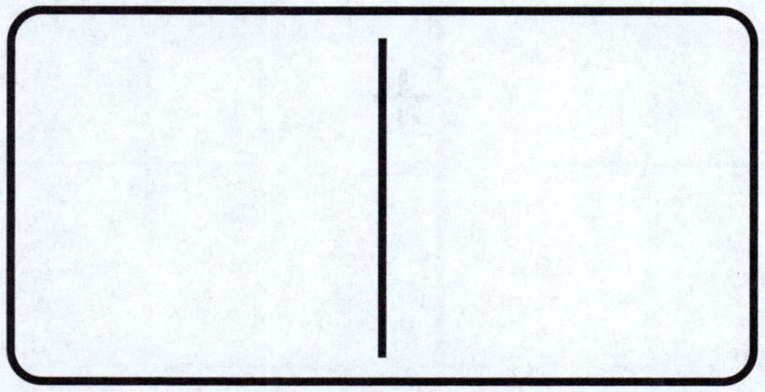

6 = 4 + 2

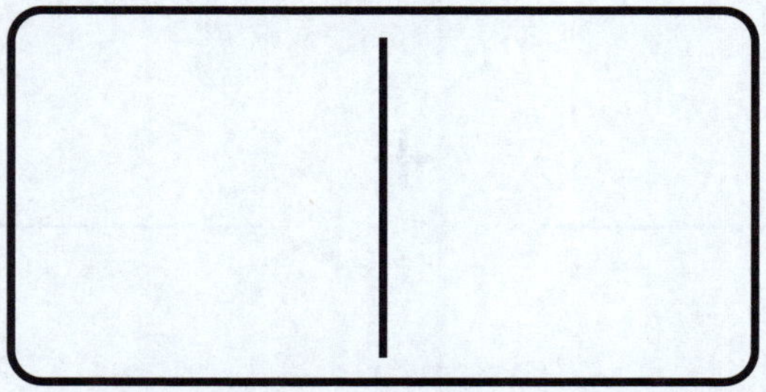

6 = ____ + ____

Have children draw dots on each domino to show number partners for 6. Then have them record the number partners for 6 as an equation.

Practice

Draw Write

7 = 2 + 5

7 = ___ + ___

7 = ___ + ___

Have children draw dots on each domino to show number partners for 7. Then have them record the number partners for 7 as an equation.

Make Connections

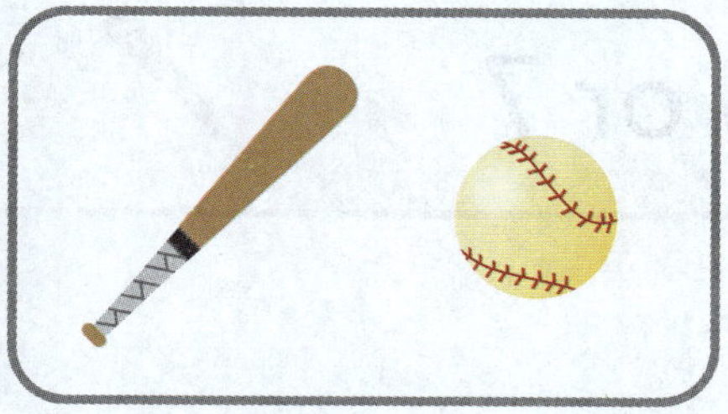

6 = ______ + ______

7 = ______ + ______

Have children draw bats and baseballs to show number partners for 6 or 7. Then have them fill in the equations.

Make 6 or 7 Activity

6 or 7 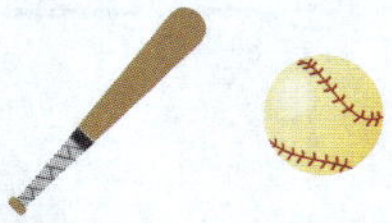

_____ = _____ + _____

_____ = _____ + _____

_____ = _____ + _____

_____ = _____ + _____

Ask children to circle 6 or 7 at the top of the page. Have them draw bats and baseballs to show different number partners for the number they circled. Then have children fill in the equations to record the number partners.

NAME:

Practice

Write Draw

Example

6

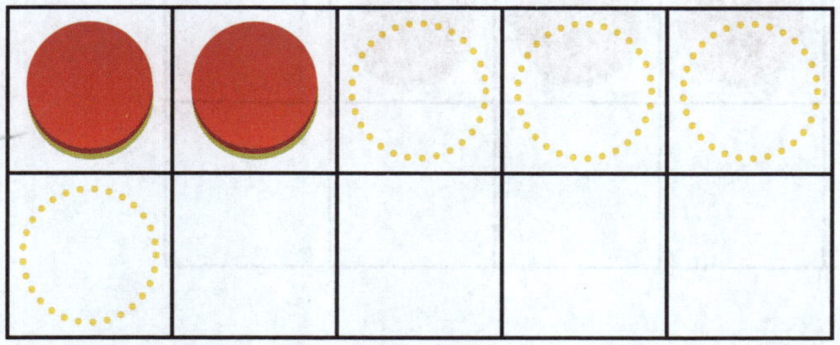

2

4

6

1

7

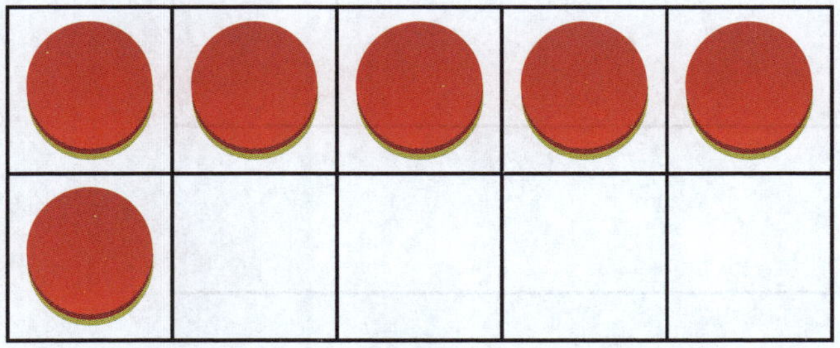

Have children trace the numbers on the left and draw counters in the 10-frames to show a total of 6 or 7. On the right, have children write the number of red counters shown and the number of counters drawn to make the total.

Practice

Write Draw

7 ______

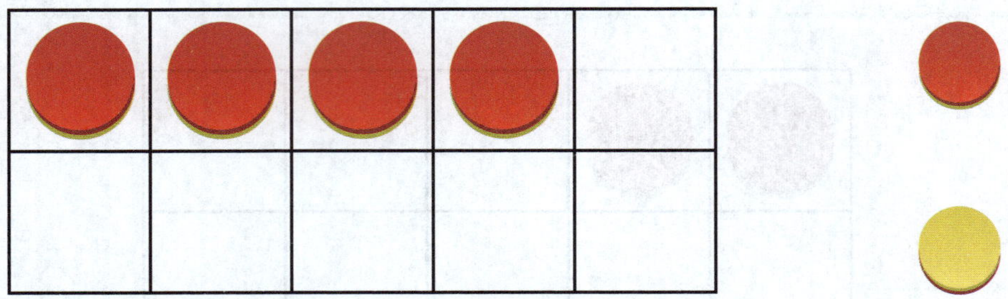

6 ______

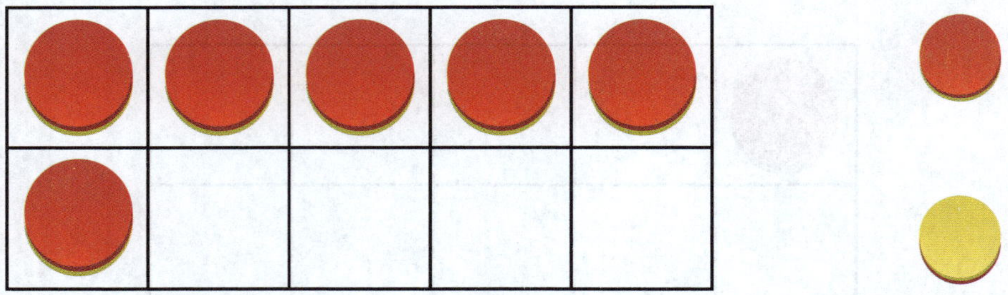

7 ______

Have children trace the numbers on the left and draw counters in the 10-frames (if needed) to make 6 or 7. On the right, have children write the number of red counters shown and the number of counters drawn to make the total.

NAME:

Analyze It

Read the problem: *The cat and dog both used counters and an equation to show number partners for 7. Do you agree with the cat, the dog, or both? Why?* Have children circle who they agree with.

Lesson Reflection

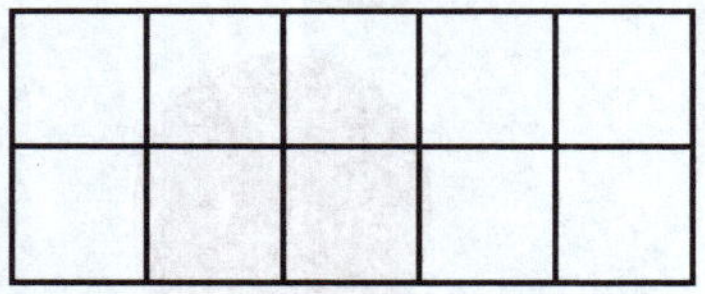

____ = ____ + ____

2 1 3

Have children use numbers, words, or drawings to show something they learned or did in this lesson to show number partners for 6 or 7.

NAME:

Practice

Circle Color

6: 7:

6	1	1	3	3	6
7	3	0	7	2	2
5	2	8	2	9	1
8	3	9	4	8	0
5	4	5	1	4	6

Have children circle as many number partners for 6 as they can find in one color and color the key for 6 with the same color. Then have them circle as many number partners for 7 as they can find in another color and color the key for 7 with the same color.

Practice

Color

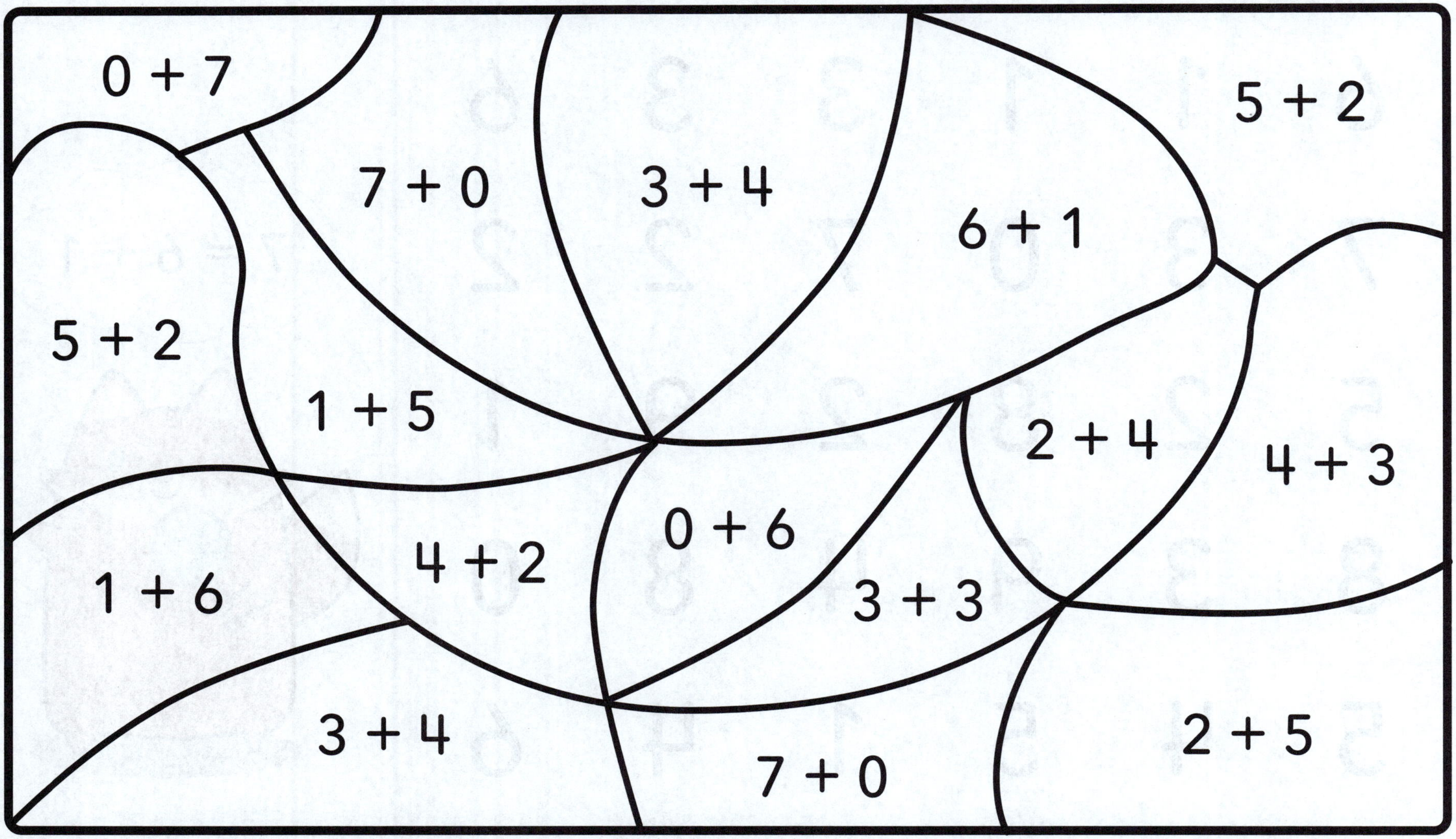

Read the following riddle: *I am a fruit that you eat at lunch. I come in a group called a bunch.* Ask children to color the spaces that show partners for 6 in yellow and spaces that show partners for 7 in blue.

Family Letters are also available in multiple languages.

LESSON 19

Compose and Decompose 8 and 9

Dear Family,

In this lesson, your child is learning to find number partners that make 8 and 9.

You can think of numbers as being made up of lesser numbers. For example, you can make 8 by putting together 4 and 4, 5 and 3, 6 and 2, 7 and 1, or 8 and 0, with the numbers in either order.

More about the Math

Recognizing number partners will help your child prepare for adding and subtracting. For example, knowing that you can break apart 8 into a group of 4 and another group of 4 lays the foundation for solving 4 + 4 = ? and 8 – 4 = ?.

In class, your child will show different ways to break apart 8 and 9 with counters in a 10-frame. Working with a 10-frame helps your child relate numbers to quantities. It also helps to develop an understanding of how numbers relate to 5 and 10, which will be important for later work with greater numbers.

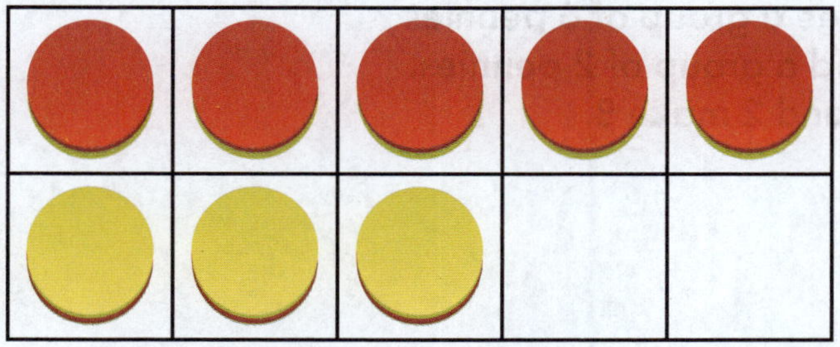

5 and 3 make 8

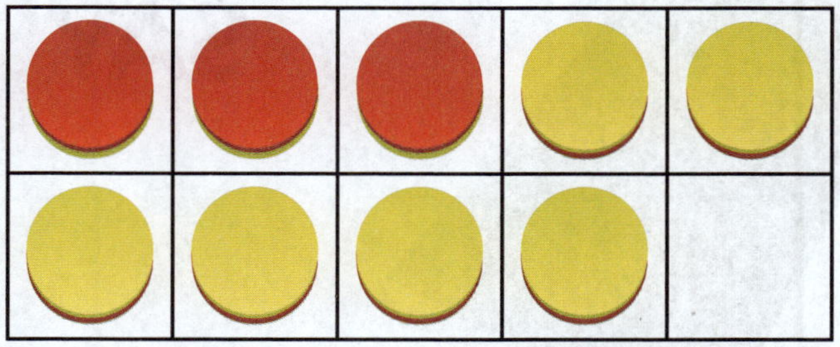

3 and 6 make 9

i-Ready Connect

Learning Games

- Hungry Guppy
- Hungry Fish

Digital Math Tools

- Counters and Connecting Cubes

Make 8 and 9

Do this activity with your child to practice making 8 and 9.

Materials: 9 pennies (or other small objects), paper, 1 cup

- Use the base of a cup to trace a circle on a piece of paper. Then place 8 pennies in the cup.
- Put the paper with the circle on a table, and spill the pennies out onto the paper.
- Ask your child to group the pennies based on how many are inside the circle and how many are outside the circle. For example, your child may see a group of 6 pennies outside the circle and a group of 2 pennies inside the circle.
- Have your child **SAY** how the groups make 8.
- Repeat several times to find different ways to make 8.
- Then repeat the activity with 9 pennies to find ways to make 9.

Math on the GO!

Conversation Starter

Look for situations to find number partners for 6 and 7 in real-world situations. For example:

- If your child has 4 grapes, how many grapes do they need to make 9?
- If you want to run 8 miles this week and you already ran 3 miles, how many miles do you still need to run to make 8?

SAY I see a group of 6 pennies and a group of 2 pennies. 6 and 2 make 8.

NAME:

Number Sense

Project the scene. Ask children: *What do you notice? What do you wonder?*

Decompose 8 and 9 into all number partners. Show number partners for 8 and 9 with equations. Begin to see patterns and relationships between number partners for 8 and 9.

Investigate It

______ = ______ + ______

After doing the Discover It activity as a class, have children complete the Investigate It activity. Ask them to write 8 or 9 in the box and then draw and write an equation to record the ways they modeled a pair of number partners for that number.

How do your models show the number partners for 8 or 9?

NAME:

Try-Discuss-Connect

8 = ______ + ______

Make sense of the problem: *There are 8 skaters. They all wear winter hats. Each hat is either red or blue. How many could be red? How many could be blue? Show how you know.* Have children color some hats red and the rest of the hats blue. Then have them fill in the equation.

Why is it okay if you and your partner showed a different number of red hats and blue hats?

Number Partner Match Up Activity

$8 =$ ______ $+$ ______

$9 =$ ______ $+$ ______

After children have completed several rounds of the Number Partner Match Up Activity, have them record one set of number partners for 8 and one set of number partners for 9 by writing on the cards. Then have children write an equation for each set of number partners.

How did you know when two cards showed number partners for 8 or 9?

NAME:

Practice

Draw Write

Example

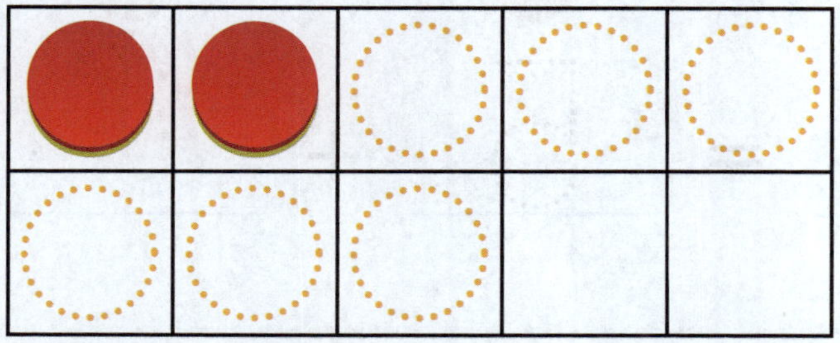

8 = 2 + 6

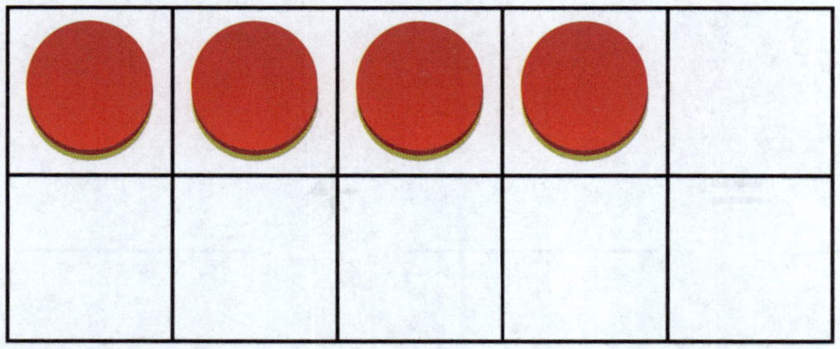

8 = ___ + ___

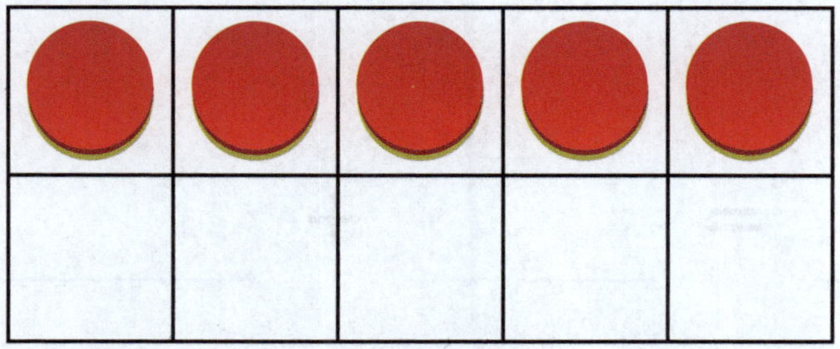

8 = ___ + ___

Have children draw counters to make 8 in each 10-frame. Then have them complete the equations to show number partners for 8.

Practice

Draw Write

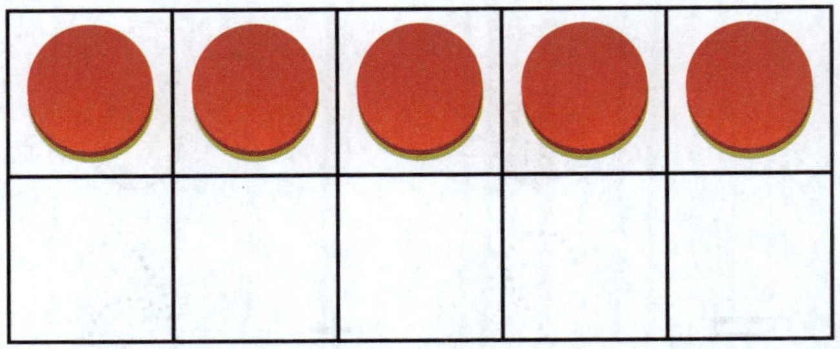

9 = 5 + ____

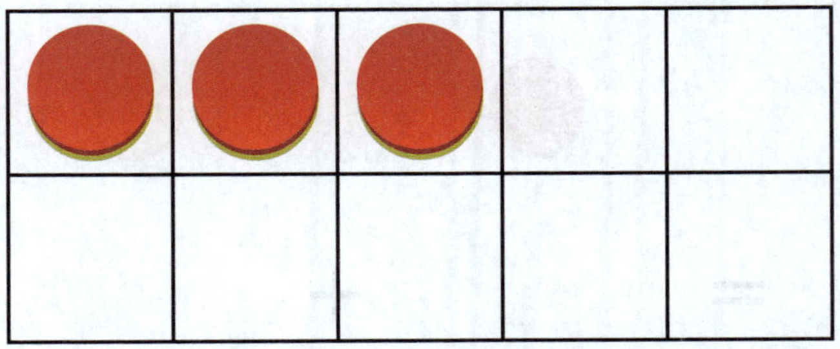

9 = ____ + ____

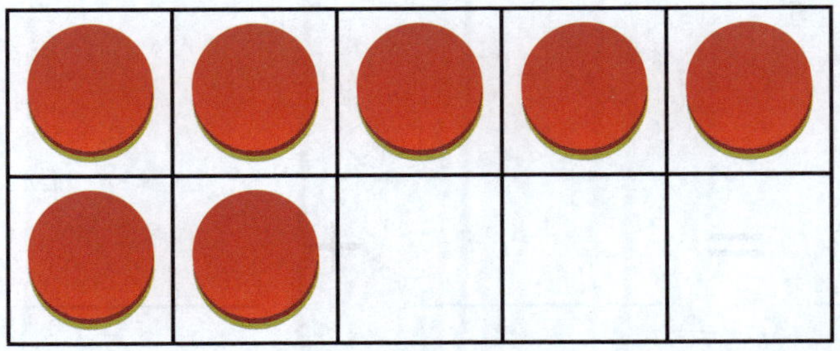

9 = ____ + ____

Have children draw counters to make 9 in each 10-frame. Then have them complete the equations to show number partners for 9.

NAME:

Try-Discuss-Connect

9 = ______ + ______

Make sense of the problem: *There are 9 snow animals. Each has either a hat or a scarf. How many could be wearing a hat? A scarf? Show how you know.* Have children draw a hat or a scarf on each snow animal. Then have them complete the equation.

What other equation can you write using the same number partners?

Number Partner Dots Activity

6: 7: 8: 9:

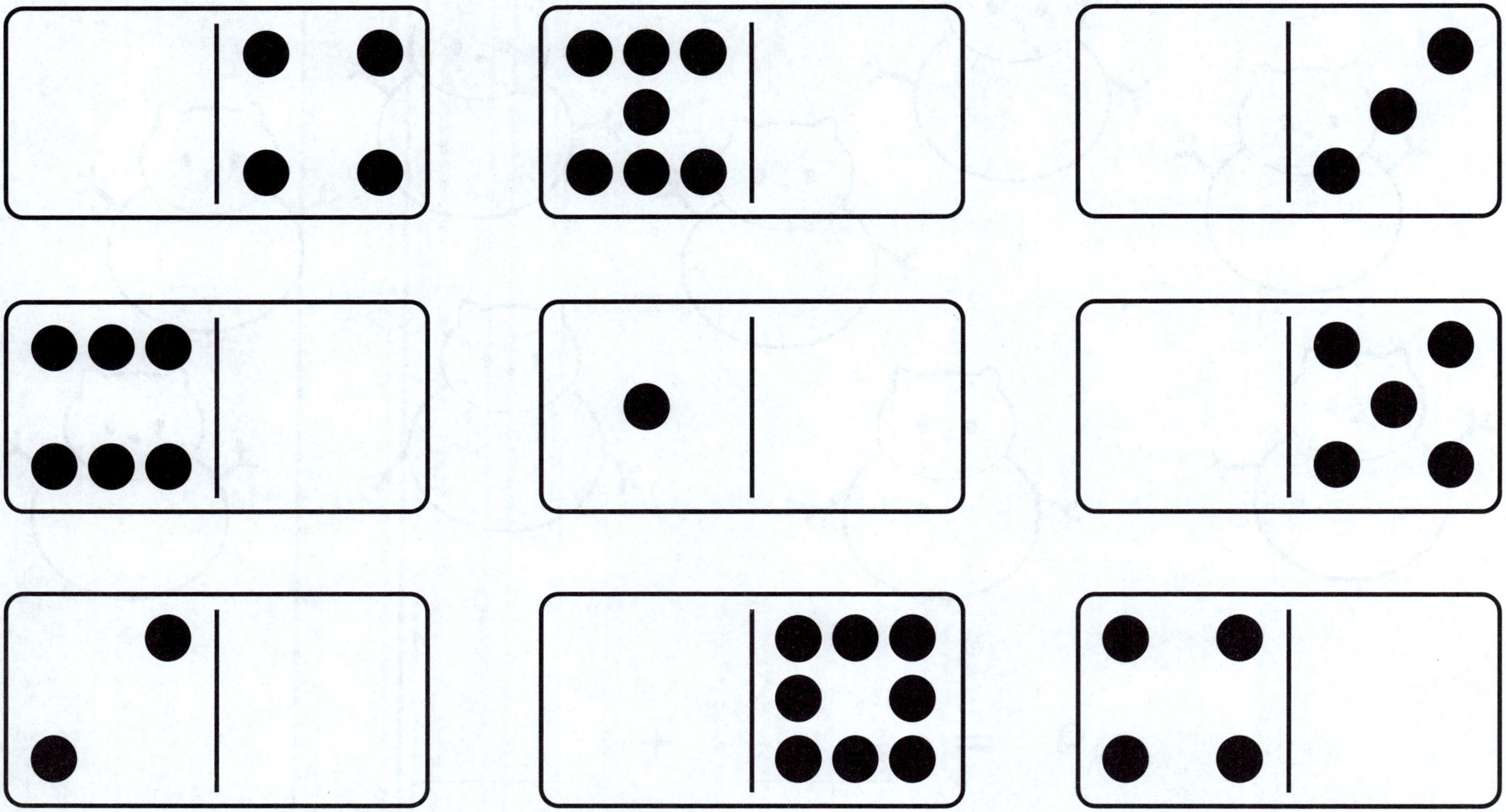

Have children use the dominoes to complete the activity. One child spins the spinner, draws dots on a domino to make the target number, and colors the domino to match the target number color. Group members take turns until they fill the workmat.

How do you know the domino shows 6, 7, 8, or 9?

NAME:

Practice

Draw Write

Example

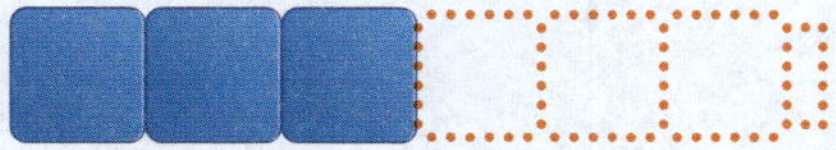

6 = 3 + 3

7 = ___ + ___

8 = ___ + ___

9 = ___ + ___

Have children draw more connecting cubes in a different color to show the total number.
Then have them write the numbers to complete the equation.

Practice

Draw Write

6 = 5 + ____

7 = ____ + ____

8 = ____ + ____

9 = ____ + ____

Have children draw more connecting cubes in a different color to show the total number. Then have them write the numbers to complete the equation.

Make Connections

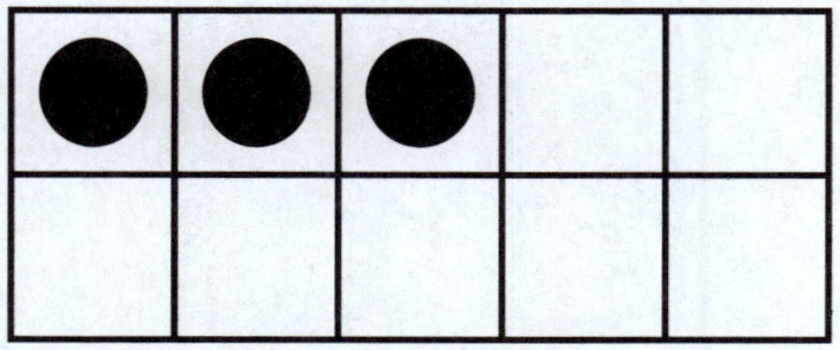
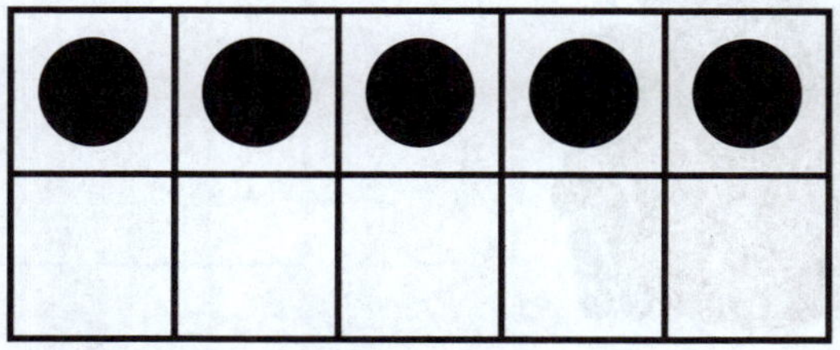
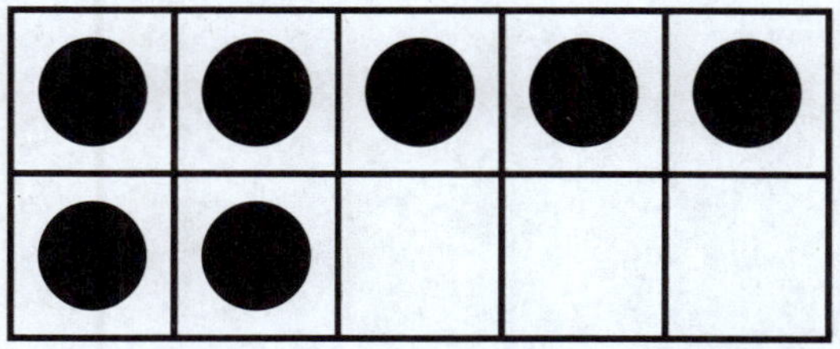

8 = ______ + ______

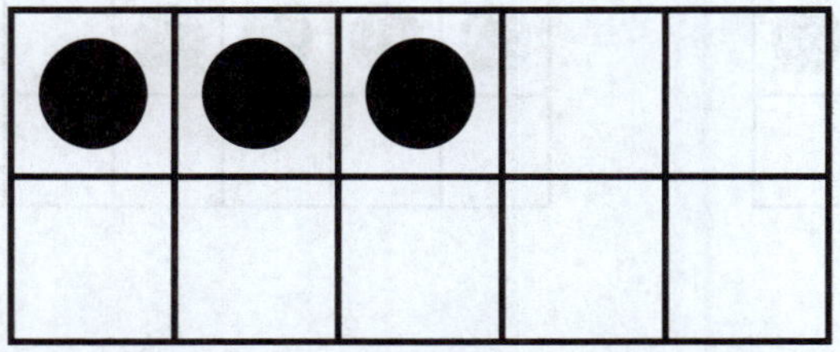
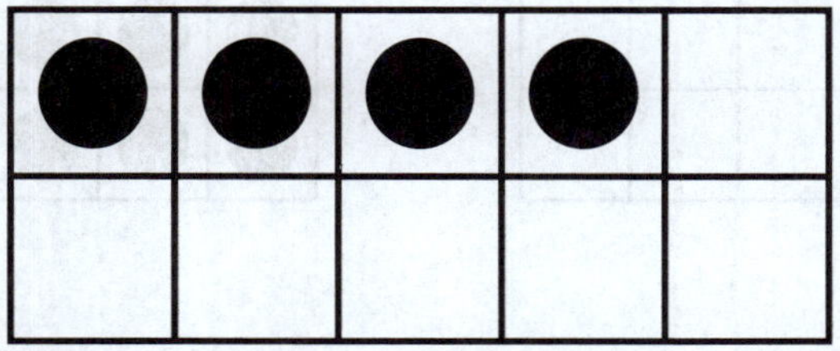
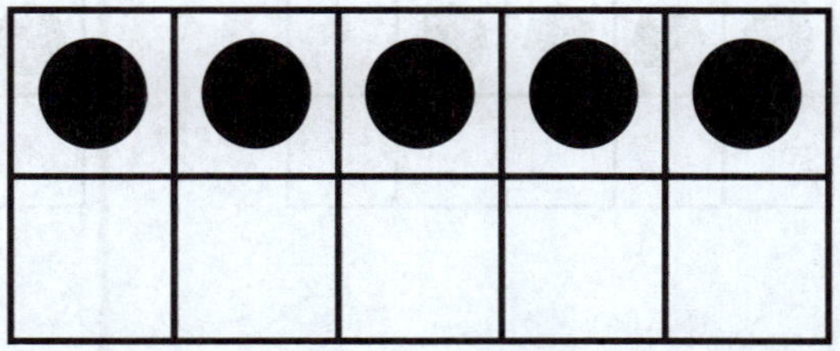

9 = ______ + ______

Have children color two of the 10-frames at the top of the page that show number partners for 8 and complete the equation. Then have them color two of the 10-frames at the bottom of the page that show number partners for 9 and complete the equation.

Color Number Partners Activity

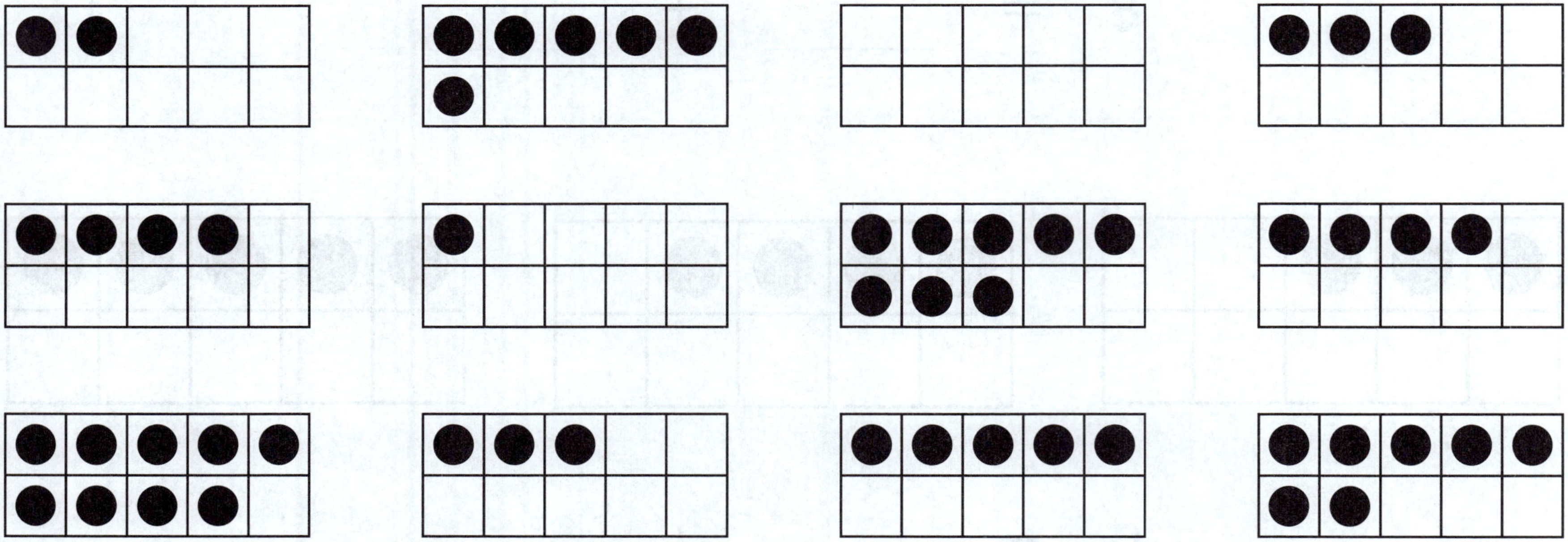

Have children write 8 or 9 at the top of the page. Ask children to color 10-frames that show number partners for the number. Have them color each pair of number partners a different color.

NAME:

Practice

Draw Write

Example

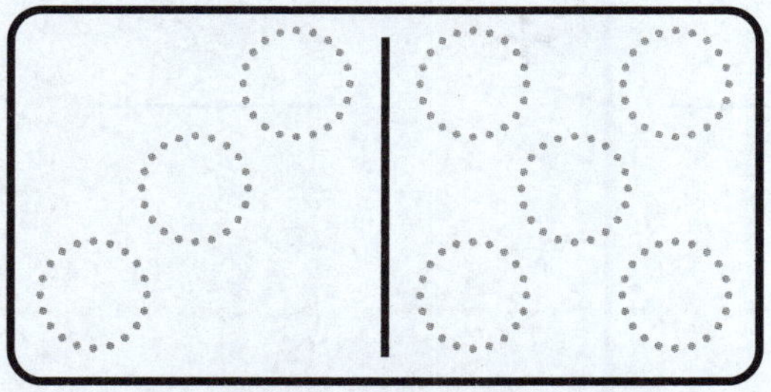

8 = 3 + 5

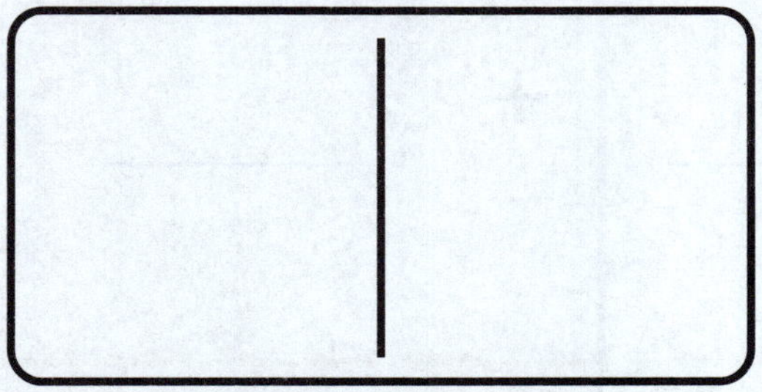

8 = ____ + ____

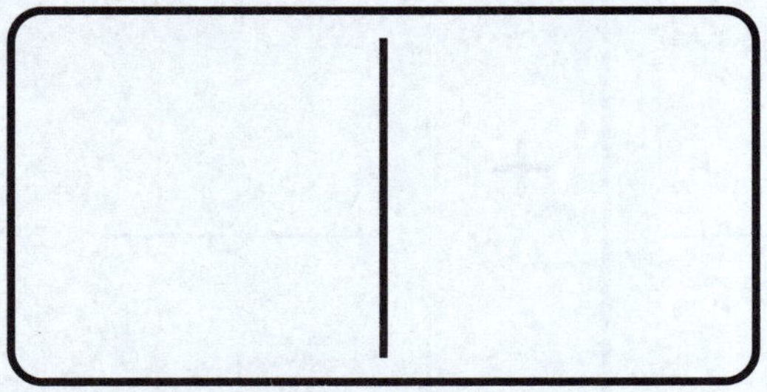

8 = ____ + ____

Have children draw dots to show number partners for 8. Then have them complete the equations to show the same number partners for 8.

Practice

Draw Write

9 = ___ + ___

9 = ___ + ___

9 = ___ + ___

Have children draw dots to show number partners for 9. Then have them complete the equations to show the same number partners for 9.

NAME:

Analyze It

Read the problem: *The cat and dog both used counters to show number partners for 9. Do you agree with the cat, the dog, or both? Why?* Have children circle who they agree with.

Lesson Reflection

_____ = _____ + _____

2 1 3

Have children use numbers, words, or drawings to show something they learned or did in this lesson to show number partners for 8 or 9.

Practice

Match

8: 9:

Have children draw lines to match birds to nests. Have them use one color for lines showing number partners for 8 and a different color for lines showing number partners for 9.

Practice

Write Color 8: 9:

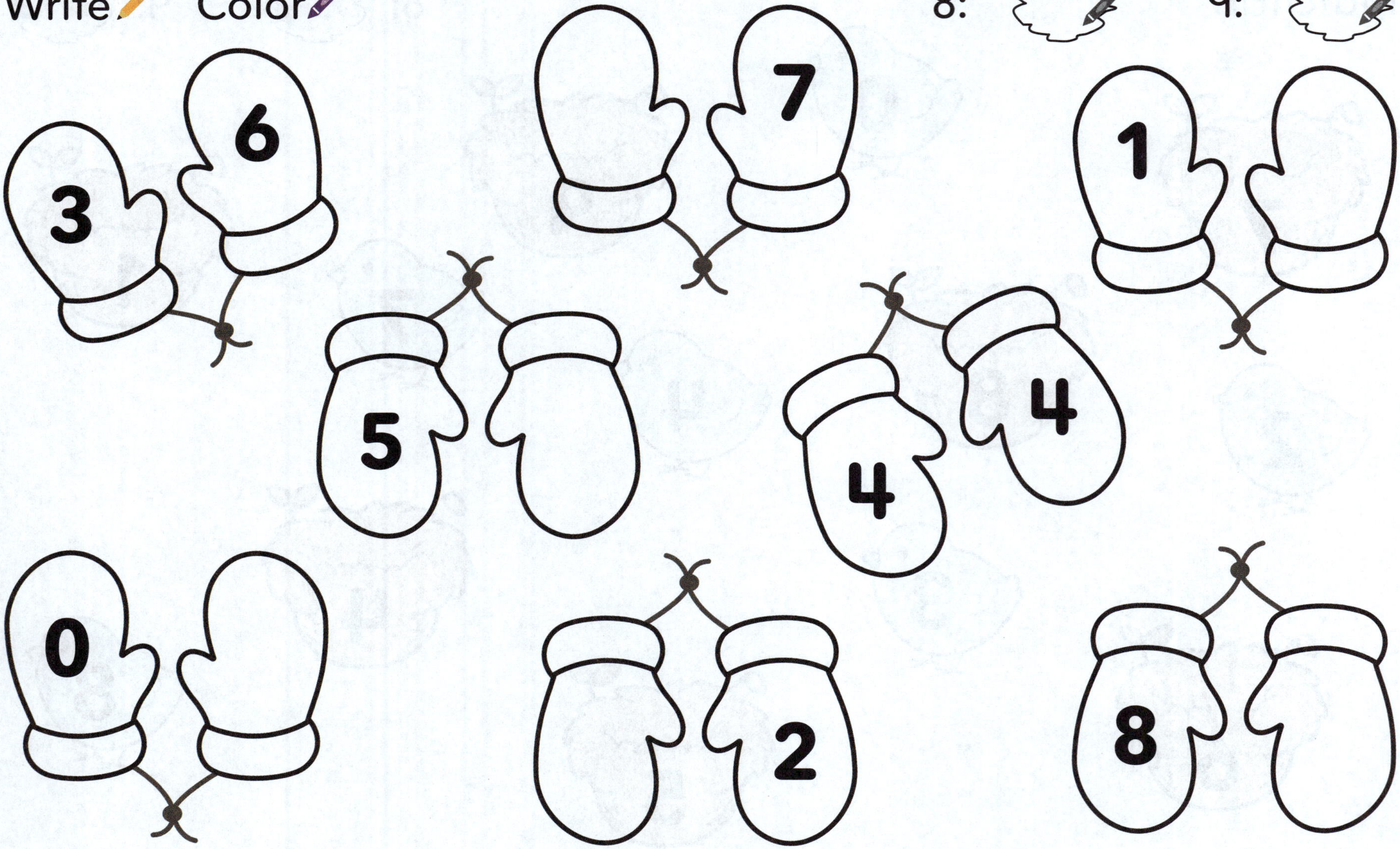

Have children write to show partners for 8 or 9 on each pair of mittens. Then have them color mittens that show number partners for 8 in one color and mittens that show number partners for 9 in another color.

NAME:

Design a Class Garden

What do you want in your garden?

Have children design a vegetable garden with more than one kind of plant. Children can show the plants they want by drawing a symbol from the class garden key inside each square.

Design a Garden with Groups

What do you want in your garden?

Have children use groups of 8 to design a new vegetable garden with more than one kind of plant. Children can show the plants they want by drawing a symbol from the class garden key inside each square.

Where did you use groups of 8 in your garden?

NAME: ______________________ UNIT 5

My Garden Information

Have children make a shopping list for their garden with groups of 8. Have them draw a symbol for each kind of plant they used and then record how many of each they need.

What is the same about your shopping lists? What is different?

Reflection

What do you notice and wonder about the class data display?

I notice:	I wonder:

Have children notice and wonder about the class data display. Have them answer one of their questions using numbers, words, drawings, objects, and/or gestures.

NAME:

Show What You Learned

Have children draw to show what they learned about numbers from 1 to 100. Prompt children to reflect on their learning by posing questions such as: *What do you know how to do well? What math could you use in your everyday life? What is a question you still have?*

Circle

4 and 1

5 and 1

6 and 0

Color

For the first problem, have children count the objects in the group and then circle the number partners that describe the group. For the next problem, have children count the shaded circles. Then have them count on, coloring more circles until they count to 20.

NAME:

Circle

15 16 17

Draw Write

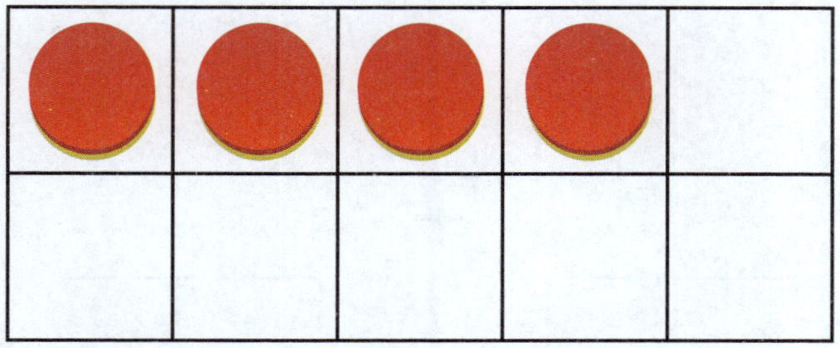

8 = ______ + ______

For the first problem, have children count the counters and then circle the number that shows how many. For the next problem, have children draw counters to make 8 in the 10-frame. Then have them complete the equation to show the number partners for 8.

Draw

19

Draw Write

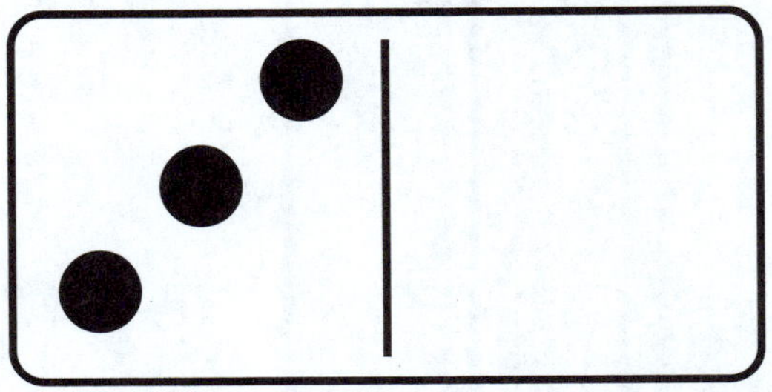

7 = ____ + ____

Draw Write

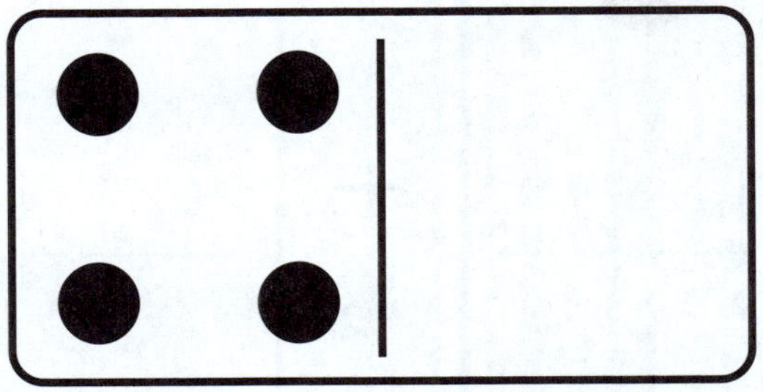

9 = ____ + ____

For the first problem, have children draw the given number of objects. For the last two problems, have children draw dots on each domino to show number partners for 7 or 9. Then have children record the number partners as an equation.

Addition and Subtraction Within 10

UNIT 6

Show What You Know

Have children draw to show what they know about addition and subtraction. Tell children that after they have completed the unit, they will draw to show what they learned.

My Words

Mathematical

addition

equal sign (=)

equation

subtraction

Academic

represent

start

Have children choose 2 to 4 words and show what they know about them using pictures, numbers, or words. Have children share their representations with peers.

To support children with word selection, ask:

- *Which words are new to you?*
- *Which words do you think are the most important? Why?*

Family Letters are also available in multiple languages.

LESSON 20

Add Within 10

Dear Family,

In this lesson, your child is solving addition problems with totals up to 10. Your child will continue to connect story problems to pictures, objects, models, and equations. In class, your child may also model addition problems with fingers, which can useful and easily available tools for adding.

More about the Math

Your child will find two numbers that add up to a given total using tools such as counters and 10-frames. Your child will also add two numbers that have a total up to 10. Working with 10-frames can help children more easily visualize numbers as quantities, which is important for building addition skills. Because a 10-frame is made up of 10 boxes arranged in 2 rows of 5, it can help your child see how the numbers being added (and the total) relate to both 5 and 10. This will be useful for understanding later work with greater numbers.

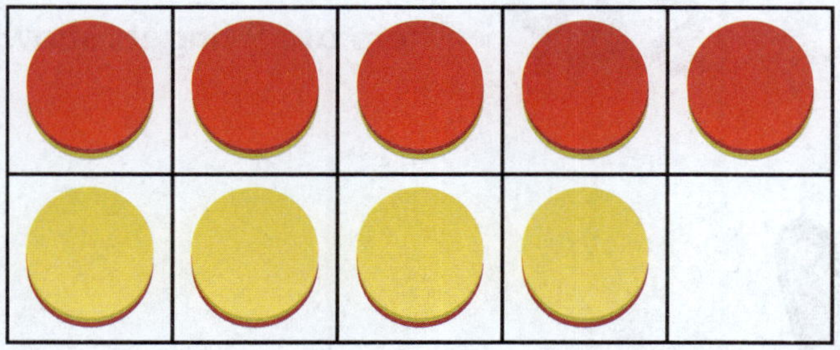

$5 + 4 = 9$

i-Ready Connect

Learning Games

- Hungry Fish
- Match

Digital Math Tools

- Counters and Connecting Cubes

ACTIVITY

Adding With Fingers

Do this activity with your child to explore adding up to 10.

- Have your child show how to use their fingers to solve 5 + 4.
- Next, place your hands under a blanket and say: *I have 5 fingers up on one hand and 4 up on the other. How many fingers do I have up?*
- Have your child model the story with their fingers to determine the total.
- Encourage your child to count and **SAY** how many fingers they are holding up.
- Allow your child to uncover your hands to see if the numbers of fingers you are both holding up match.
- Repeat with more simple stories using other number combinations (for example, 7 + 1, 6 + 3, 8 + 2, and so on).

5 + 4

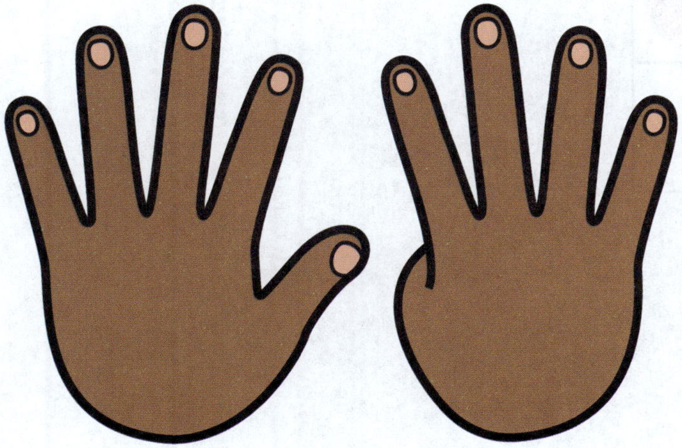

SAY There are 9 fingers showing!

Math on the GO!

Conversation Starter

Look for opportunities to add up to 10 in real-world situations. For example:

- If there are 3 dogs at the park and 4 dogs join them, how many dogs are at the park now?
- If your child borrowed 5 books from the library on Monday and borrowed 2 more books from the library on Tuesday, how many books have they borrowed?

NAME:

Number Sense

Project the scene. Ask children: *What do you notice? What do you wonder?*

Solve addition problems up to 10 using manipulatives.

Investigate It

1	2	3	4	5	6	7	8	9	10

______ + ______ = ______

1	2	3	4	5	6	7	8	9	10

______ + ______ = ______

After doing the Discover It activity as a class, have children complete the Investigate It activity and record two of their results.

How can you use a number path to solve an addition problem?

NAME:

Try-Discuss-Connect

1	2	3	4	5	6	7	8	9	10

_____ + _____ = _____

Make sense of the problem: *There are 9 soccer balls. Some are black and white. Some are colorful. Use the number path to show how many of each. Then write an equation to match.*

How many soccer balls could be black and white? How many could be colorful?

Addition Tales Activity

____ + ____ = 5

____ + ____ = 8

____ + ____ = 6

____ + ____ = 9

____ + ____ = 7

____ + ____ = 10

Have children tell an addition story problem to their partner. Have partners solve the problem and record an equation to match.

How did you find an answer to the story problems?

NAME:

Practice

Match

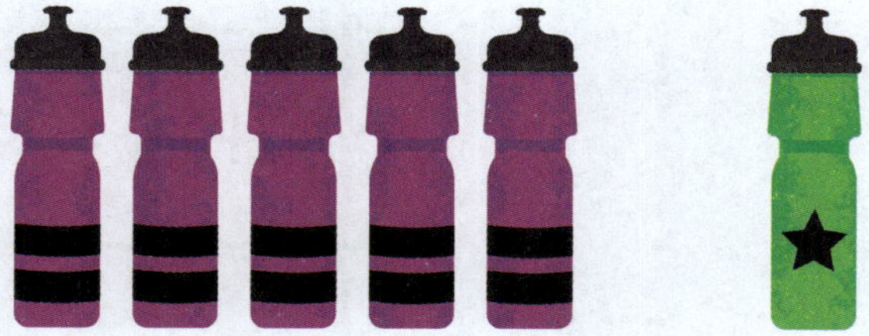

$5 + 1 = 6$

$6 + 2 = 8$

$3 + 4 = 7$

Have children describe the two groups and the total in each picture. Read each equation aloud together. Then have children draw lines to match each picture to an equation.

Practice

Match

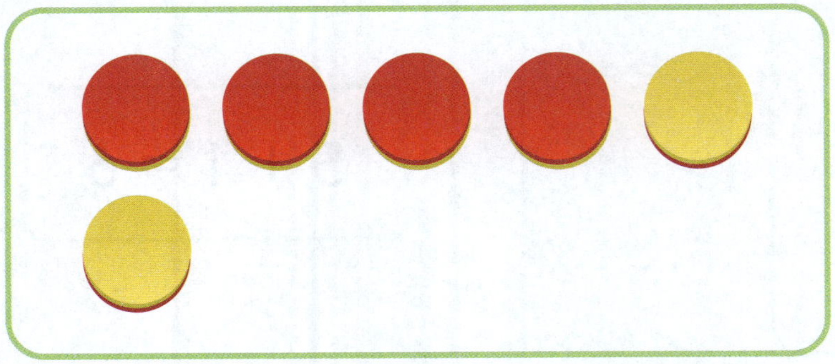

3 + 6 = 9

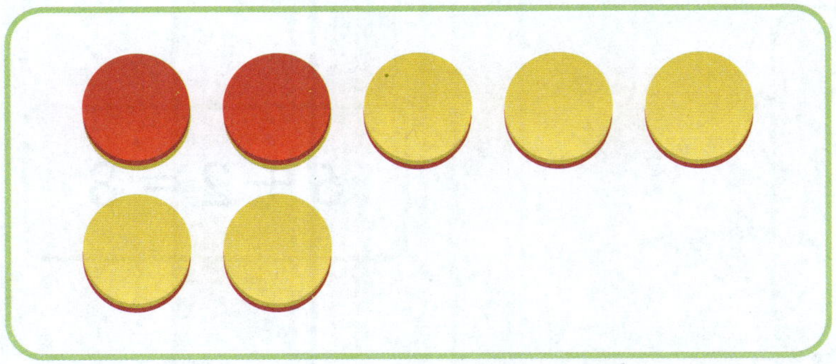

4 + 2 = 6

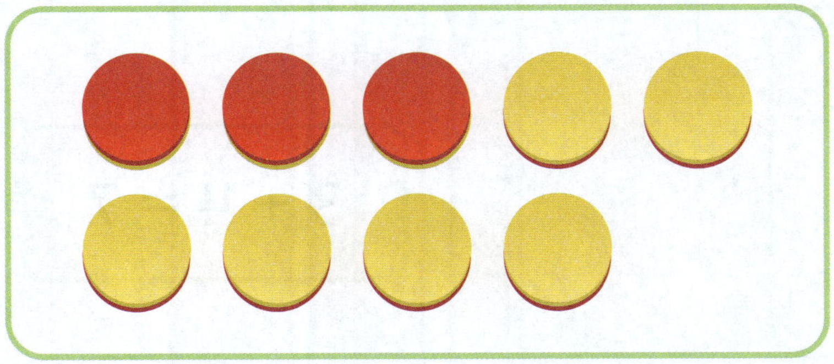

2 + 5 = 7

Have children describe the counters and the total in each group. Read each equation aloud together. Then have children draw lines to match each group of counters to an equation.

NAME:

Try-Discuss-Connect

_____ ◯ _____ ◯ _____

Make sense of the problem: *There are 7 juice boxes. Some are apple juice and some are grape juice. How many of each could there be?* Have children color some juice boxes one color and the rest another color to show how many of each kind and then write an equation.

How did you decide how many juice boxes are apple juice and how many are grape juice?

Number Partner Search Activity

6	0	1	2	3	4	5	6	7	8	9
7	0	1	2	3	4	5	6	7	8	9
8	0	1	2	3	4	5	6	7	8	9
9	0	1	2	3	4	5	6	7	8	9

Have children use the spinner to find a target number. Using a different color for each set, children color the number partners with the same total. Once all number partners are found for a number, have children circle the number at the beginning of the row.

How did you choose numbers that add up to the number on the spinner?

NAME:

Practice

Draw Write

Example

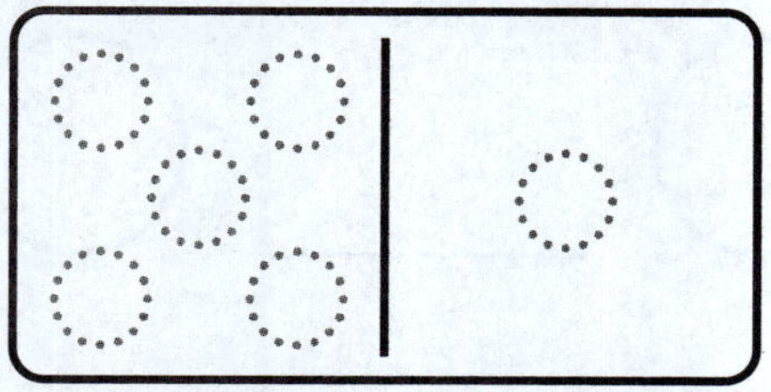

5 (+) 1 (=) 6

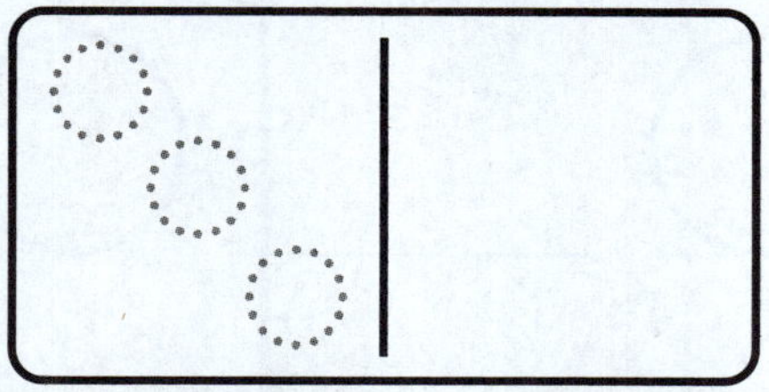

3 ○ ___ ○ 7

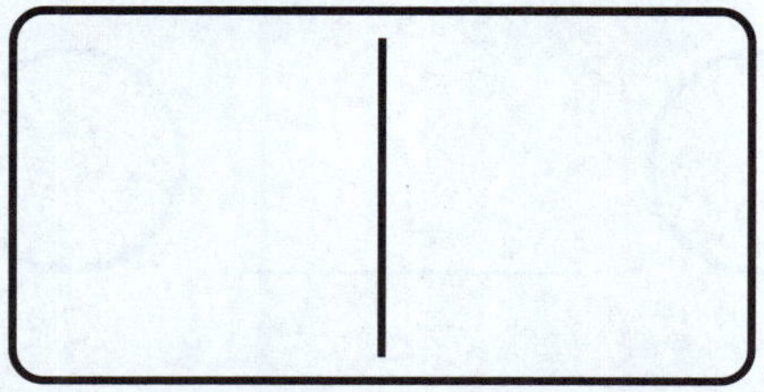

___ ○ 4 ○ 8

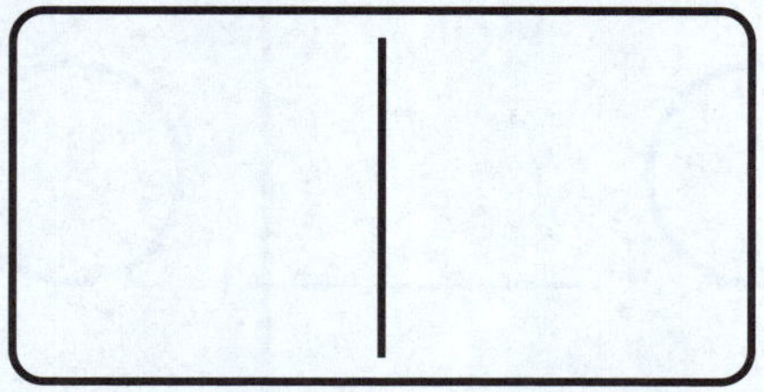

7 ○ ___ ○ 9

Have children draw dots on each domino to show number partners for the total. Then have them write an equation that represents the dots on each domino.

Practice

Draw Write

____ ○ ____ ○ 6

____ ○ ____ ○ 7

____ ○ ____ ○ 8

____ ○ ____ ○ 9

Have children draw dots on each domino to show possible number partners for the total.
Then have them write an equation that represents the dots on each domino.

NAME:

Make Connections

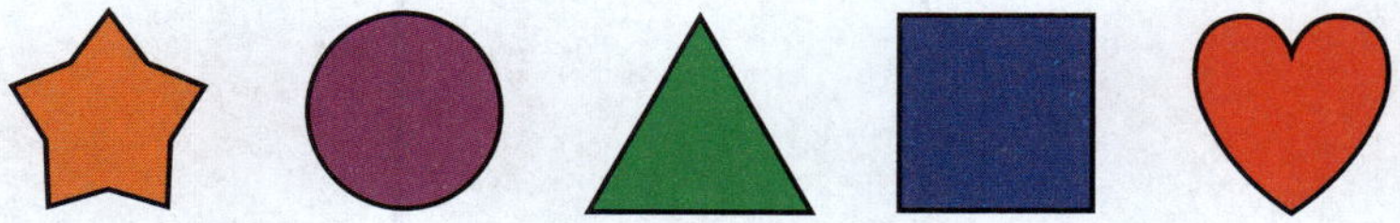

6

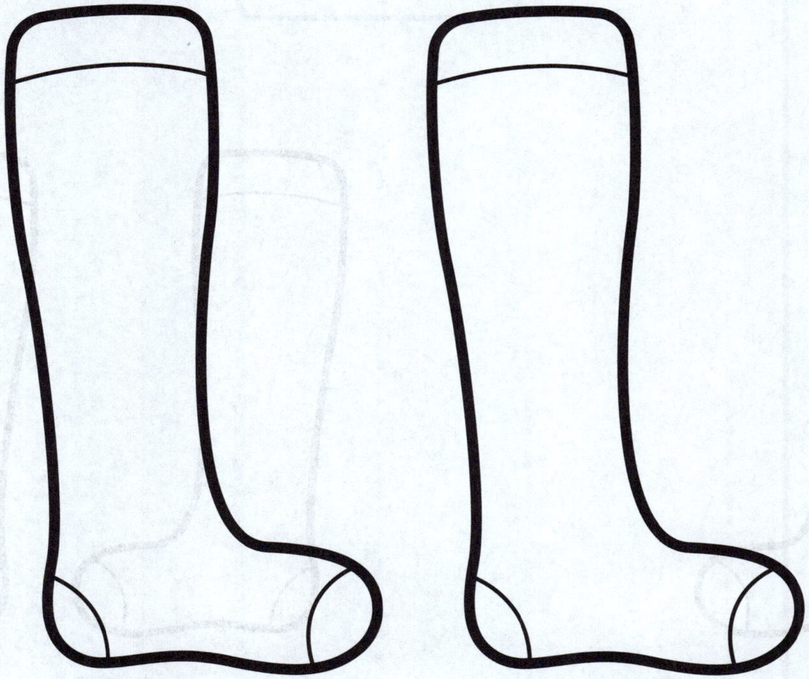

Say: *Everyone on the soccer team decorated their pair of socks with 6 shapes.* Have children draw shapes on the socks to show 6. Then have them write an equation for the total number of shapes on the socks.

Shape Number Partners Activity

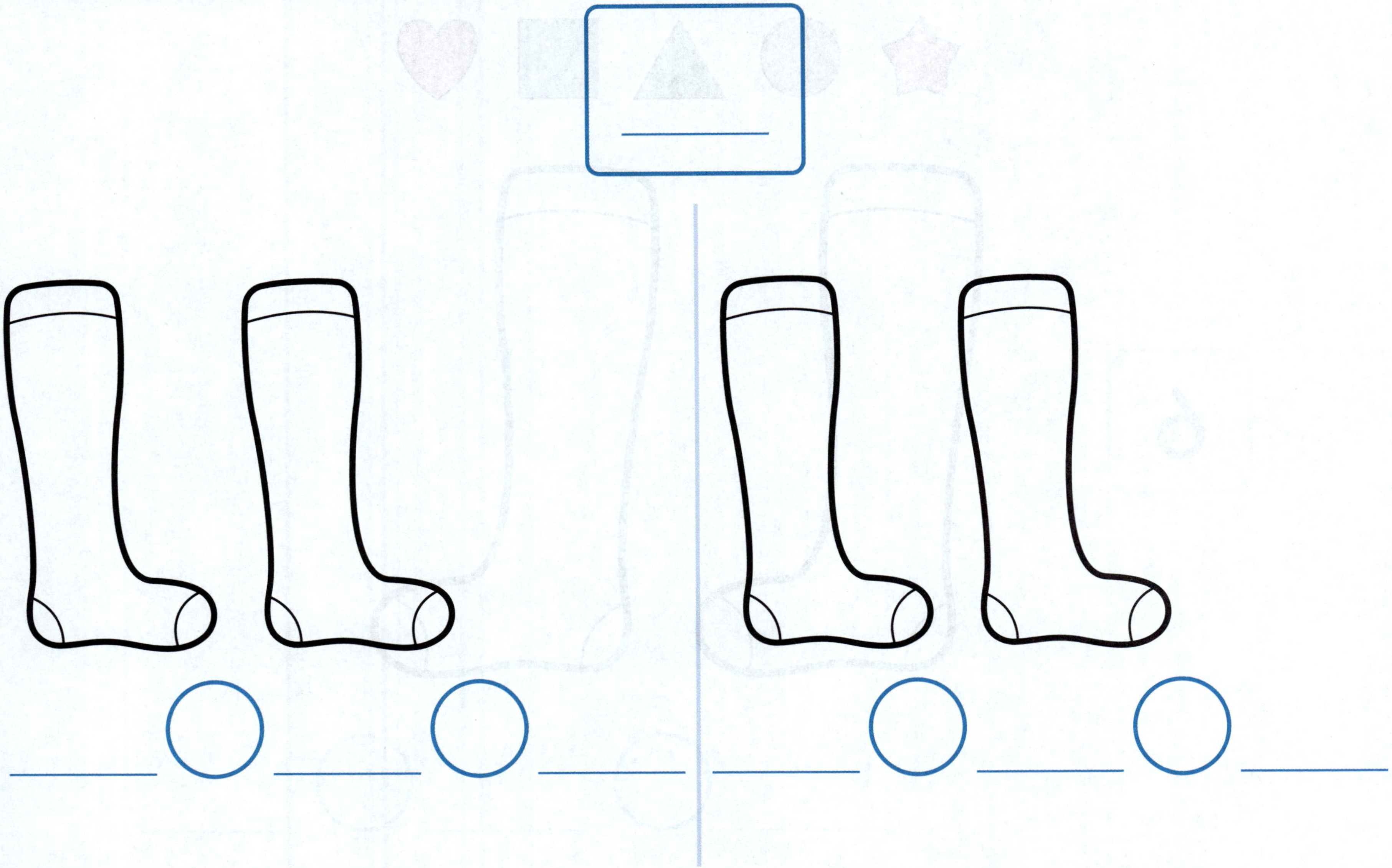

Tell children to write 7, 8, 9, or 10 in the box at the top. Then have them draw that many shapes on each pair of socks, in different ways, to show this number. Have children write an equation to record the number partners shown on each pair of socks.

NAME:

Practice

Write

Example

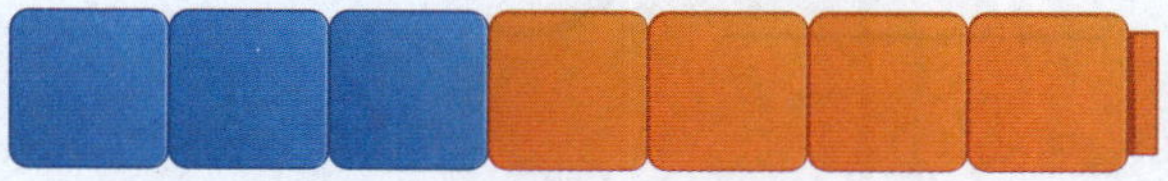

3 + 4 = 7

___ ◯ ___ ◯ ___

___ ◯ ___ ◯ ___

___ ◯ ___ ◯ ___

Have children fill in the equation for each cube train.

Practice

Write

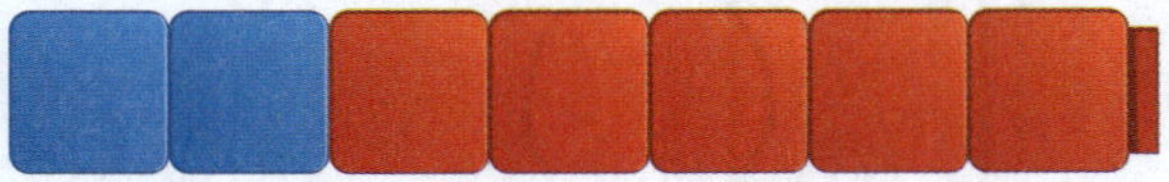

Have children fill in the equation for each cube train.

Analyze It

9

$3 + 6 = 9$

$5 + 4 = 9$

Read the problem: *The cat and dog both say their connecting cubes and equation show number partners for 9. Do you agree with the cat, the dog, or both? Why?* Have children circle who they agree with.

Lesson Reflection

1	2	3	4	5	6	7	8	9	10

___ + ___ = ___

Have children use numbers, words, or drawings to show something they learned or did in this lesson to add within 10.

NAME:

Practice

Circle Color

6 7 8 9 10

Have children circle 6, 7, 8, 9, or 10. Then have them color ways to make the circled number, using a different color for each pair of numbers.

Practice

Color

6: 7: 8: 9:

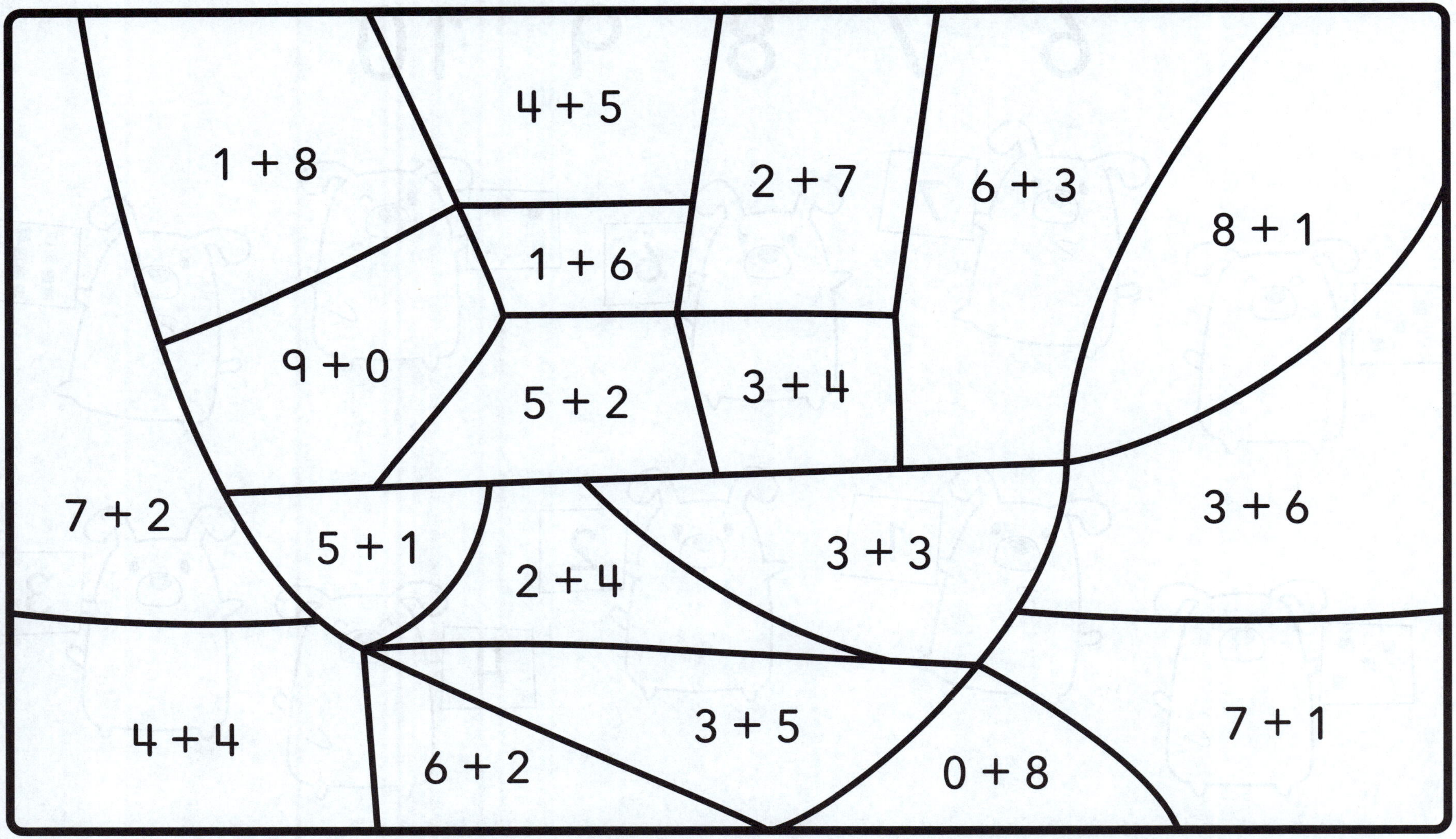

Read the following riddle: *You cannot pick me up, but I can float.* Have children color the spaces that show totals of 6, 7, 8, and 9, each in a different color.

Family Letters are also available in multiple languages.

Subtract Within 10

Dear Family,

In this lesson, your child is solving subtraction problems that involve taking away part of a group of up to 10 objects and finding how many are left. There is a continued focus on connecting story problems about subtraction to pictures, objects, models, and equations.

More about the Math

Your child will examine various models for subtracting, including using a number path. Your child will color the number path to show the first number in a subtraction equation. Then they will cross out numbers to show the second number in the subtraction equation. The answer to the subtraction problem is the number of spaces colored that are not crossed out.

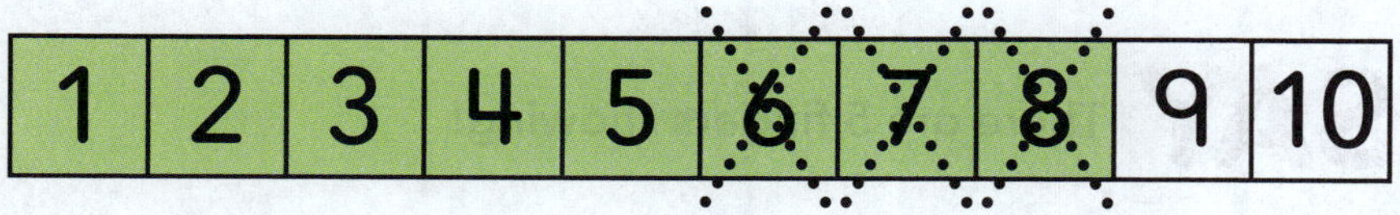

$8 - 3 = 5$

Your child will also use 10-frames to model subtraction problems by putting counters in the 10-frame to model the first number and then taking counters off the 10-frame to model the second number. The counters that remain in the 10-frame show the answer to the subtraction problem.

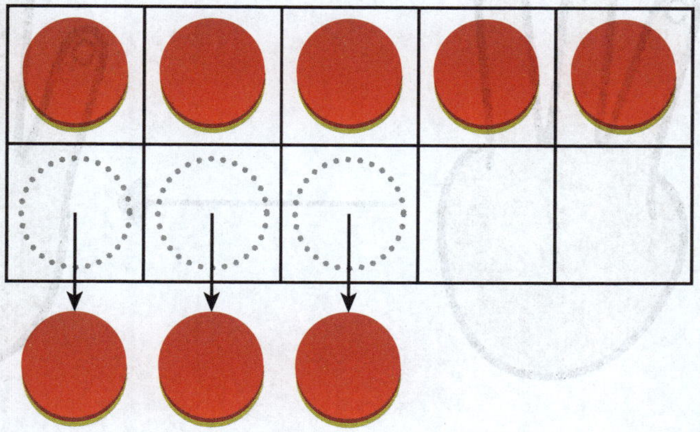

$8 - 3 = 5$

i-Ready Connect

Learning Games

 Hungry Guppy

 Hungry Fish

Digital Math Tools

Counters and Connecting Cubes

ACTIVITY

Subtracting with Fingers

Do this activity with your child to explore subtracting from 10 or less.

- Have your child show how to use their fingers to solve 8 – 3. Discuss how each number is represented with their fingers.
- Say: *I have 8 grapes. I eat 3 of them. How many grapes are left? How can we use fingers to model the problem?* Encourage your child to show 8 fingers to represent the 8 grapes.
- Ask: *Now, how can you model the 3 grapes I ate?* Have your child put down 3 fingers.
- Encourage your child to count and **SAY** how many fingers are up now.
- Ask: *What do the fingers that are up represent?* Discuss that the remaining fingers represent 5 grapes that are left.
- Repeat with more simple stories using other number combinations (for example, 7 – 1, 6 – 3, 8 – 2, and so on).

SAY There are 5 fingers showing!

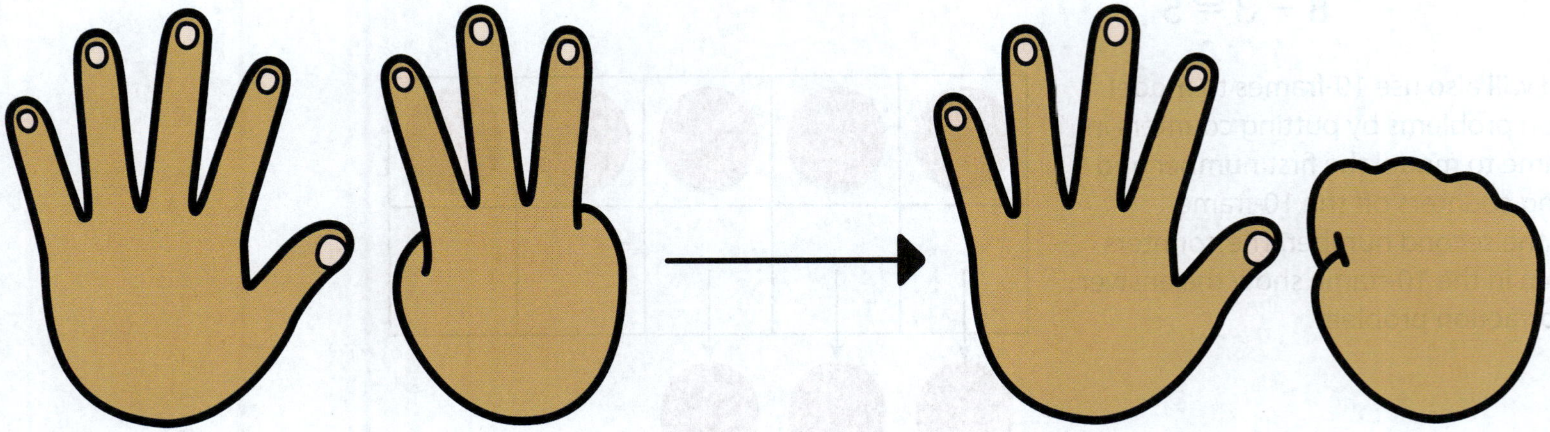

Math on the GO!

Conversation Starter

Look for opportunities to subtract from 10 or less in real-world situations. For example:

- If there are 9 peas on your plate and you eat 4 of them, how many peas are on your plate now?
- If your child has borrowed 7 books from the library and then returned 5 of the books, how many books do they still need to return to the library?

NAME:

Number Sense

Project the scene. Ask children: *What do you notice? What do you wonder?*

Solve subtraction problems from 10 or less using manipulatives.

Investigate It

1	2	3	4	5	6	7	8	9	10

______ ( ) ______ ( ) ______

1	2	3	4	5	6	7	8	9	10

______ ( ) ______ ( ) ______

After doing the Discover It activity as a class, have children complete the Investigate It activity and record two of their results.

How can you use a number path to solve a subtraction problem?

NAME:

Try-Discuss-Connect

1	2	3	4	5	6	7	8	9	10

______ ◯ ______ ◯ ______

Make sense of the problem: *There are 8 ducks at the park. Then 5 fly away. How many ducks are at the park now? Show your thinking on the number path. Then write an equation to match.*

How can you find the number of ducks that are at the park now?

Take-Away Tales Activity

_____ − _____ = _____ _____ − _____ = _____

_____ − _____ = _____ _____ − _____ = _____

_____ − _____ = _____ _____ − _____ = _____

After children complete the Take-Away Tales Activity, have them fill in the equations to record their results.

What ways do you solve subtraction equations?

NAME:

Practice

Match

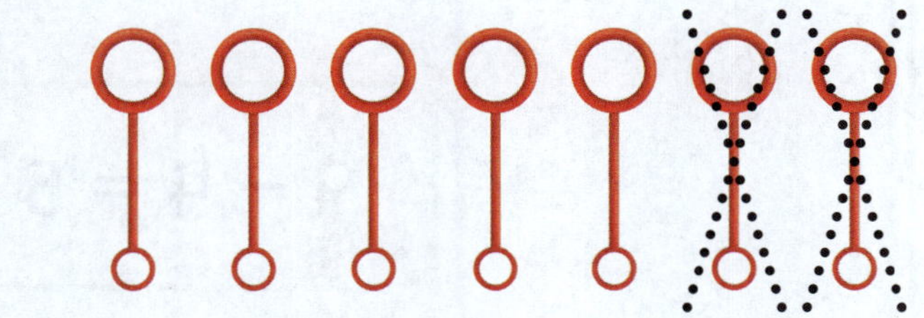

$6 - 4 = 2$

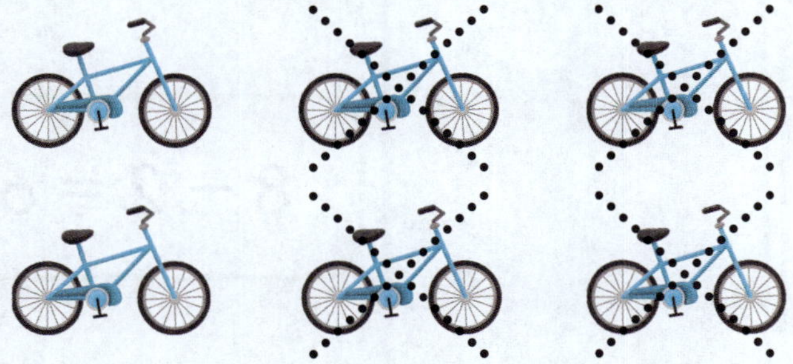

$8 - 5 = 3$

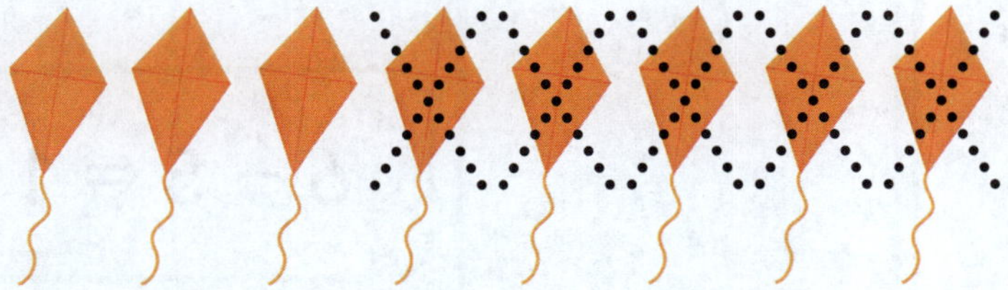

$7 - 2 = 5$

Have children describe the subtraction story in each picture. Then have them draw lines to match each picture to an equation.

Practice

Match

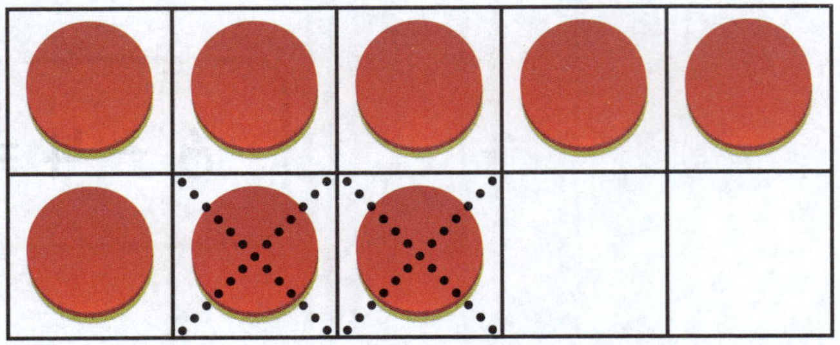

$9 - 4 = 5$

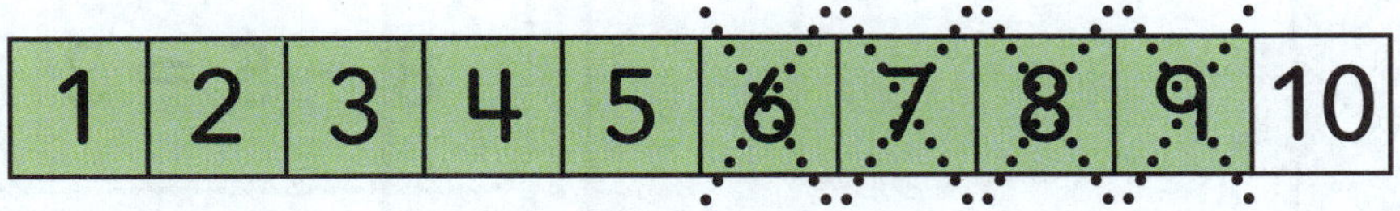

$8 - 2 = 6$

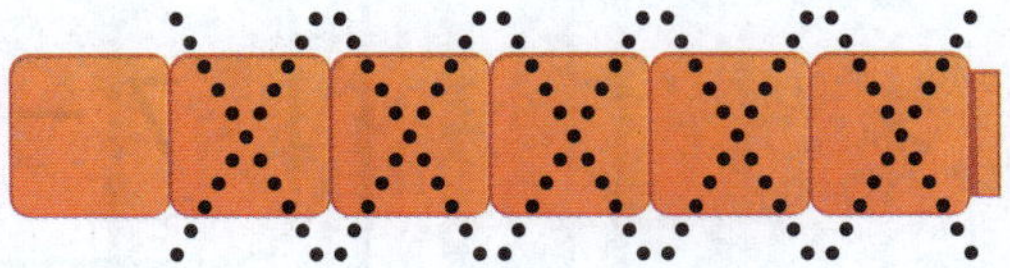

$6 - 5 = 1$

Have children describe the subtraction story in each picture. Then have them draw lines to match each picture to an equation.

NAME:

Try-Discuss-Connect

_____ ◯ _____ ◯ _____

Make sense of the problem: *There are 9 balloons. Some of the balloons pop. How many balloons are left?* Have children cross out some balloons to show how many balloons pop. Then have them fill in the equation.

How many balloons pop? How did you decide how many balloons are left?

Flip and Solve Activity

______ − ______ = ______   ______ − ______ = ______

______ − ______ = ______   ______ − ______ = ______

______ − ______ = ______   ______ − ______ = ______

______ − ______ = ______   ______ − ______ = ______

As children complete the Flip and Solve Activity, have them record their equations.

How do you know when you have solved a subtraction problem correctly?

NAME:

Practice

Cross Out   Write

Example

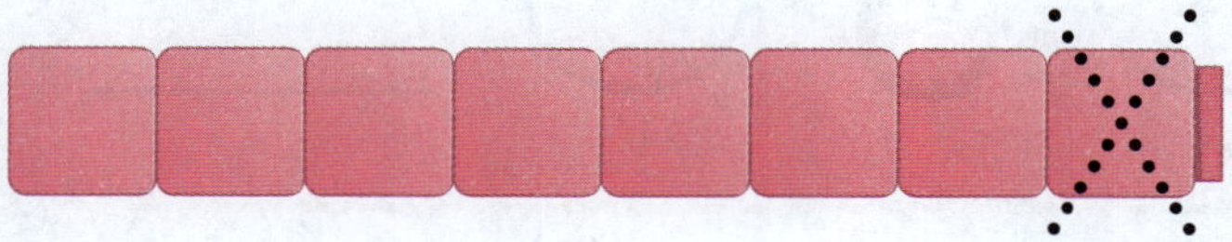

8 ○ 1 ○ 7

(traced: 8 − 1 = 7)

6 ○ 3 ○ ____

9 ○ 3 ○ ____

7 ○ 5 ○ ____

Have children cross out cubes to model each subtraction problem on a cube train.
Then have them complete each equation.

Practice

Cross Out ✗ Write

9 ○ 5 ○ ____

6 ○ 1 ○ ____

8 ○ 4 ○ ____

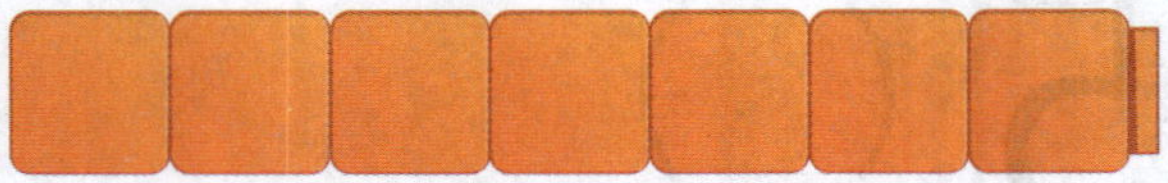

7 ○ 4 ○ ____

Have children cross out cubes to model each subtraction problem on a cube train.
Then have them complete each equation.

NAME:

Make Connections

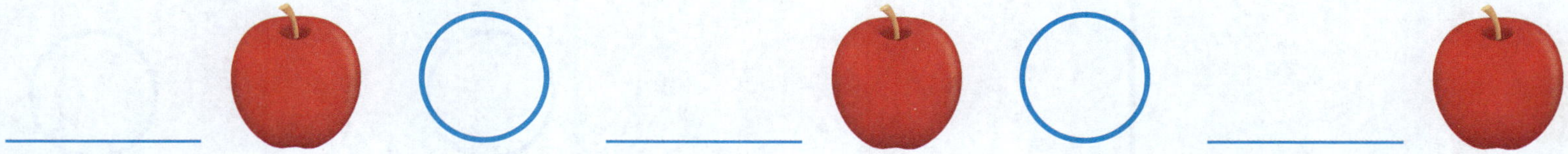

Have children cross out some apples. Then have them tell a subtraction story problem and write an equation for the situation.

Fruit Baskets Activity

____ ◯ ____ ◯ ____

____ ◯ ____ ◯ ____

____ ◯ ____ ◯ ____

Have children draw up to 10 of each fruit in its own basket. Then have them cross out some of the fruits in each basket to show some being eaten. Have children tell a subtraction story problem and write an equation for each situation.

Practice

Write

Example

1	2	3	4	~~5~~	~~6~~	7	8	9	10

6 − 2 = 4

1	2	3	4	5	~~6~~	~~7~~	~~8~~	9	10

___ ◯ ___ ◯ ___

1	2	3	~~4~~	~~5~~	~~6~~	~~7~~	~~8~~	~~9~~	10

___ ◯ ___ ◯ ___

1	~~2~~	~~3~~	~~4~~	~~5~~	~~6~~	~~7~~	8	9	10

___ ◯ ___ ◯ ___

Have children write an equation for each number path.

Practice

Write

1	2	~~3~~	~~4~~	~~5~~	~~6~~	~~7~~	~~8~~	9	10

1	2	~~3~~	~~4~~	~~5~~	~~6~~	~~7~~	~~8~~	~~9~~	10

1	2	~~3~~	~~4~~	~~5~~	~~6~~	7	8	9	10

1	2	3	4	~~5~~	~~6~~	~~7~~	8	9	10

Have children write an equation for each number path.

NAME:

Analyze It

$$8 - 3 = 5$$

Read the problem: *The cat and dog both modeled the equation with tools. Do you agree with the cat, the dog, or both? Why?* Have children circle who they agree with.

Lesson Reflection

1	2	3	4	5	6	7	8	9	10

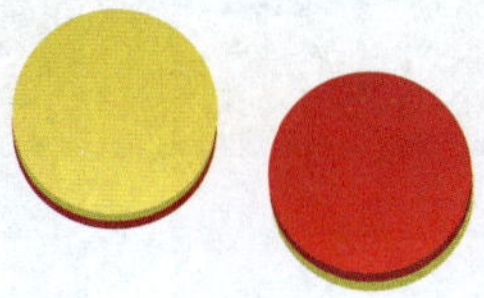

____ – ____ = ____

Have children use numbers, words, or drawings to show something they learned or did in this lesson to subtract within 10.

NAME:

Practice

Cross Out ✗ Write

Have children cross out some stickers and write a subtraction equation for each type of sticker.

Practice

Color

1: 2: 3: 4: 5:

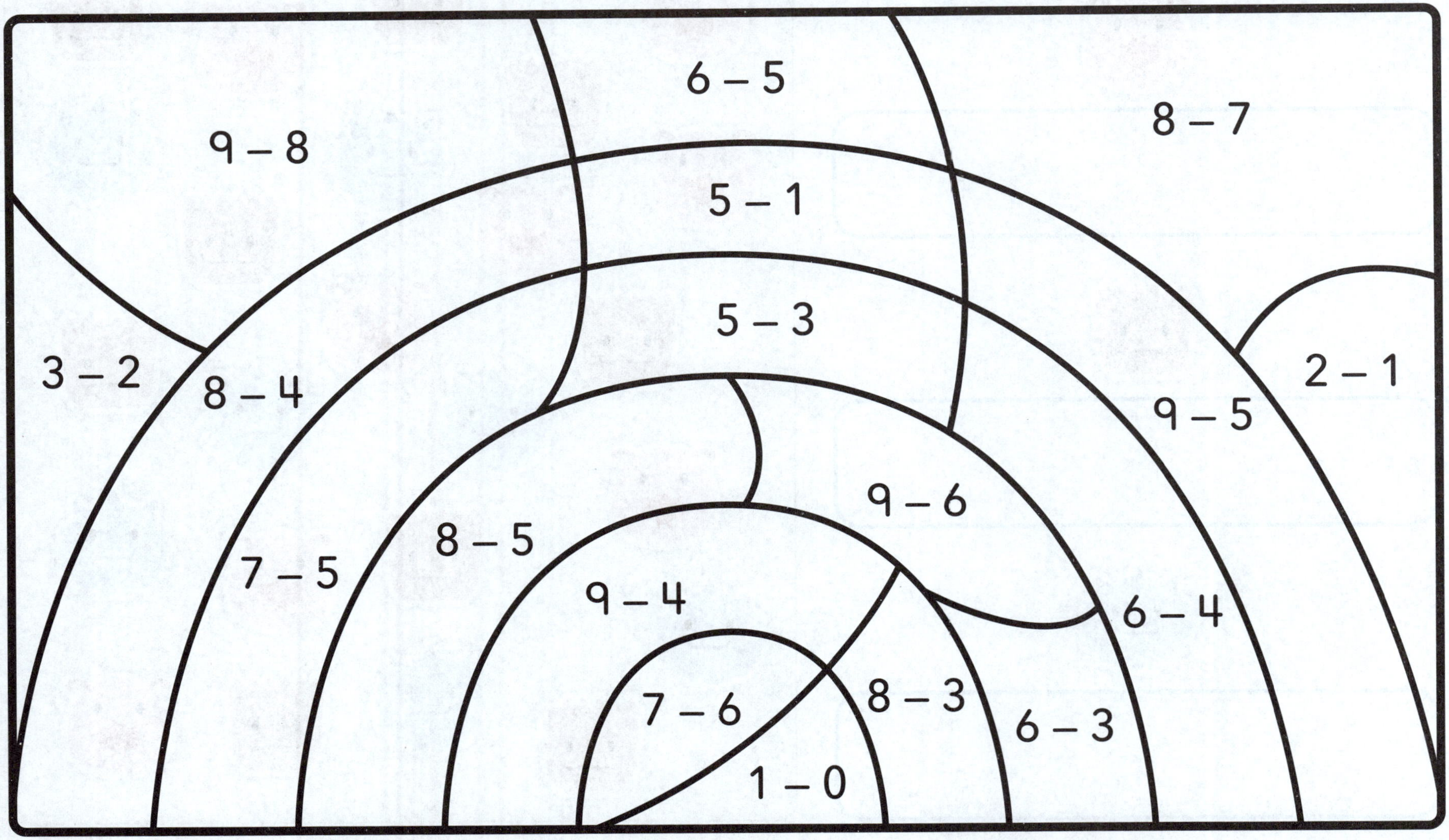

Read the following riddle: *I am a bow, but I cannot be tied. What am I?* Ask children to color the key for each number in a different color. Then have them find how many in each space of the hidden picture and use the key to color the space with the matching color.

Family Letters are also available in multiple languages.

LESSON 22

Add and Subtract to Solve Word Problems

Dear Family,

In this lesson, your child is learning more about solving addition and subtraction story problems. Your child may listen to a math story problem or tell their own story. Then they will use quick drawings to show what is happening in the problem and find the answer.

i-Ready Connect

Learning Games

Hungry Guppy

Digital Math Tools

Counters and Connecting Cubes

More about the Math

Earlier in Kindergarten, your child used their fingers and objects like counters and cubes to help them add and subtract. In this lesson, your child will use drawings as a way to show and solve problems.

There are 4 green caterpillars.

5 brown caterpillars join them.

How many caterpillars are there now?

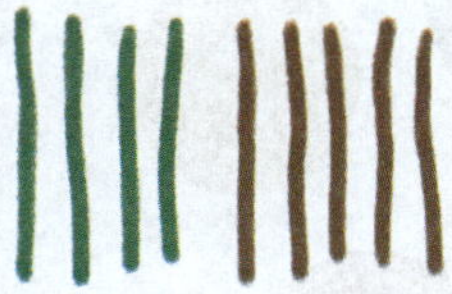

$4 + 5 = 9$

Your child has already solved problems when they knew whether to add or subtract. Now your child will decide how to solve problems. As children build this skill, they begin to recognize when to add and when to subtract.

Add or Subtract

Do this activity with your child to explore adding and subtracting to solve story problems.

Materials: 10 small objects, such as buttons or paper clips

- Tell an addition or subtraction story problem. For example, say: *There are 5 big fish and 3 small fish. How many fish are there?* Choose numbers so that all the numbers in the problem, including the number you ask your child to find, are 10 or less.
- Give your child the 10 objects. Ask them to use the objects to show your story problem and find the answer. Ask them whether they added or subtracted to solve the problem. Have your child **SAY** what they added or subtracted and the answer.
- Switch roles. Ask your child to tell an addition or subtraction story problem. Use the objects to show the story problem they tell. Ask your child whether you correctly solved the problem.

SAY 5 plus 3 equals 8. There are 8 fish.

Math on the GO!

Conversation Starter

Look for opportunities to add and subtract in real-world situations. For example:

- If you have 4 markers and 6 pencils, ask your child how many markers and pencils you have altogether.
- If you have 7 apples in a bowl and you want to eat 1 of them, ask your child how many apples will still be in the bowl.

NAME:

LESSON 22

Number Sense

Project the scene. Ask children: *What do you notice? What do you wonder?*

Draw to represent addition and subtraction situations. Solve story problems for numbers up to 10.

Investigate It

$8 + 2 =$ ______	$6 - 5 =$ ______	$10 - 4 =$ ______
$5 + 3 =$ ______	$6 + 3 =$ ______	$8 - 4 =$ ______
$1 + 7 =$ ______	$9 - 2 =$ ______	$7 - 4 =$ ______

After doing the Discover It activity as a class, have children complete the Investigate It activity. Have one partner choose an equation and tell a matching story problem. Have the other partner find the matching equation. Then both partners solve the problem.

How did you know which equation matched the story?

NAME:

Try-Discuss-Connect

____ ◯ ____ ◯ ____

____ ◯ ____ ◯ ____

Say: *There are 4 caterpillars. 4 more join them. How many caterpillars are there now?* Have children draw to represent the story problem and write an equation to match. Repeat with this problem: *There are 8 butterflies. Then 1 flies away. How many butterflies are there now?*

What did you do to solve the addition and subtraction story problems?

Draw to Represent Activity

____ ◯ ____ ◯ ____

____ ◯ ____ ◯ ____

____ ◯ ____ ◯ ____

Have children record their work throughout the Draw to Represent Activity. Have them draw to represent and solve their story problems and write an equation to match.

How do your drawings represent each story problem?

Practice

Match Write

1 + 5 = ______

9 − 7 = ______

3 + 6 = ______

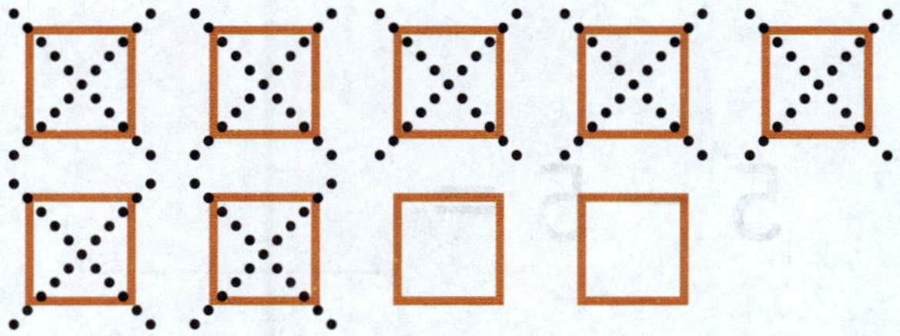

Have children draw lines to match each equation with the drawing that shows the addition or subtraction. Then have them use the drawing to solve.

Practice

Match Write

$8 - 2 =$ ______

$3 + 7 =$ ______

$5 - 5 =$ ______

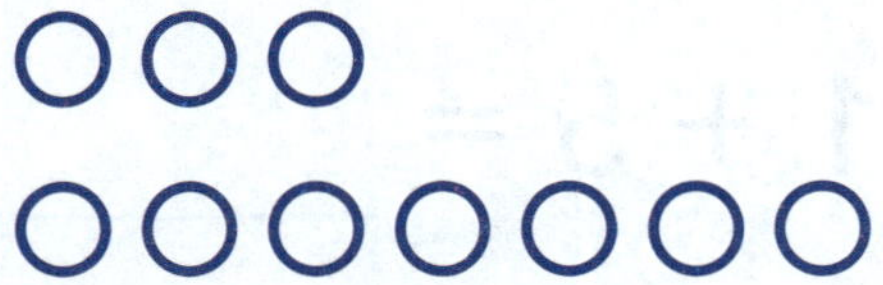

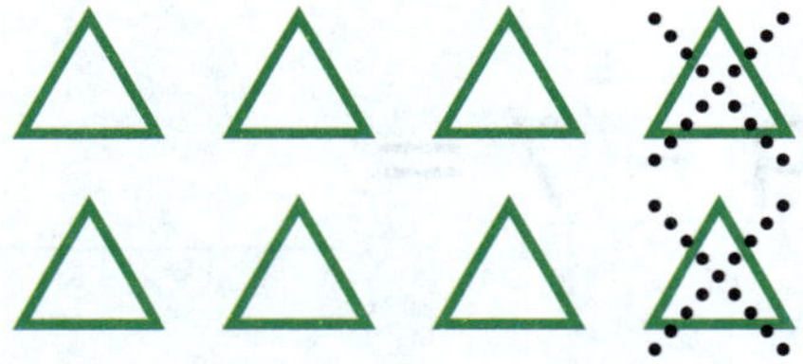

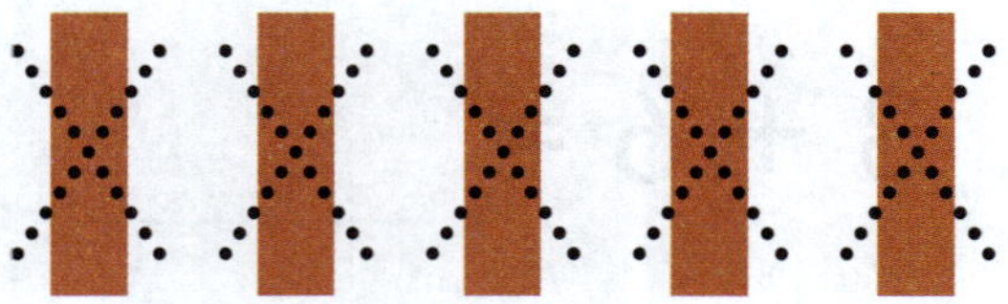

Have children draw lines to match each equation with the drawing that shows the addition or subtraction. Then have them use the drawing to solve.

NAME:

Try-Discuss-Connect

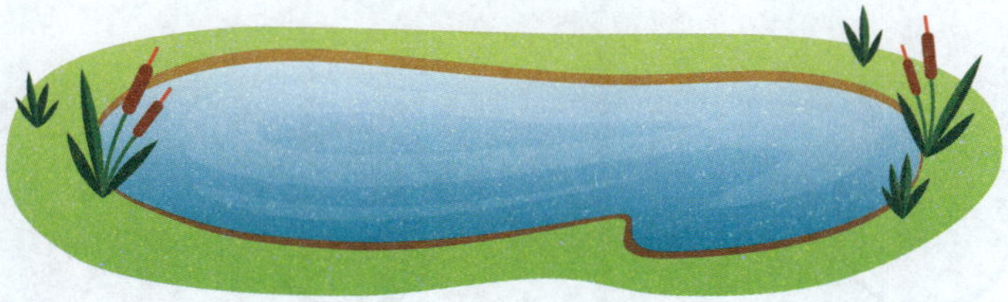

Say: *There are 9 fish. Some fish swim away. How many fish are left?* Have children represent the problem and write an equation to match. Repeat. Say: *There are 7 turtles. Some are on a log and some are on the grass. How many turtles are on the log and how many are on the grass?*

How did you decide to represent the story problems?

Model and Draw a Story Problem Activity

_____ ◯ _____ ◯ _____

_____ ◯ _____ ◯ _____

As children complete their first two rounds of the Model and Draw a Story Problem Activity, have them draw and write equations to show the story problems they modeled and solved using counters.

How did you decide how to solve the problems?

NAME: ____________________

Practice

Write

Example

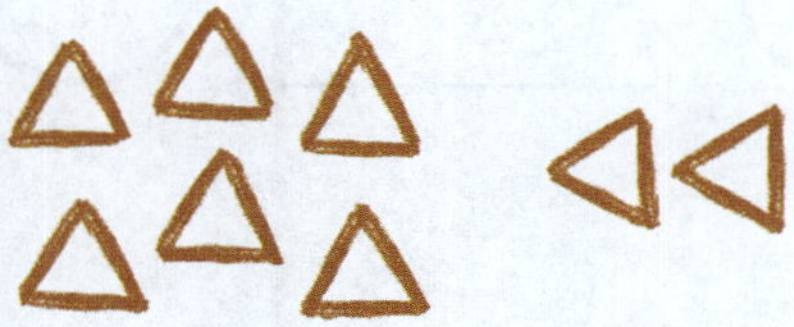

6 + 2 = 8

____ ◯ ____ ◯ ____

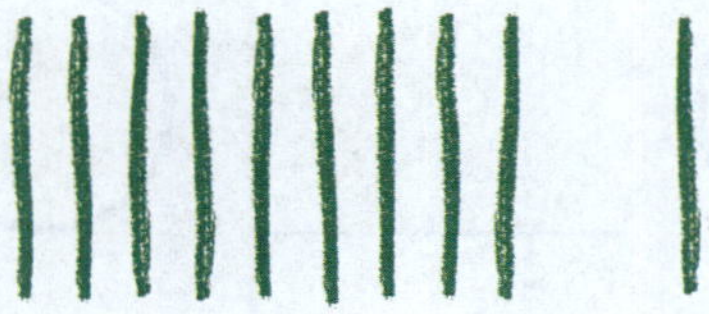

____ ◯ ____ ◯ ____

Tell children: *Some children drew to represent their story problems.* Have children write an equation to match the drawing that represents each story problem.

Practice

Write

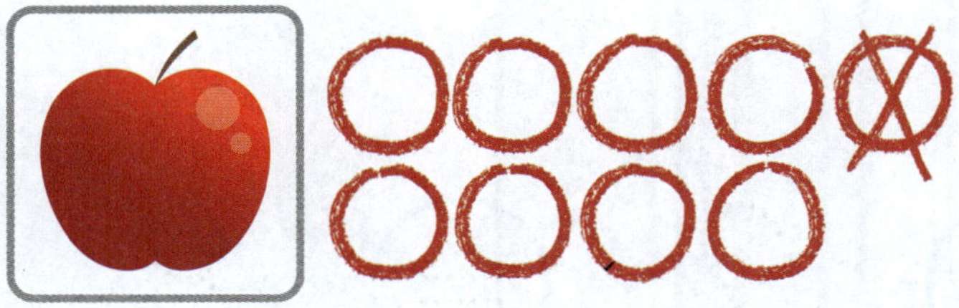

____ ◯ ____ ◯ ____

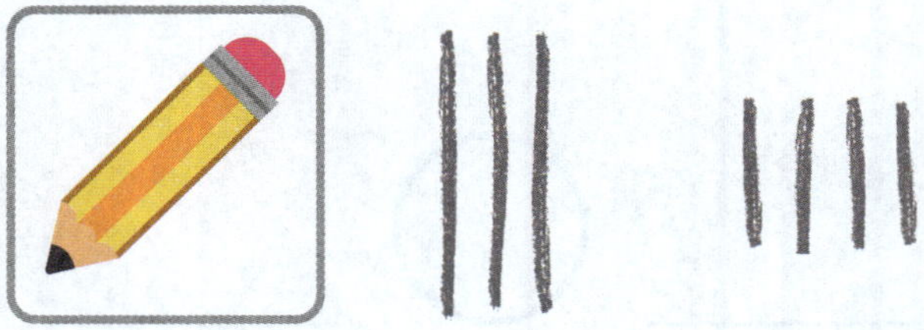

____ ◯ ____ ◯ ____

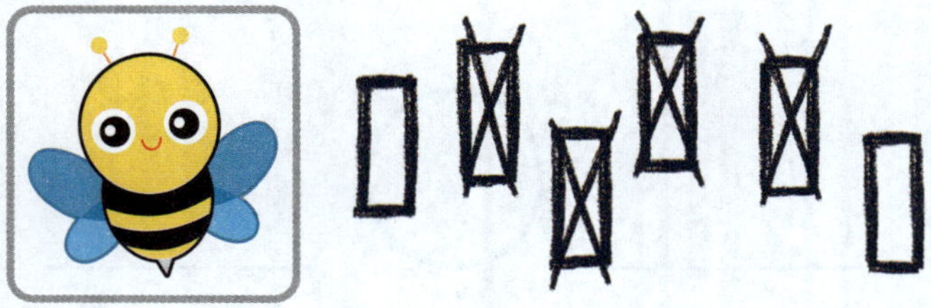

____ ◯ ____ ◯ ____

Tell children: *Some children drew to represent their story problems.* Have chilDSNdren write an equation to match the drawing that represents each story problem.

NAME:

Make Connections

Have children tell a story problem to a partner. Then have them draw to show their story problem and write an equation to match.

Represent a Problem Activity

Have children draw to represent a story problem where something is added or subtracted. Have them write an equation that matches the problem. Have them repeat for each space and then tell at least one of their problems to a friend.

NAME:

Practice

Draw Write

Example

$9 - 3 =$ 6

$3 + 5 =$ ____

$7 - 2 =$ ____

Have children think of a story problem to match each equation. Have them draw to represent their story problem, then complete the equation.

Practice

Draw Write

$1 + 5 =$ ____

$9 - 7 =$ ____

$3 + 6 =$ ____

Have children think of a story problem to match each equation. Have them draw to represent their story problem, then complete the equation.

Analyze It

$7 - 2 =$ ______

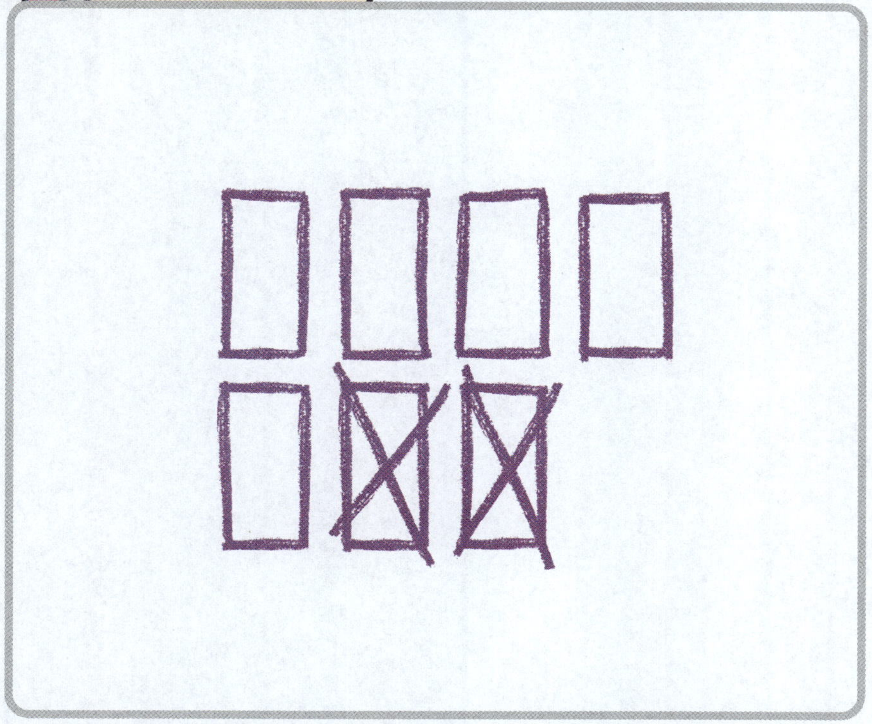

Read the problem: *There are 7 butterflies in the garden. Then 2 fly away. How many butterflies are in the garden now? The cat and dog both think they have modeled the problem. Do you agree with the cat, the dog, or both? Why?* Have children circle who they agree with.

Lesson Reflection

Have children use numbers, words, or drawings to show something they learned or did in this lesson to show how to add and subtract to solve story problems.

NAME:

Practice

Cut Glue

$4 - 1 = 3$	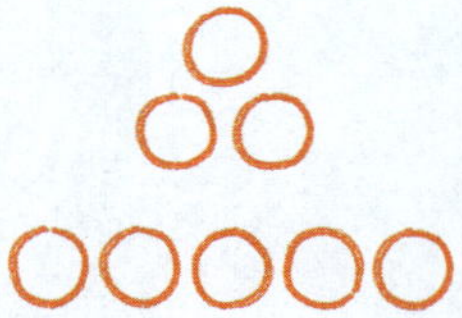
$9 + 0 = 9$	
$3 + 5 = 8$	

Have children cut out the 6 boxes that show equations and drawings. Ask them to use the pictures to think of a story problem to match each equation. Then have them glue the equation next to the picture, along with the drawing that shows how to solve it.

This page serves as the back of the cut and glue activity on the previous page.

NAME:

Plan Two Dance Groups

Where will your dancers start?

_____ ◯ _____ ◯ _____

Have children show two groups of dancers that total 10 on the grid. Ask children to write an equation to show the number of dancers in each group and the total number of dancers.

Plan Two Dance Moves

What move will your dancers make?

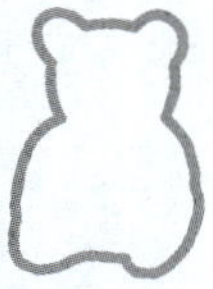

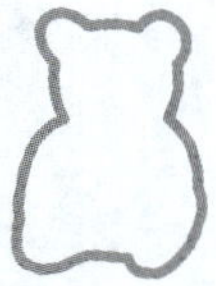

Have children choose two dance moves and draw the symbols. Then have them show where each dancer will stand and what dance move they will do. Ask children to write an equation that shows their dancers.

How did you decide how many dancers to have on stage and what dance move each will do?

NAME:

My Dance Information

Have children draw the symbol of each dance move they used in this part of the dance. Then have children write how many dancers did each dance move. Finally, have them circle their favorite dance move.

What is the same? What is different?

Reflection

What do you notice and wonder about the class data display?

I notice:

I wonder:

Have children notice and wonder about the class data display. Have them answer one of their questions and use numbers, words, drawings, objects, and/or gestures to show their reasoning.

NAME:

Show What You Learned

Have children draw to show what they learned about addition and subtraction. Prompt children to reflect on their learning by posing questions such as: *What do you know how to do well? What math could you use in your everyday life? What is a question you still have?*

Write

____ ○ ____ ○ ____

Write

____ ○ ____ ○ ____

Draw Write

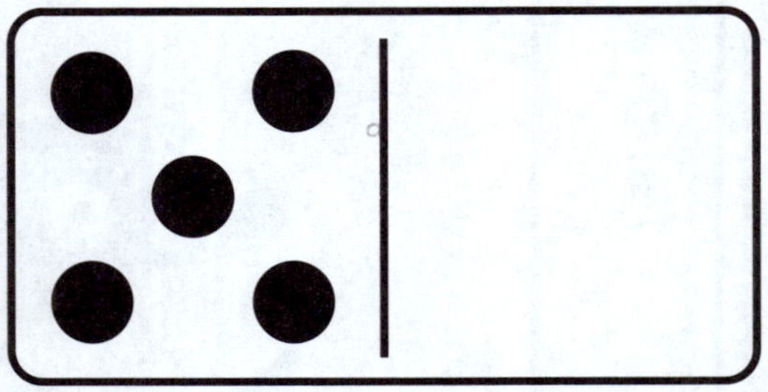

____ ○ ____ ○ 6

For the first two problems, tell children: *Some children drew to represent their story problems.* Have them write an equation to match each drawing. For the next problem, have them draw dots on the domino to show the number partner for the total and then complete the equation to match.

NAME:

Color

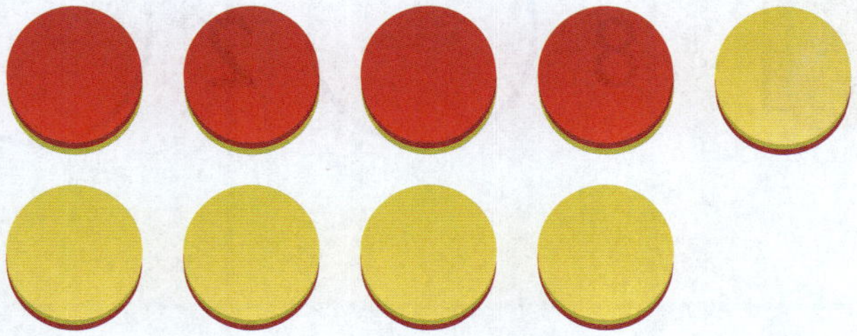

$4 + 4 = 8$

$4 + 5 = 9$

$5 + 5 = 10$

Color

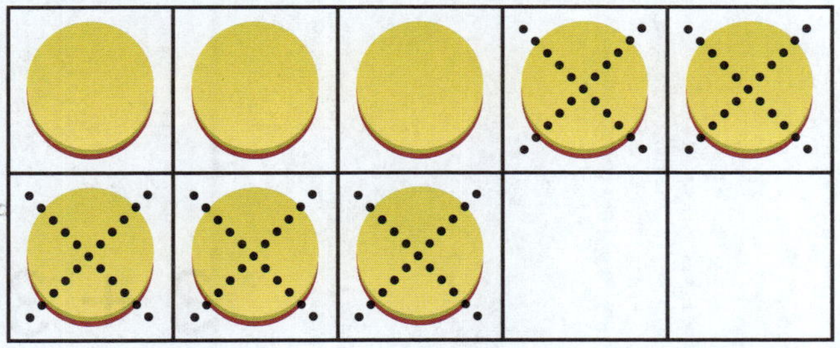

$8 - 5 = 3$

$10 - 2 = 8$

$7 - 4 = 3$

For each problem, have children describe the addition or subtraction story in the picture. Then read each equation aloud and have children color the equation that matches the picture.

Cross Out Write

8 ◯ 2 ◯ ____

Write

1	2	3	4	5	6	7	8	9	10

$6 - 2 =$ ____

Write

$3 + 3 =$ ____

For the first problem, have children cross out cubes to model the subtraction and then complete the equation.
For the next two problems, have children complete the equation for each picture.

Teen Numbers and Shapes

UNIT 7

Show What You Know

Have children draw to show what they know about teen numbers and shapes. Tell children that after they have completed the unit, they will draw to show what they learned.

My Words

Mathematical
compose
flat
solid
teen numbers
ten

Academic
build
describe

Have children choose 2 to 4 words and show what they know about them using pictures, numbers, or words. Have children share their representations with peers.

To support children with word selection, ask:
- *Which words are new to you?*
- *Which words do you think are the most important? Why?*

Family Letters are also available in multiple languages.

LESSON 23

Compose and Decompose Teen Numbers with Tools and Drawings

Dear Family,

In this lesson, your child is learning to use tools and drawings to put together and break apart teen numbers. Your child will see that all teen numbers are made up of 10 ones and some more ones.

16

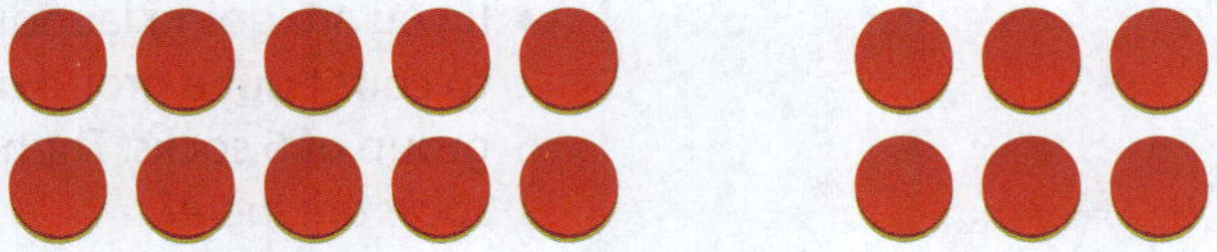

10 6

i-Ready Connect

Digital Math Tools

Counters and Connecting Cubes

More about the Math

Previously, your child has counted teen numbers and learned that teen numbers are the numbers from 11 to 19. In this lesson, your child will count out a teen number of objects and group the objects to see them as 10 ones and some more ones. Your child will describe the groups they make by drawing pictures and by writing.

Your child will also count objects in a drawing and then separate them into a group of 10 ones and a group of some more ones.

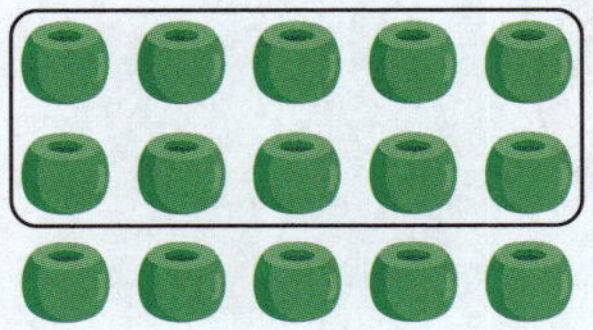

15

10 + 5

As children build these skills throughout this lesson, they will begin to recognize the groups that each teen number can be broken into. For example, 15 always makes a group of 10 ones and a group of 5 ones.

ACTIVITY

Making Groups

Do this activity with your child to explore how to put together a group of 10 ones and some more ones to make a teen number.

Materials: 19 small household objects, 1 cup

- Put 10 objects in front of your child. Put the rest of the objects in a cup.
- Tell your child to take a handful of objects from the cup and arrange the objects into a group beside the group of 10 objects.
- Ask your child to **SAY** how many objects are in each group.
- Ask your child to find how many objects there are by counting on from 10.
- Repeat several times to practice making different teen numbers.

SAY **One group has 10.**
One group has 3.
There are 13 pennies.

Math on the GO!

Conversation Starter

Look for opportunities to put together and break apart teen numbers in real-world situations. For example:

- If your child has 17 books, ask them to separate them into a pile of 10 books and a pile of some more books.
- If you are doing laundry, ask your child to count out a group of 10 socks and a group of 6 socks. Then ask: *how many socks are there?*

NAME:

Number Sense

Project the scene. Ask children: *What do you notice? What do you wonder?*

Compose and decompose teen numbers into 10 ones and some more ones. Understand that teen numbers can always be composed of 10 ones and some more (1 to 9) ones.

Investigate It

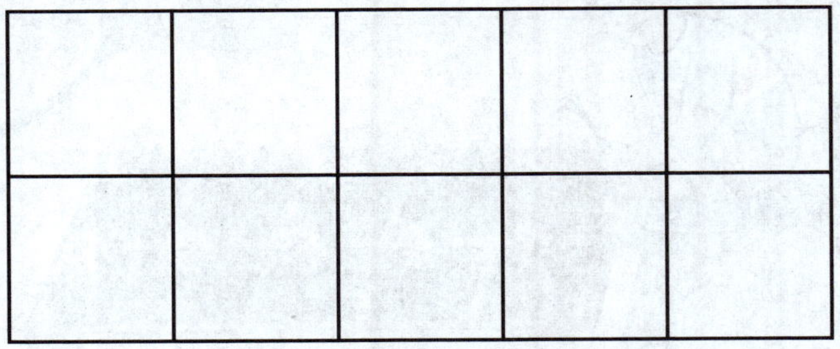

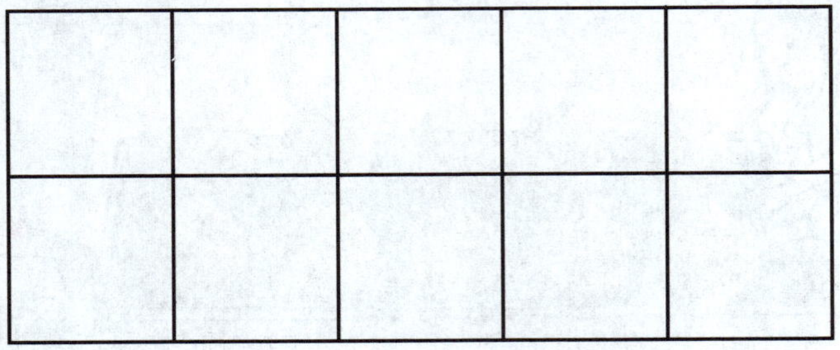

After doing the Discover It activity as a class, have children complete the Investigate It activity and record two of the bags of cubes they count by coloring the 10-frames and then writing the number.

How does using 10-frames help you count the cubes?

NAME:

Try-Discuss-Connect

______

Make sense of the problem: *Count the beans and write the number. Then use the 10-frames to show how many.* Have children place counters in the 10-frames to show the number.

How did you decide how to arrange your counters?

Group and Count Activity

Have children use the 10-frames throughout the Group and Count Activity. After they have completed the activity, have them record one turn by writing the card number in the box, drawing in the 10-frames, and writing the number of counters next to each 10-frame.

How did you use addition to describe the counters in the 10-frames?

NAME:

Practice

Draw Write

Example

17

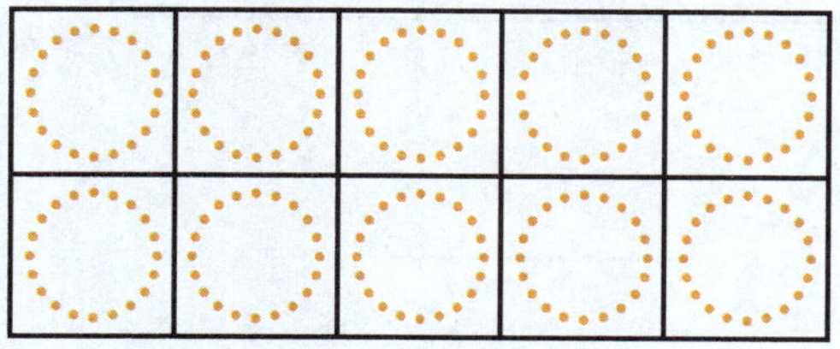

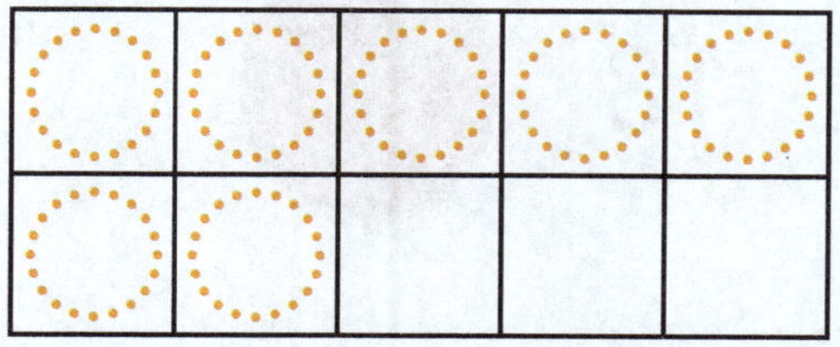

10 7

12

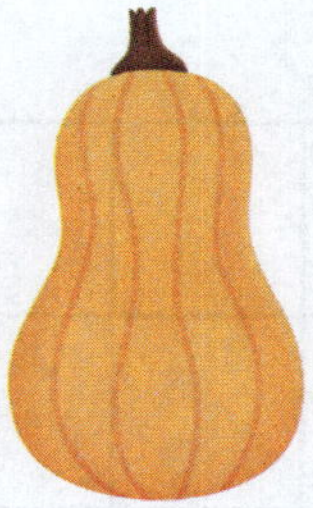

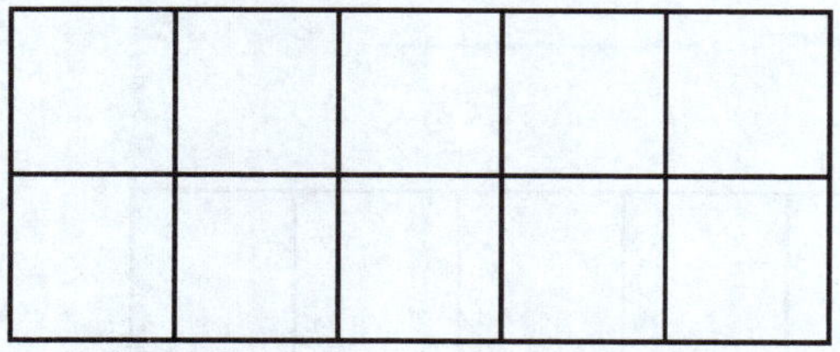

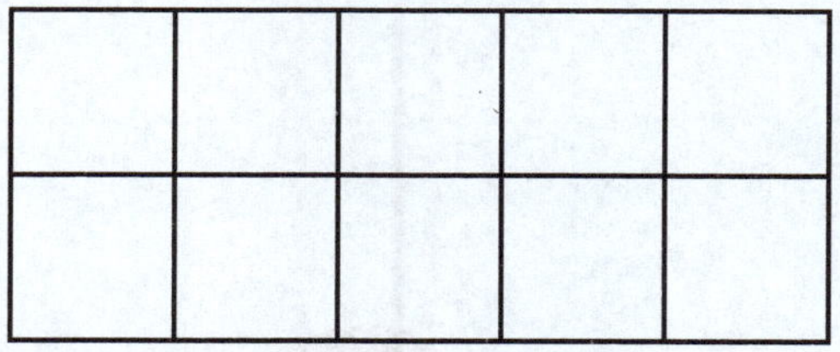

10 ___

Have children fill in the 10-frames to show each number of vegetables as 10 vegetables and some more vegetables. Then have them write the number of vegetables in each 10-frame.

Practice

Draw Write

18 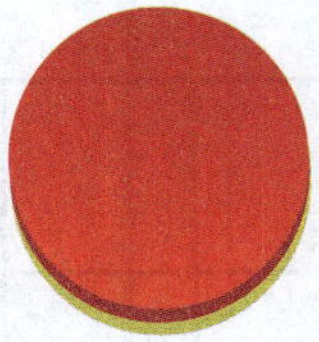

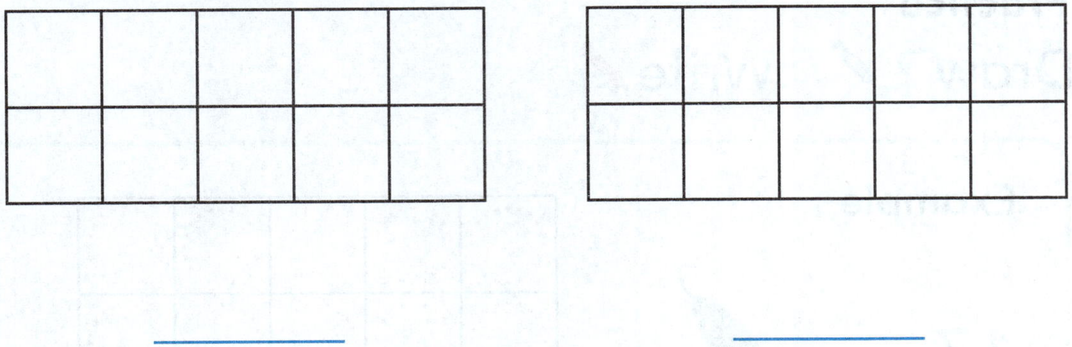

15 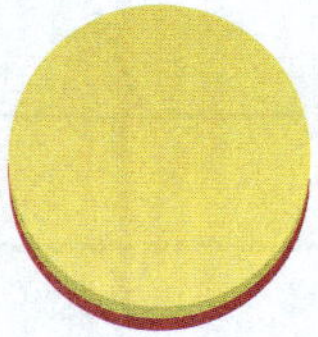

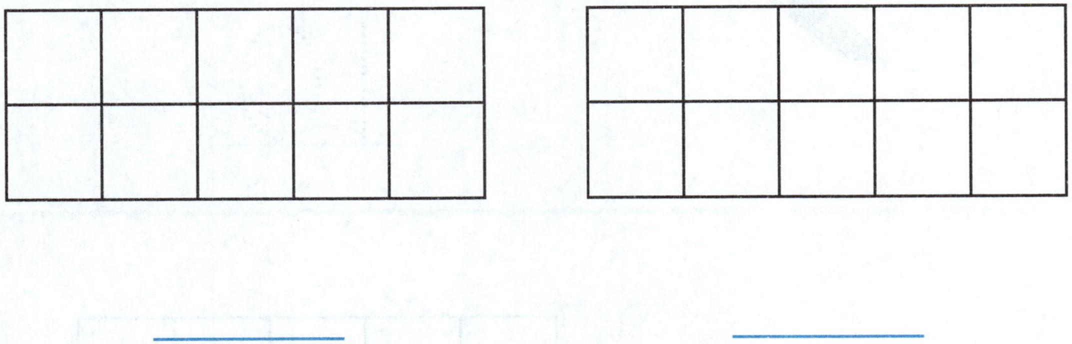

11 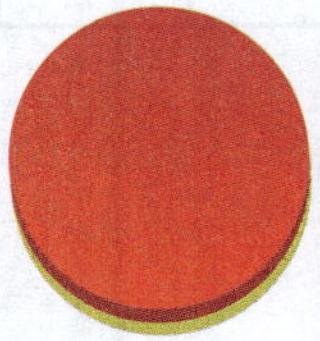

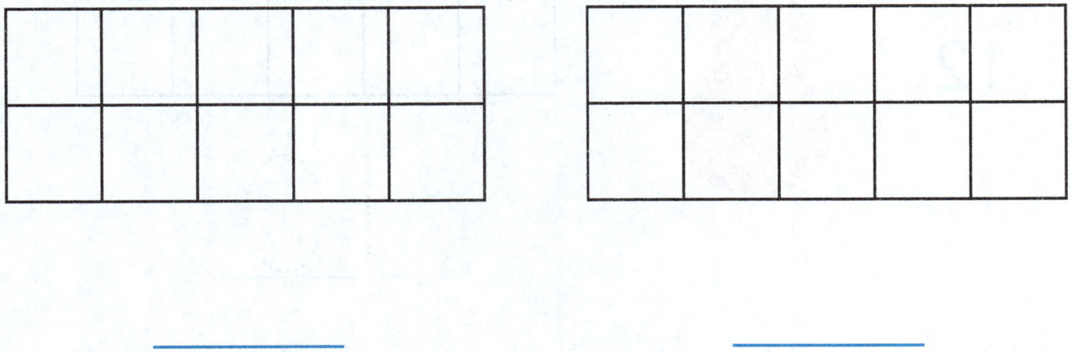

Have children draw counters in the 10-frames to show each number of counters as 10 counters and some more counters. Then have them write the number of counters in each 10-frame.

NAME:

Try-Discuss-Connect

______

10 + ______

Make sense of the problem: *Student gardeners put melons into boxes. Choose and write a teen number of melons. Then draw to fill one box and put some more in another box.* Have children write the number of melons, draw melons in the boxes, and complete the expression.

How do you know you drew the right number of melons?

Circle and Count Activity

_____ + _____

Have children draw dots to show a teen number. Ask children to circle some dots to show one way to help count the dots. Then have them fill in the blank to describe the number of dots.

How did you organize the dots to help you count?

NAME:

Practice

Circle Write

Example

12 13 14

10 + ____

17 18 19

10 + ____

16 17 18

10 + ____

11 12 13

10 + ____

Have children circle 10 peppers and then circle the teen number that tells how many peppers. Then have them complete the addition that describes the peppers as a group of 10 peppers and some more peppers.

Practice

Circle Write

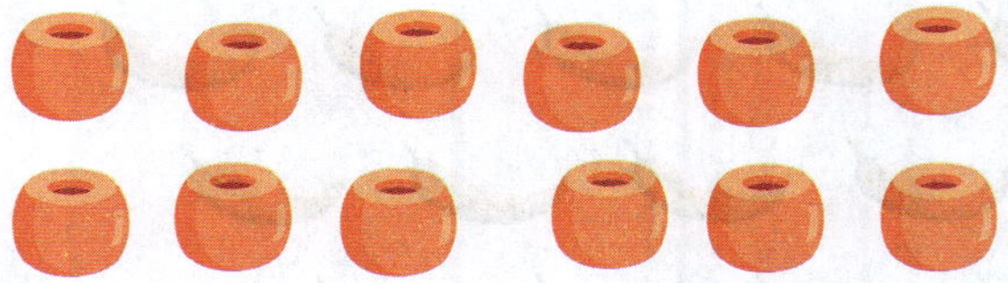

11 12 13

10 + ___

15 16 17

10 + ___

13 14 15

10 + ___

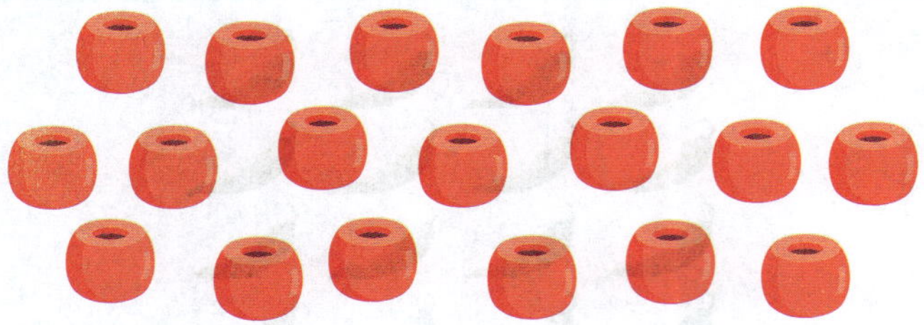

17 18 19

10 + ___

Have children circle 10 beads and then circle the teen number that tells how many beads. Then have them complete the addition that describes the beads as a group of 10 beads and some more beads.

NAME:

Make Connections

____

19

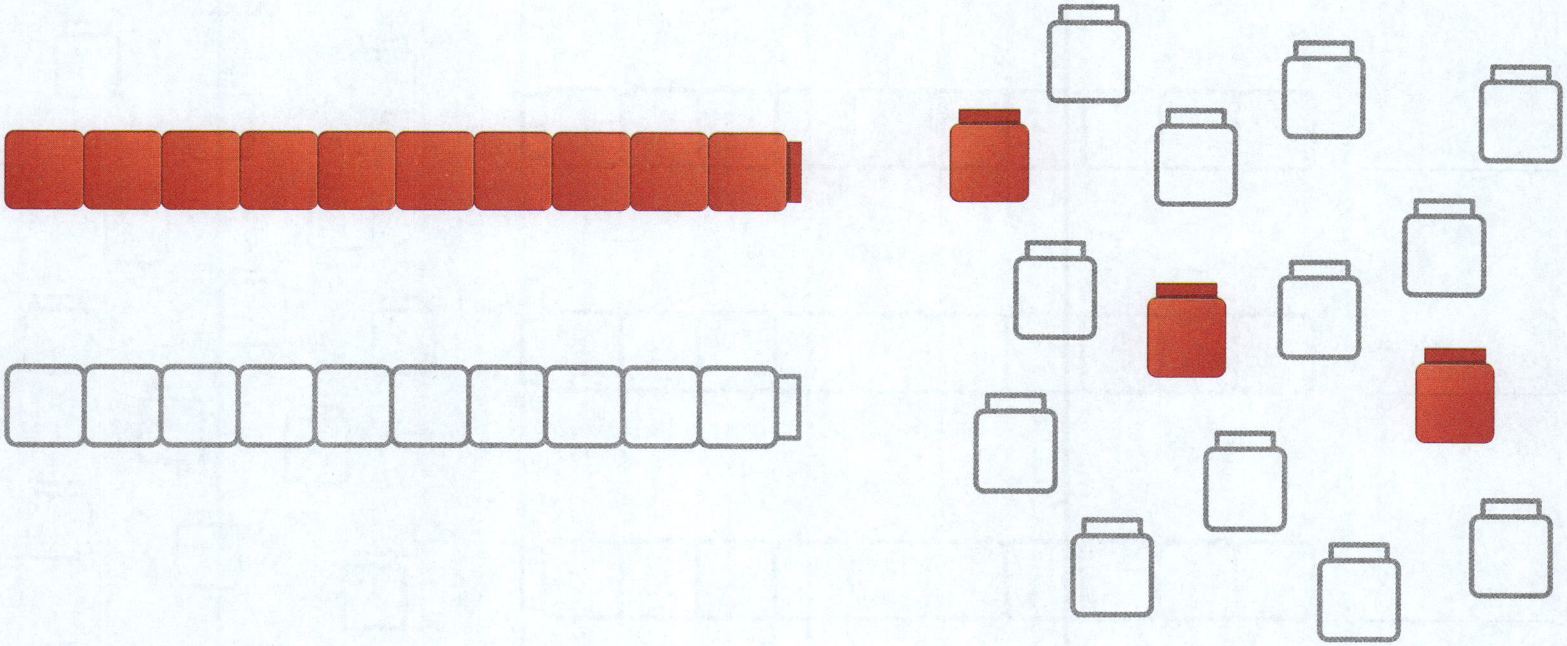

Have children count the red cubes and write the number of red cubes. Then have them read the number next to the second cube train and color the cube train and a group of ones to make the number.

Color and Count Activity

Have children write a teen number on the first line. Then have them color the first train of 10 cubes and use the same crayon to color a group of ones to make the teen number. Repeat, using a different teen number and crayon each time.

NAME:

LESSON 23

Practice

Draw Write

Example

16  10 + 6

11 ___ + ___

18 ___ + ___

Have children draw to show each number as a group of 10 ones and some more ones. Then have them fill in the blanks to describe their drawing.

Practice

Draw Write

______  ______ + ______

______  ______ + ______

______  ______ + ______

Ask children to write a teen number. Have them draw to show the number as a group of 10 ones and some more ones. Then have them fill in the blanks to describe their drawing.

Analyze It

18

Read the problem: *The cat and dog both think they have arranged their buttons to show 18 as a group of 10 ones and some more ones. Do you agree with the cat, the dog, or both? Why?* Have children circle who they agree with.

Lesson Reflection

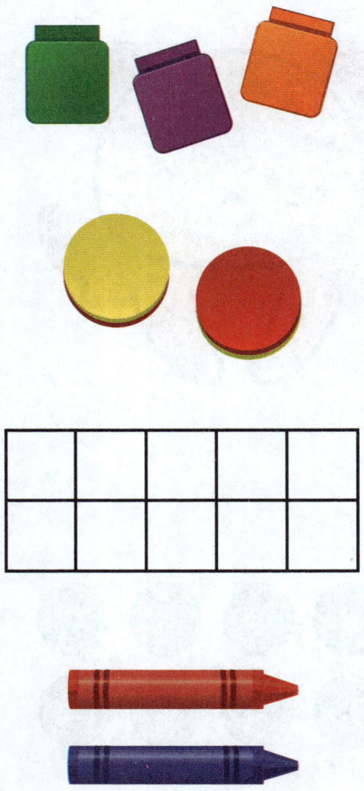

10 + 6

Have children use numbers, words, or drawings to show something they learned or did in this lesson to put together and break apart teen numbers using tools and drawings.

Practice

Color

11:

12:

14:

15:

17:

19:

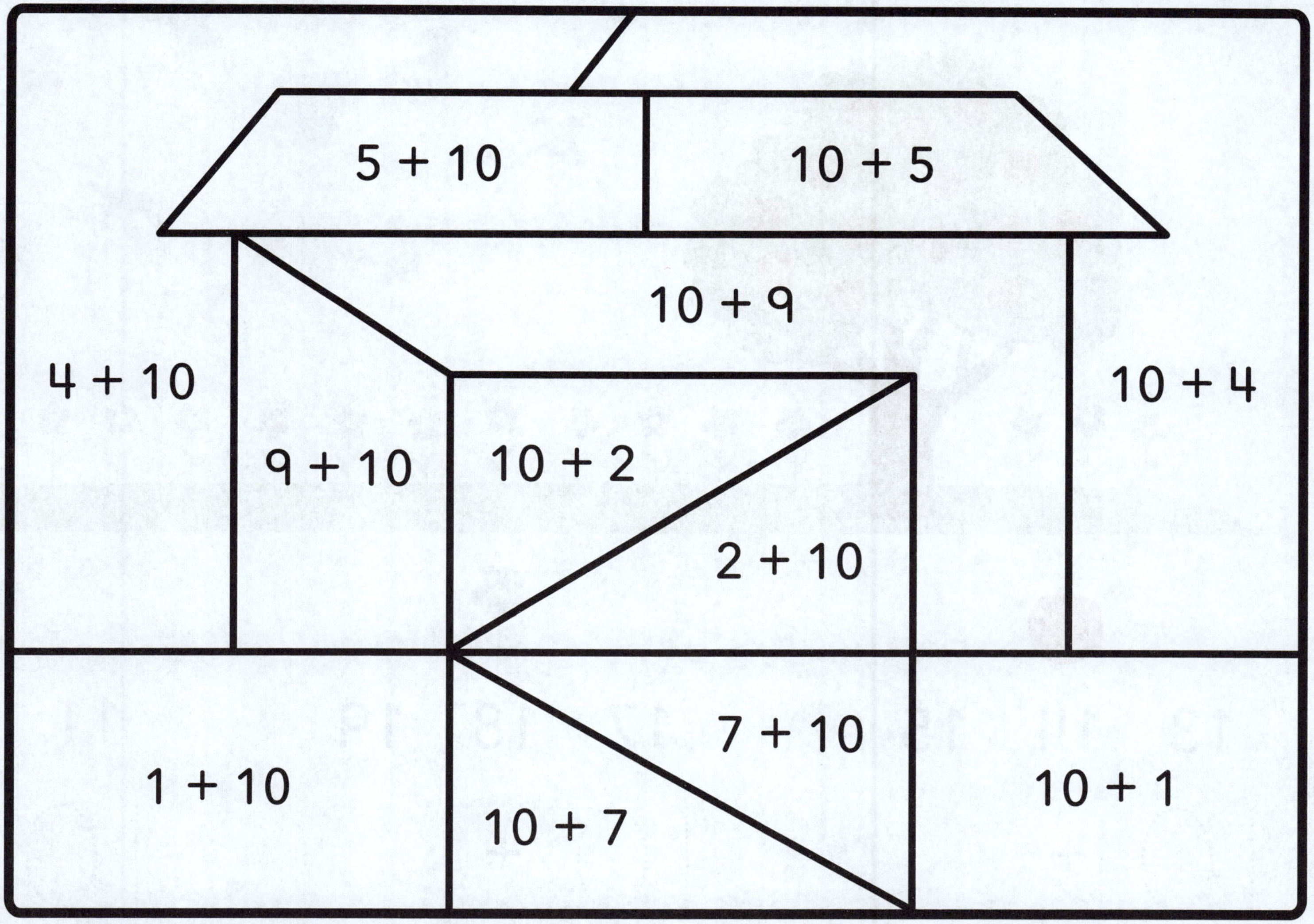

Ask children to color the key for each teen number in a different color. Then have them find how many in each space of the hidden picture and use the key to color the space with the matching color.

Practice

Draw Circle Write

13 14 15

10 + ____

17 18 19

10 + ____

11 12 13

10 + ____

Have children draw circles to show the apples, flowers, and birds as groups of 10 ones and some more ones. Then have them circle the numbers that tell how many and fill in the blanks to describe the groups.

Family Letters are also available in multiple languages.

Build with Shapes

Dear Family,

Your child is learning to model recognizable objects using flat or solid shapes.

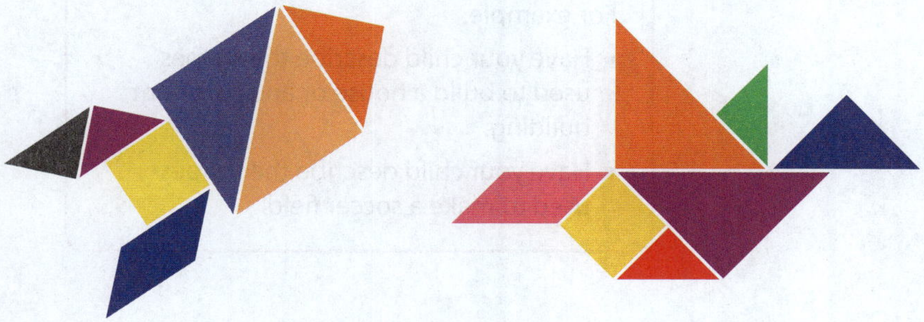

More about the Math

Flat, or two-dimensional, shapes can be used to make a picture of an object. For example, tangrams are flat puzzle blocks shaped like triangles, squares, and parallelograms. They can be used to represent two-dimensional shapes and make many different pictures.

Solid, or three-dimensional, shapes can be used to model objects. For example, building blocks can be used to make many different structures.

Learning to use shapes to model real-world objects will help your child build a foundation for work in later grades with area and volume.

Build with Shapes

Do this activity with your child to explore building with solid shapes.

Materials: common three-dimensional objects such as building blocks, boxes, and cans

- With your child, collect several three-dimensional objects shaped like cubes, rectangular prisms, cones, and cylinders. Include several objects for each shape.
- Invite your child to use the three-dimensional objects to build a bridge. Ask: *What shapes did you use to build the bridge?*
- Have your child **SAY** the names of the shapes used to build the bridge. Encourage your child to use positional language such as *above, below, next to, in front of,* or *behind.*

SAY **I used 2 cubes, 1 cylinder, 1 cone, and 1 rectangular prism.**

Math on the GO!

Conversation Starter

Look for opportunities to find two-dimensional or three-dimensional shapes that make up objects in the world. For example:

- Have your child describe the shapes used to build a house or an apartment building.
- Have your child describe the shapes used to make a soccer field.

NAME:

LESSON 24

Number Sense

Project the scene. Ask children: *What do you notice? What do you wonder?*

Identify shapes as flat or solid. Make a picture with flat shapes and build objects with solid shapes.

Investigate It

Flat	Solid

After doing the Discover It activity as a class, have children complete the Investigate It activity and glue a card that shows a flat shape on the left part of the page and a card that shows a solid shape on the right part of the page.

How do you know whether a shape is flat or solid?

NAME:

LESSON 24

Try-Discuss-Connect

Make sense of the problem: *An artist puts shapes together to make animals. What is one way the artist can put shapes together to make an animal?* Have children choose an animal and put shapes together to make the animal.

What animal did you make? What shapes did you use to make the animal?

Tangram Puzzle Pictures Activity

After children have completed several puzzles in the Tangram Puzzle Pictures Activity, have them record the tangram puzzle they made by tracing an outline of the picture.

Can you use different shapes to make a picture of the same object? How do you know?

NAME:

Practice

Match

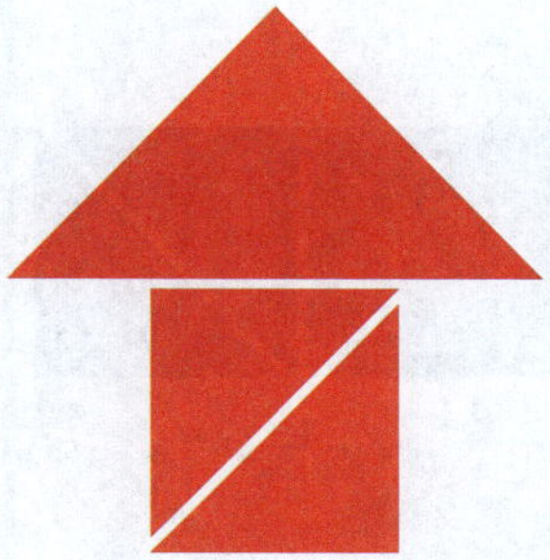

Have children match each set of shapes to the picture the shapes can make. Allow children to use tangrams as needed.

Practice

Match

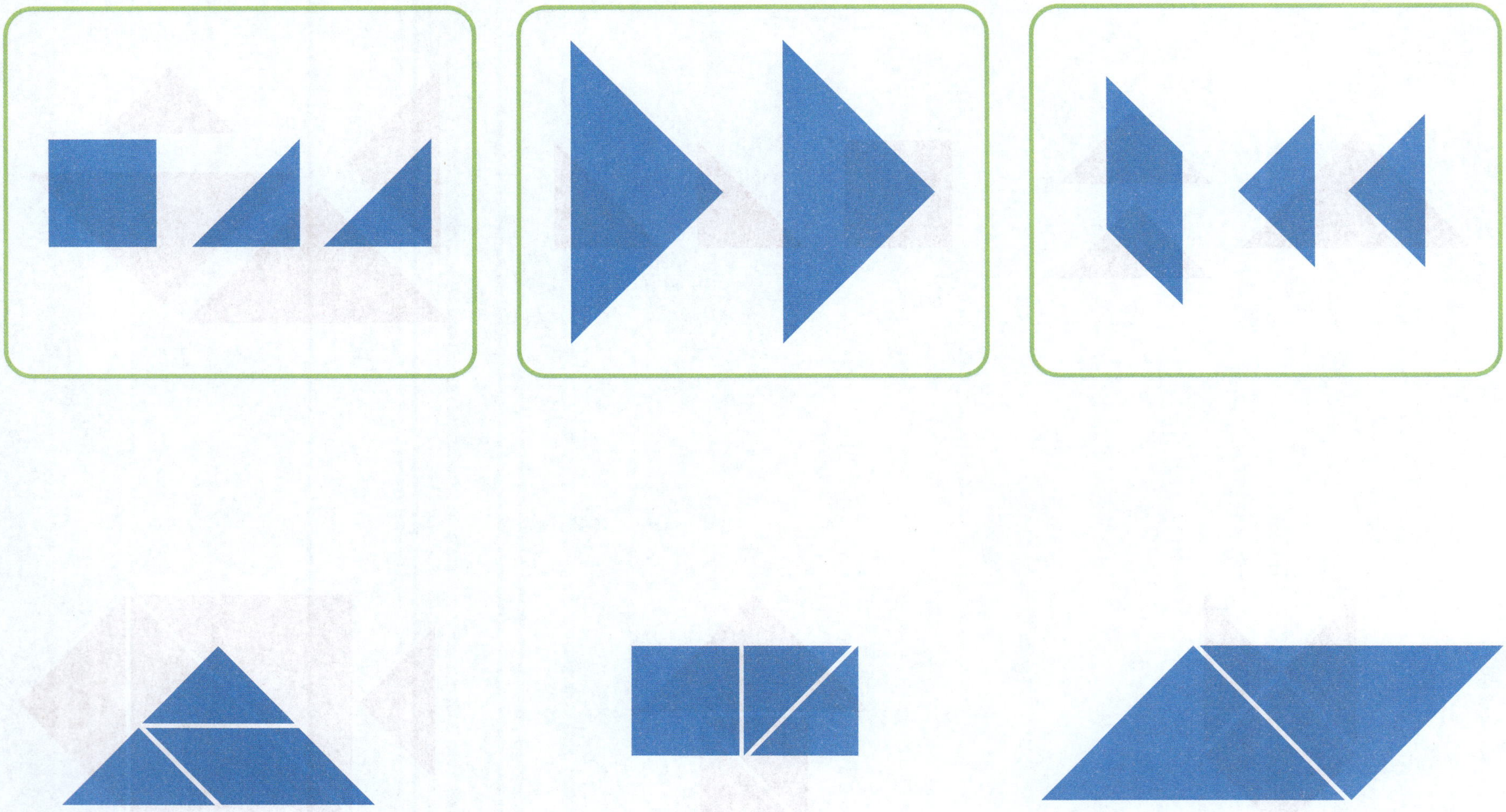

Have children match each set of shapes to the picture the shapes can make. Allow children to use tangrams as needed.

NAME:

Try-Discuss-Connect

Make sense of the problem: *Look at the two building blocks. What can you build by putting these blocks together? How would you place them?* Have children draw to show how they can put the blocks together to make something recognizable.

How would you put the blocks together? What could you make?

Build Solid Objects Activity

After children have completed several rounds of the Build Solid Objects Activity, have them circle the picture of one of the objects they made. Then have them discuss with a partner which shapes they used to make the object.

How did you know which solid shapes to use to build the object?

NAME:

Practice

Circle

Example

Have children circle the object that is made from the given solid shapes.

Practice

Circle

Have children circle the object that is made from the given solid shapes.

NAME:

Make Connections

Have children circle three shapes that have something in common. Then have children use items that match the shapes they circled and combine them to build something.

Build with Shapes Activity

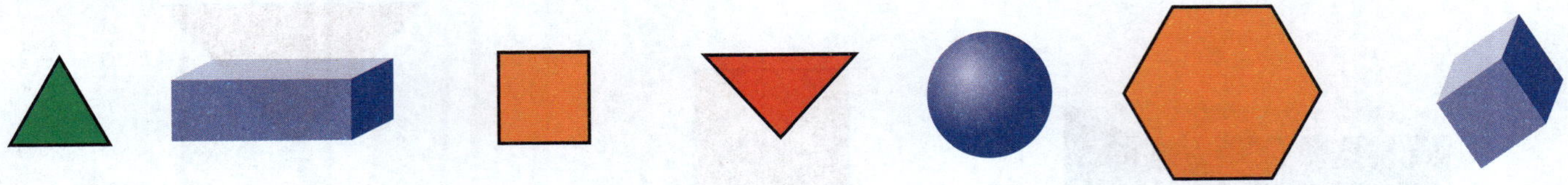

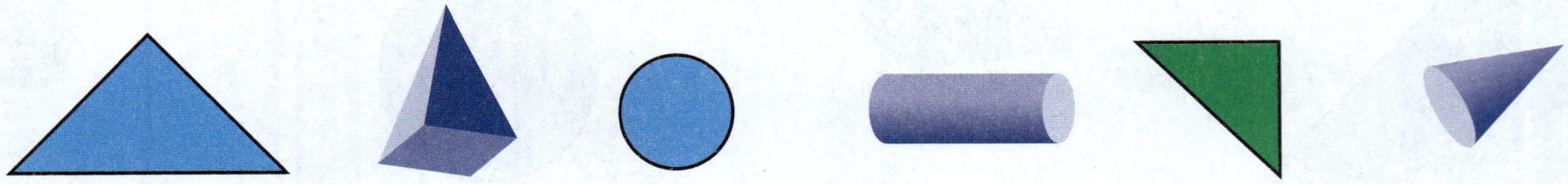

Have children use three or more of the shapes to build anything they want using materials from the previous sessions. Then have children draw a representation of what they made and circle the shapes they used.

NAME:

Practice

Match

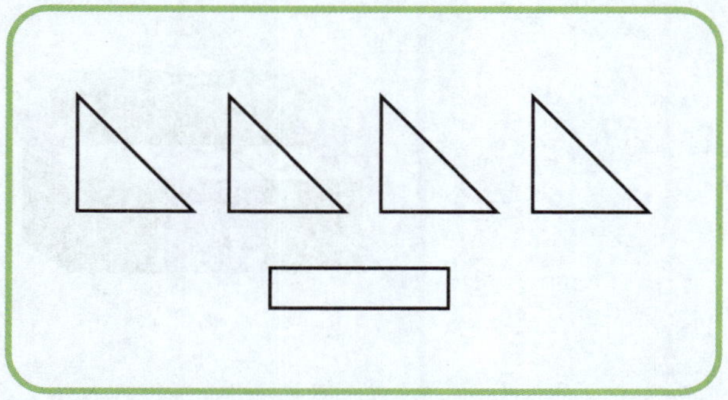

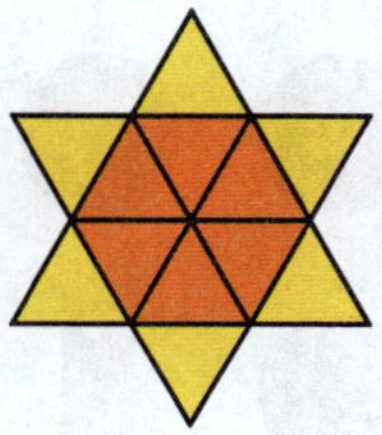

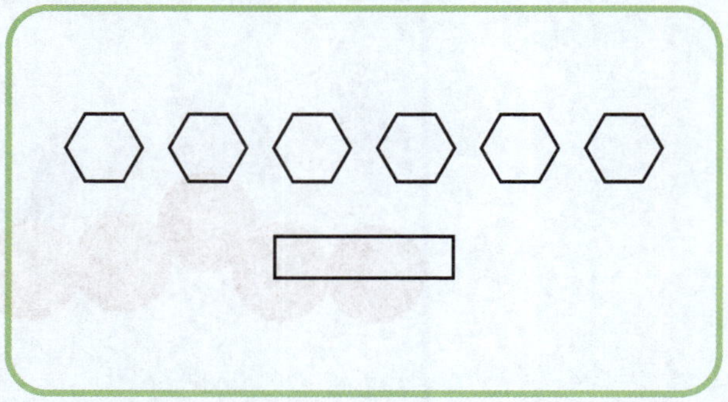

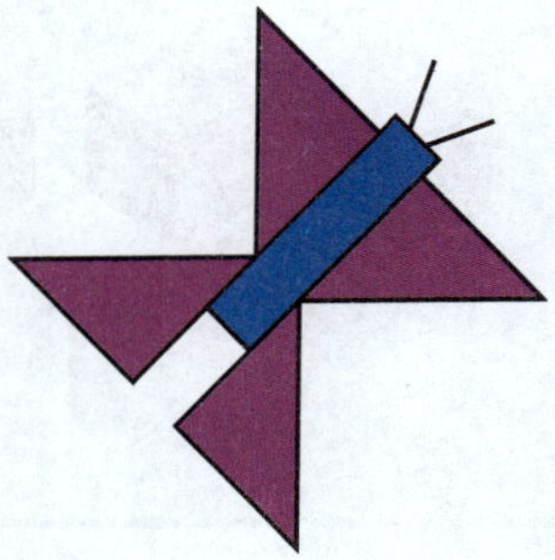

Have children look at the different shapes used to make each object. Then have them draw lines to match each group of shapes to the object they can make.

Practice

Match

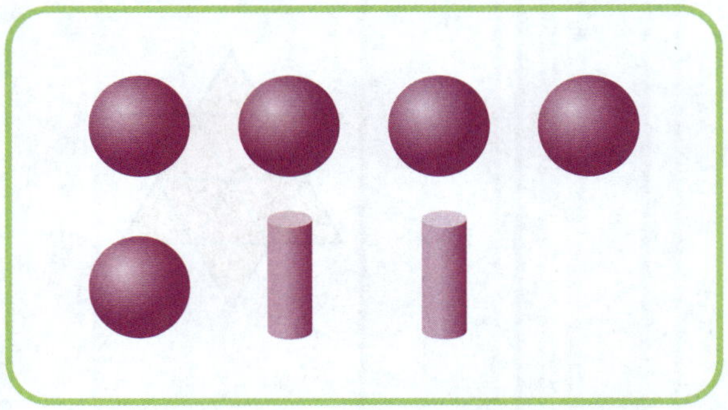

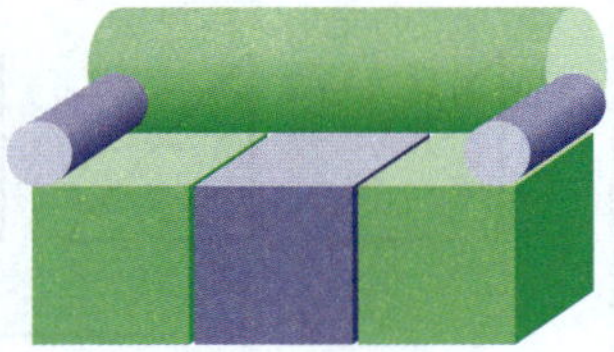

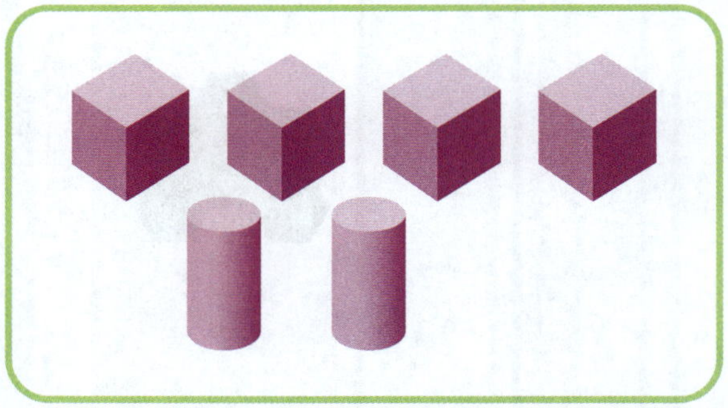

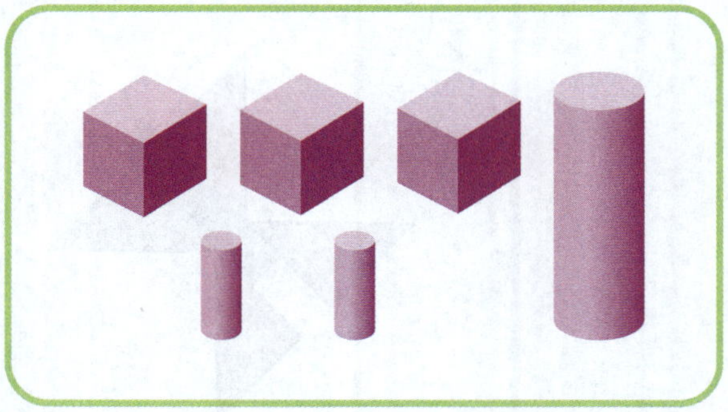

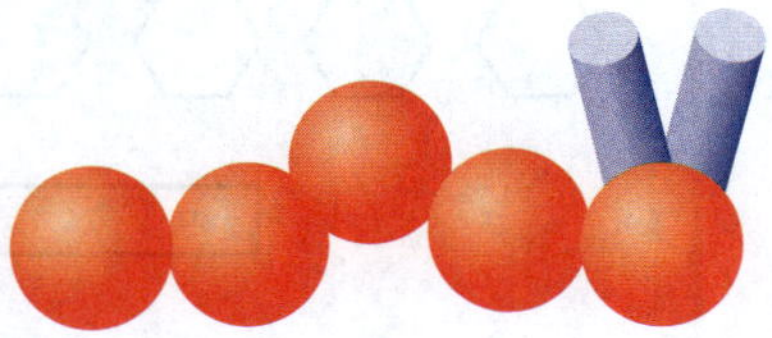

Have children look at the different shapes used to make each object. Then have them draw lines to match each group of shapes to the object they can make.

NAME:

Analyze It

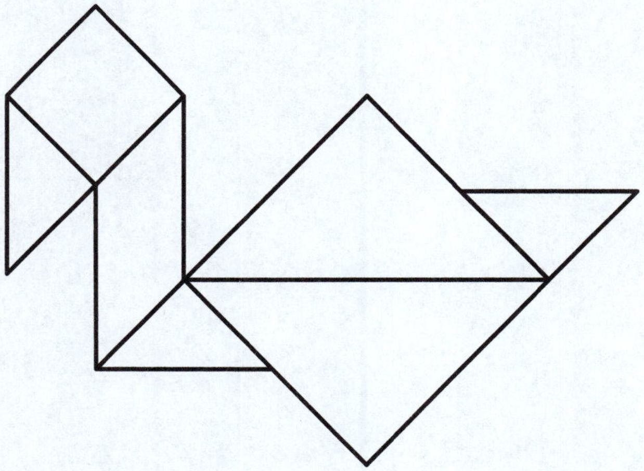

Read the problem aloud: *The cat and dog both think they used the tangram pieces to make a bird. Do you agree with the cat, the dog, or both? Why?* Have children circle the character or characters they agree with.

Lesson Reflection

Have children use numbers, words, or drawings to show something they learned or did in this lesson to build objects from shapes.

Practice

Color

Have children color triangles and squares to make their own picture or pattern.

Practice

Draw

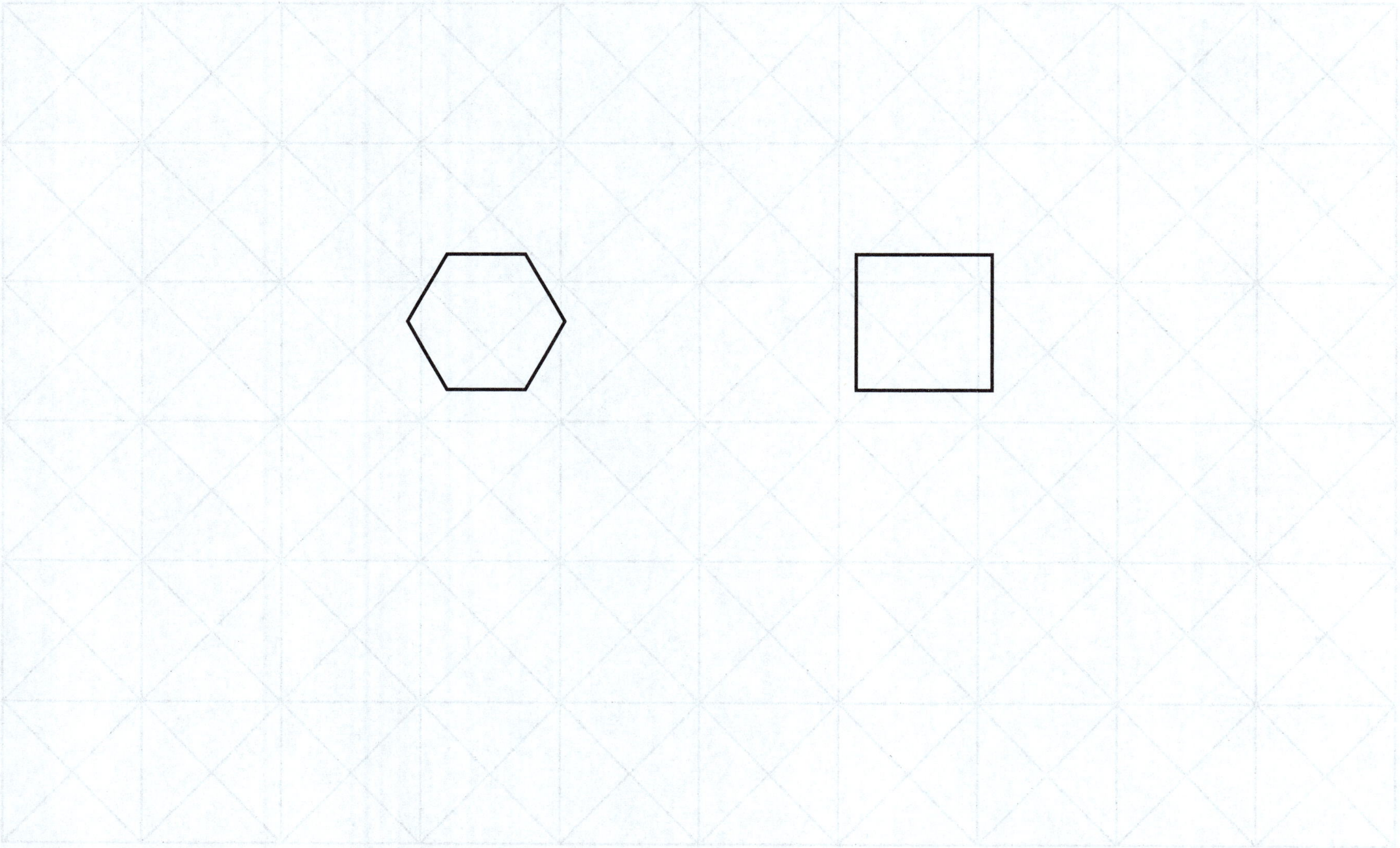

Have children draw shapes they know to make a picture that includes the hexagon and square.

LESSON 25

Family Letters are also available in multiple languages.

Compose and Decompose Teen Numbers with Symbols

Dear Family,

Your child is learning to write equations to show how teen numbers can be put together from, or broken apart into, 10 ones and some more ones. They continue to develop their understanding that all teen numbers are made up of 10 ones and some more ones.

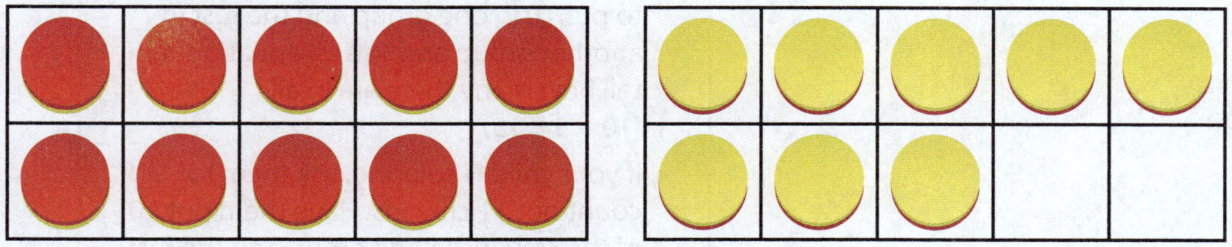

10 ones and 8 more ones

10 + 8 = 18

More about the Math

Your child has used objects and drawings to show how to put together and break apart teen numbers. Now your child will use what they know about addition to write addition equations to describe how they broke apart or put together a teen number.

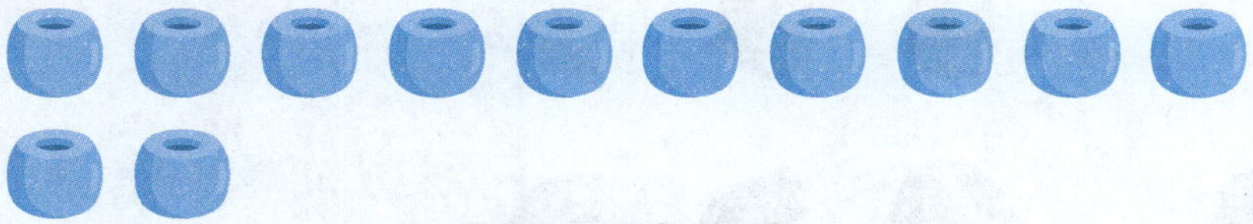

12 = 10 + 2

As children build these skills, they will begin to recognize patterns in putting together and taking apart teen numbers. For example, they will see that all teen numbers can be broken apart into 10 ones and some more ones.

i-Ready Connect

Digital Math Tools

Counters and Connecting Cubes

ACTIVITY

Break Apart

Do this activity with your child to explore how to use equations to describe breaking a teen number into a group of 10 ones and some more ones.

Materials: 19 small objects, such as pebbles or pennies

- Choose a number from 11 to 19. Ask your child to count out that many objects and place them in a pile.
- Have your child show how to break that number into a group of 10 ones and a group of some more ones.
- Ask your child how many objects are in each group.
- Ask your child to **SAY** an addition equation to describe adding the two groups to make the teen number.

SAY 10 plus 6 is equal to 16.

Math on the GO!

Conversation Starter

Look for opportunities to use equations to describe putting together and breaking apart teen numbers in real-world situations. For example:

- As you prepare dinner or a snack, make a pile of 15 items (such as pieces of carrots or small crackers). Ask your child to put 10 in one group and the rest in another group and use an equation to tell how many there are in all. ($10 + 5 = 15$)
- If your child is coloring, ask them to count out 11 crayons. Have them put 10 of the crayons in one group and the rest in another group and use an equation to describe how they broke apart the number 11. ($11 = 10 + 1$)

NAME:

LESSON 25

Number Sense

Project the scene. Ask children: *What do you notice? What do you wonder?*

Compose and decompose teen numbers into 10 ones and some more ones. Record composing and decomposing teen numbers with drawings and equations.

Investigate It

______

______ + ______

After doing the Discover It activity as a class, have children complete the Investigate It activity and draw or write to show two cards they matched.

In the game, how did you make sure the cards matched?

NAME:

Try-Discuss-Connect

Make sense of the problem: *A family counted 12 snail shells in the tide pools. Write an equation to show what the family found.* Have children write an addition equation that shows the number of snail shells.

How did you decide what equation to write?

Model Teen Numbers Activity

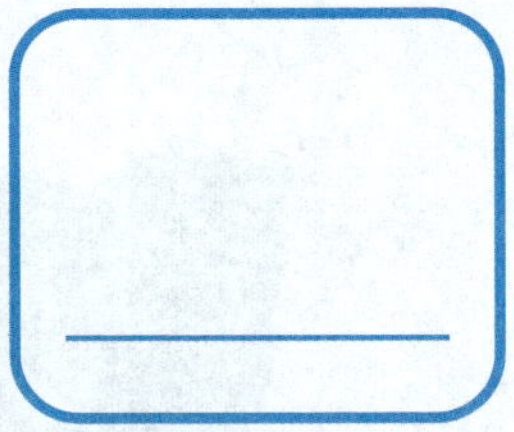

10 + ______ ◯ ______

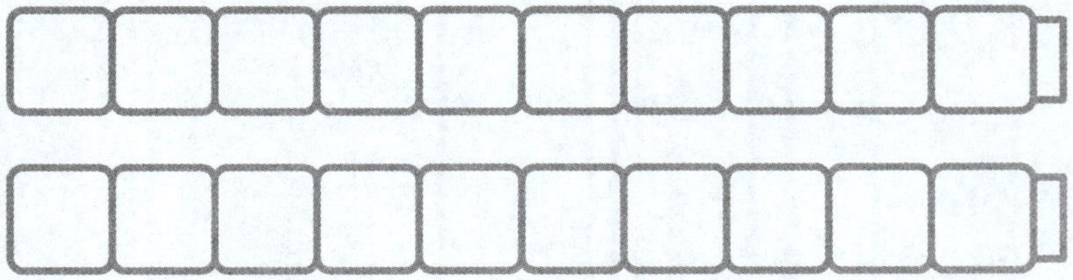

After children have completed one round of the Model Teen Numbers Activity, have them record their results by writing the number, writing an equation, coloring connecting cubes, and drawing counters in the 10-frames.

How do you know when a model shows a teen number?

NAME:

Practice

Match

$10 + 7 =$ ______

$10 + 4 =$ ______

$10 + 6 =$ ______

Have children match each group to the equation that shows the same quantities. Then have them complete the equations.

Practice

Match

$10 + 8 =$ ______

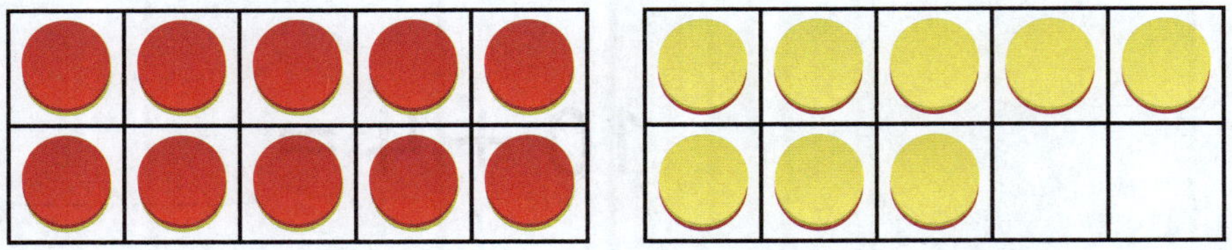

$10 + 2 =$ ______

$10 + 5 =$ ______

Have children match each group to the equation that shows the same quantities. Then have them complete the equations.

NAME:

Try-Discuss-Connect

Make sense of the problem: *A scientist has a collection of fossils. One case is full. The other case is not full. How many fossils could they have?* Have children draw to solve the problem and write an equation to match.

Do you and your partner have the same equation? How are they the same or different?

Make Teen Numbers Activity

______

10 + ______ = ______

______

10 + ______ = ______

______

10 + ______ = ______

______

10 + ______ = ______

______

10 + ______ = ______

______

10 + ______ = ______

After children have completed several rounds of the Make Teen Numbers Activity, have them record three rounds by writing the teen numbers, coloring counters in the 10-frames, and writing an equation.

How do you know what teen number you make when you add some ones to 10 ones?

NAME:

Practice

Write

Example

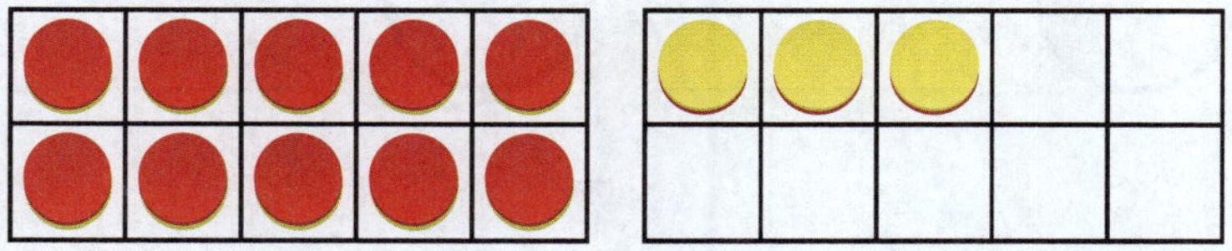

10 + 3 = 13

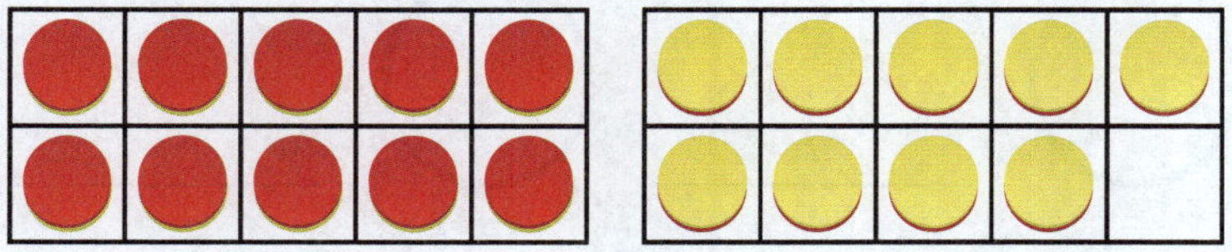

___ ◯ ___ ◯ ___

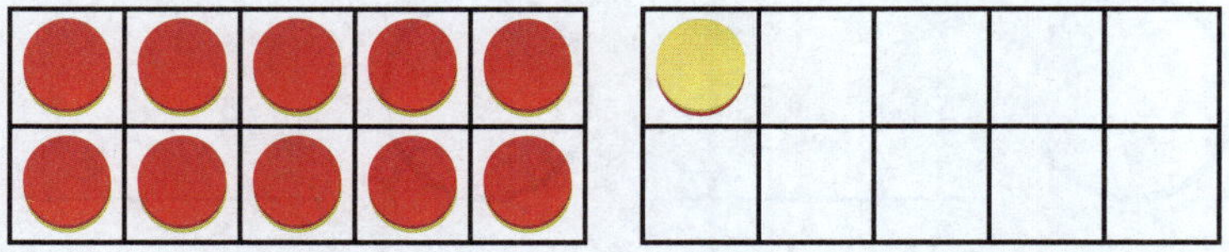

___ ◯ ___ ◯ ___

Have children write equations to show 10 ones plus some more ones.

Practice

Draw Write

Have children draw counters and write equations to show 10 ones plus some more ones.

NAME:

Make Connections

10 ◯ ______ ◯ ______

Have children use one crayon to color the first swatch and 10 sea stars. Have them use a different crayon to color the second swatch and any number of the remaining sea stars. Then have them write an equation to describe the number of sea stars they colored.

Show Teen Numbers Activity

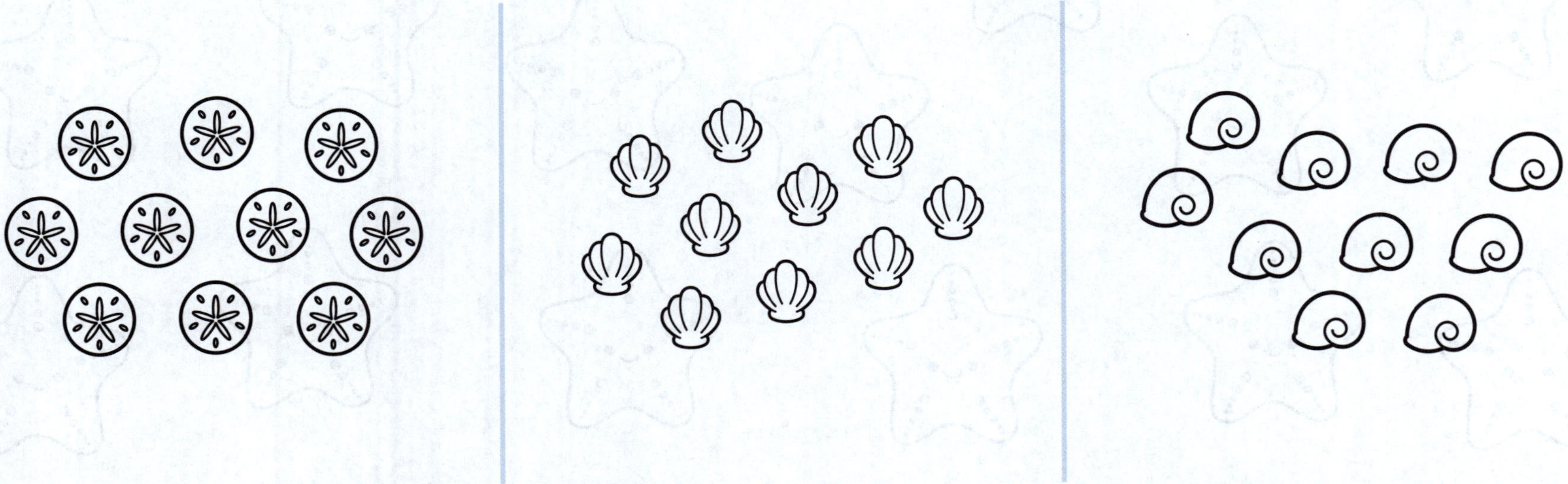

Ask children to color a group of 10 and draw some more to make a teen number. Have them color to complete the key and write an equation to match. Repeat for the other two groups, using different colors.

Practice

Color

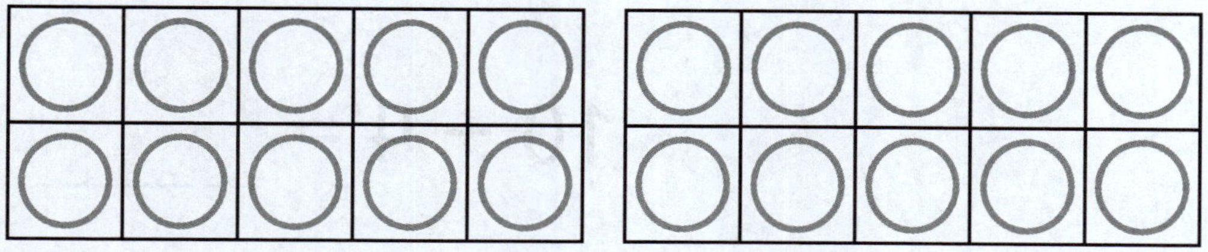

10 + 5 = ______

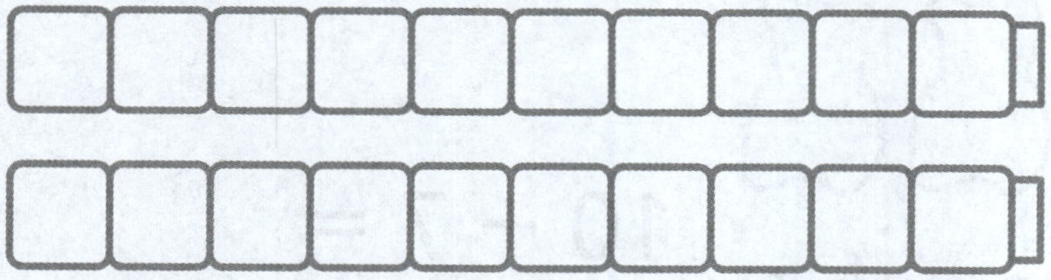

10 + 9 = ______

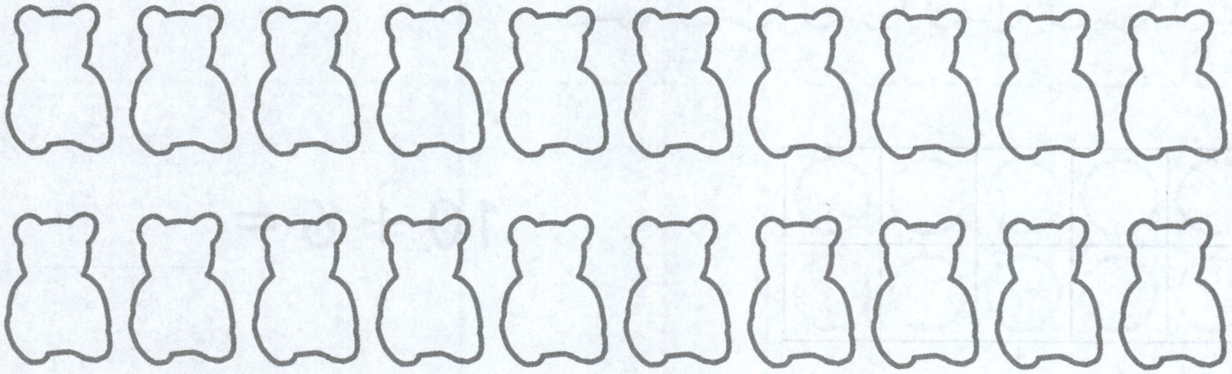

10 + 3 = ______

Have children color to model each equation and write the teen number.

Practice

Color

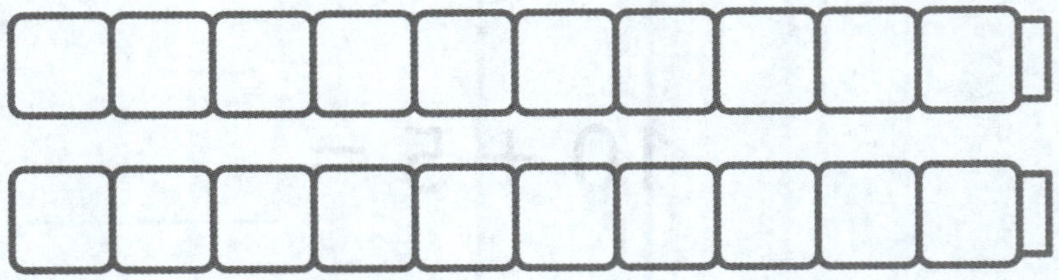

$10 + 4 =$ ______

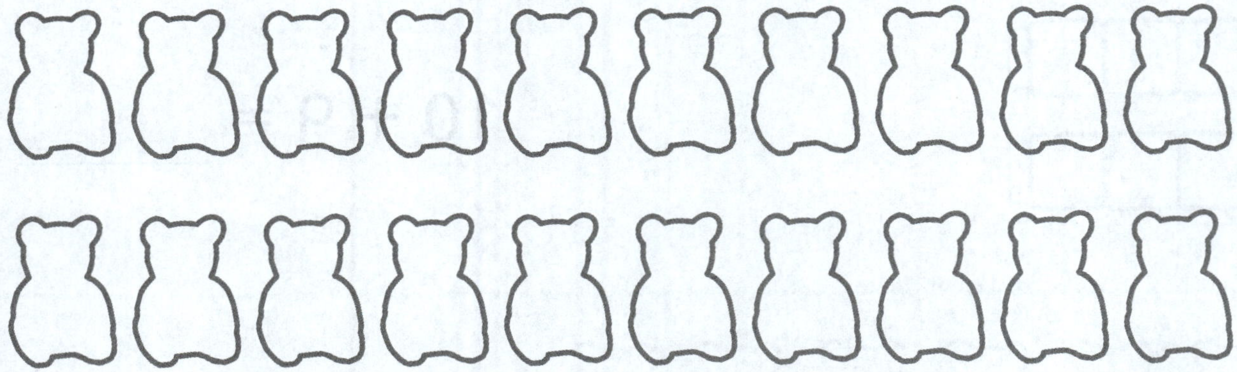

$10 + 7 =$ ______

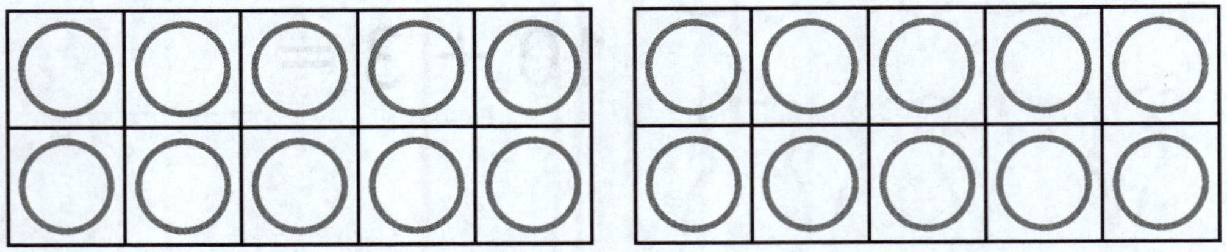

$10 + 6 =$ ______

Have children color to model each equation and write the teen number.

NAME:

Analyze It

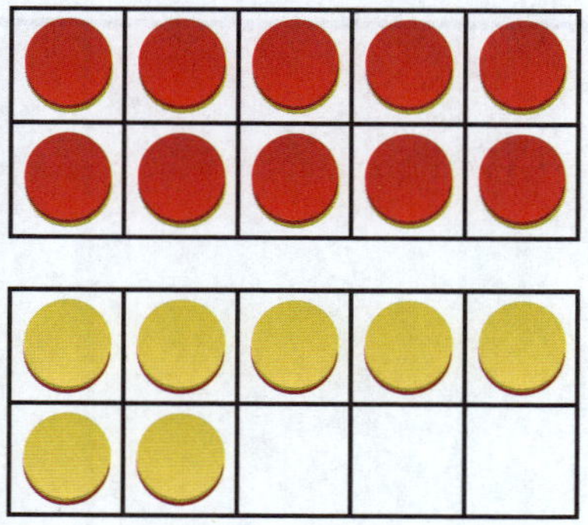

$17 = 10 + 7$

$10 + 7 = 17$

Read the problem aloud: *The cat and dog both wrote equations to represent the model. Do you agree with the cat, the dog, or both? Why?* Have children circle who they agree with.

Lesson Reflection

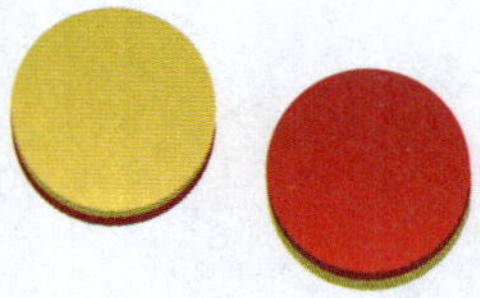

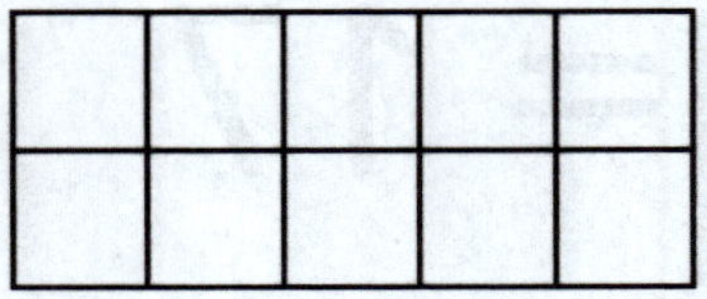

_____ + _____ = _____

Have children use numbers, words, or drawings to show something they learned or did in this lesson to compose and decompose teen numbers.

Practice

Color Write

10 + ______ = ______

10 + ______ = ______

10 + ______ = ______

10 + ______ = ______

Have children color the marbles in a bag and then use the same crayon to color some more of the marbles to make a teen number. Color to complete the key and write an equation to match. Repeat for each bag.

Practice

Color 12: 13: 15: 18: 19:

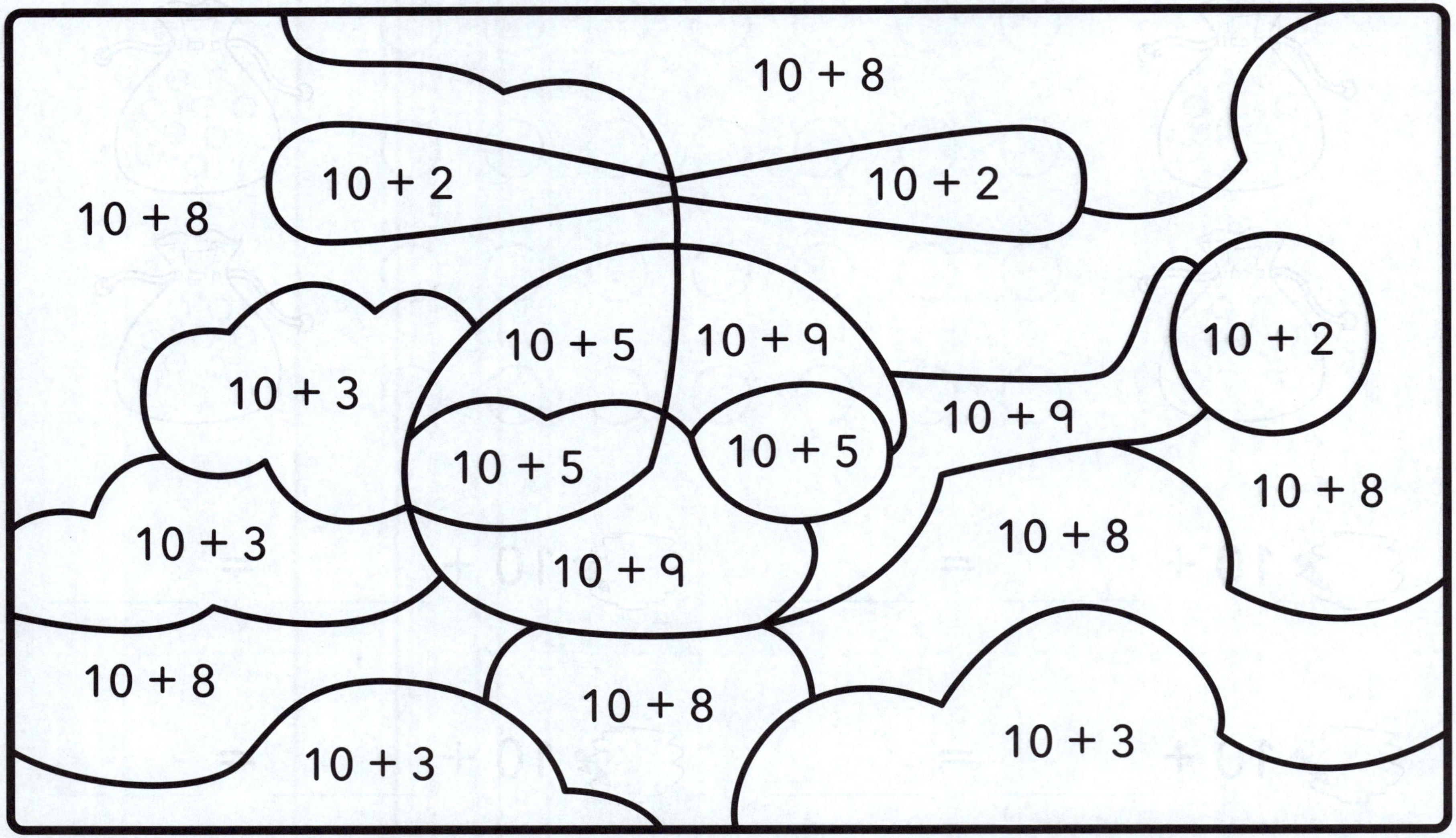

Read the following riddle: *I have blades but I am not grass. I can fly but I do not have wings.* Ask children to color the key for each number in a different color. Then have them find how many in each space of the hidden picture and use the key to color the space..

NAME:

Design Birdhouses

What flat shapes did you use for your birdhouse pictures?

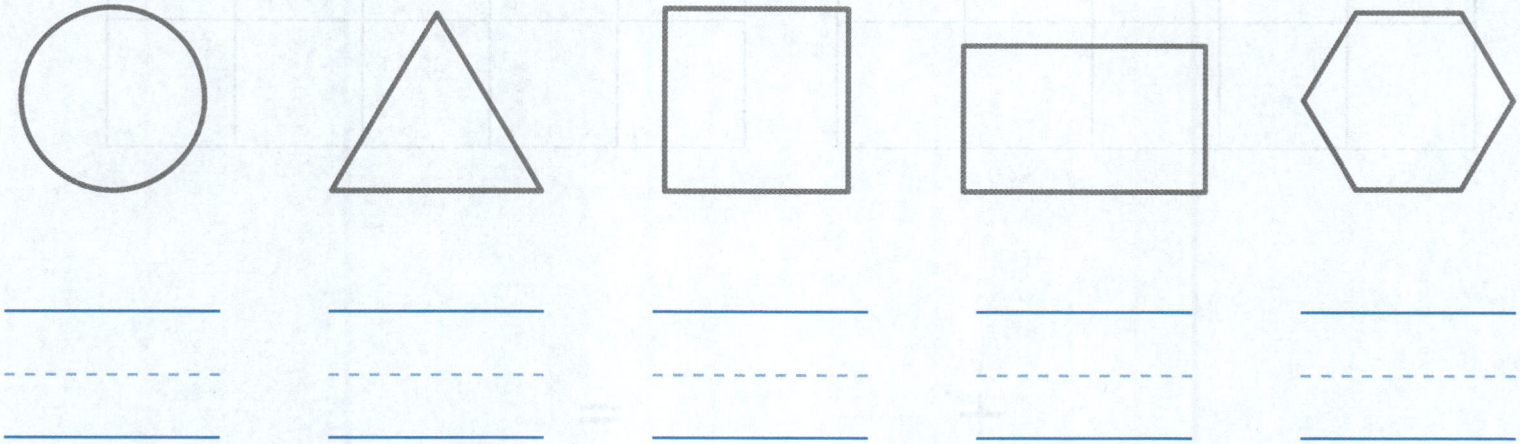

Have children put flat shapes together to design different birdhouses. Then have children color each kind of shape they used and write the number of each kind.

Design a Birdhouse for Groups

How many bird families can live in your birdhouse?

______ + ______ = ______

Have children make a design for a birdhouse with a teen number of holes. Then have children fill in the 10-frames and complete the equation to show the number of holes as 10 ones and some more ones.

How is your birdhouse the same as your partner's? How is it different?

NAME:

My Birdhouse Information

11	12	13
14	15	16
17	18	19

Have children circle the number of bird families that can live in their birdhouse. Have them write the number. Then have them trace over the first ten lines and draw some more lines to show their number using short lines.

What is the same? What is different?

Reflection

What do you notice and wonder about the class data display?

I notice:

I wonder:

Have children notice and wonder about the class data display. Have them answer one of their questions and use numbers, words, drawings, objects, and/or gestures to show their reasoning.

NAME:

Show What You Learned

Have children draw to show what they learned about teen numbers and shapes. Prompt children to reflect on their learning by posing questions such as: *What do you know how to do well? What math could you use in your everyday life? What is a question you still have?*

Circle

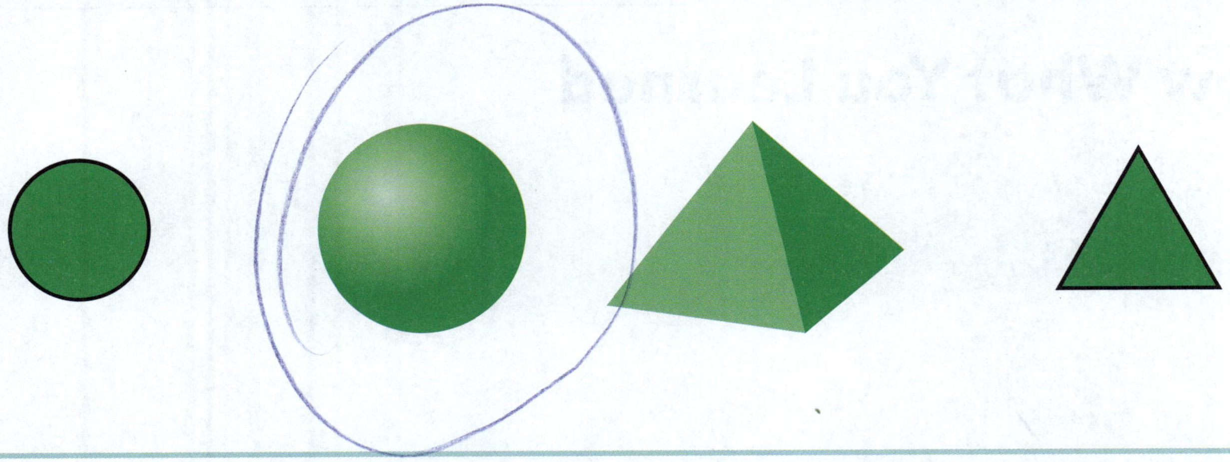

Write

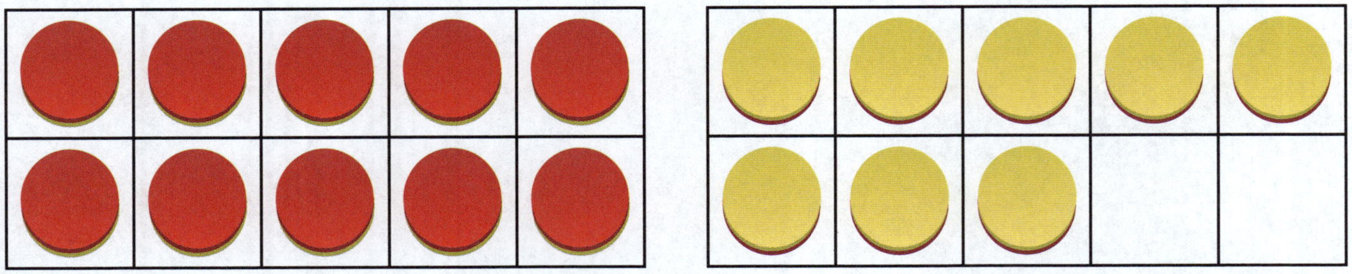

10 + 8 = 18

For the first problem, have children circle the solid shapes.
For the next problem, have children write an equation to show 10 ones plus some more ones.

NAME:

Draw Circle Write

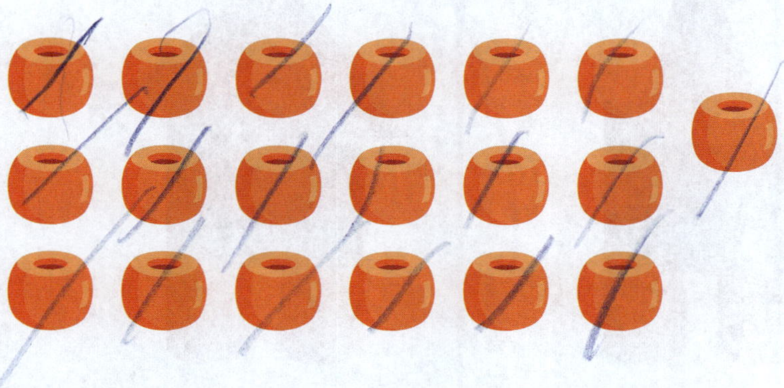

17 18 19

10 + ____ = ____

Circle

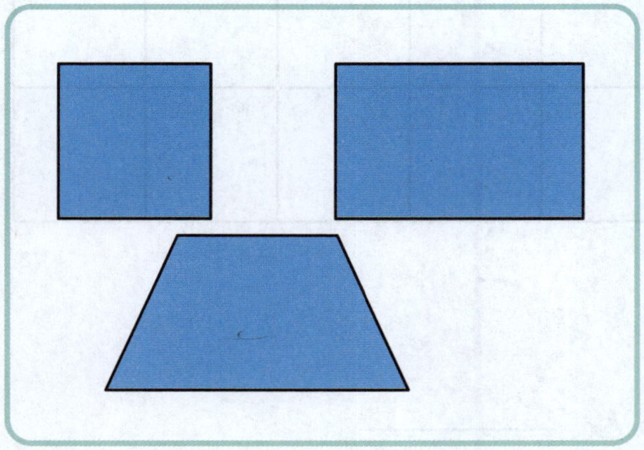

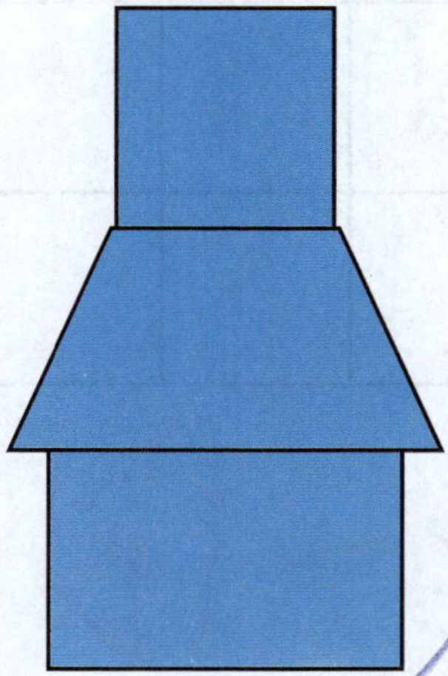

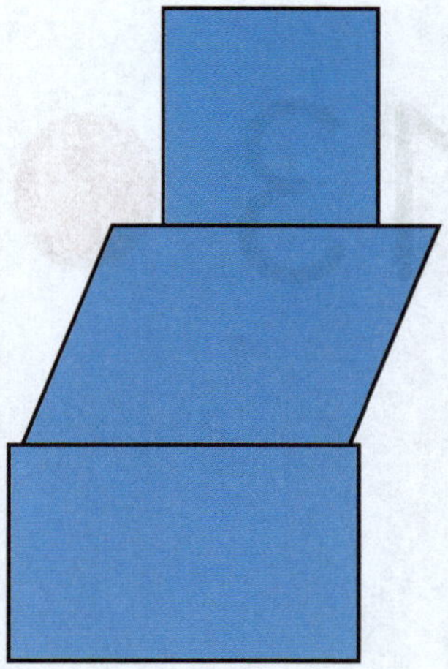

For the first problem, have children circle 10 beads, circle the teen number that tells how many, and complete the addition that describes them. For the next problem, have children circle the picture that the set of shapes can make. Allow them to use tangrams as needed.

Circle

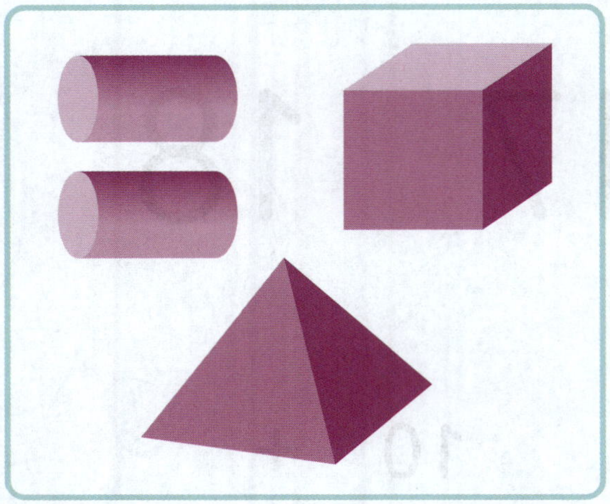

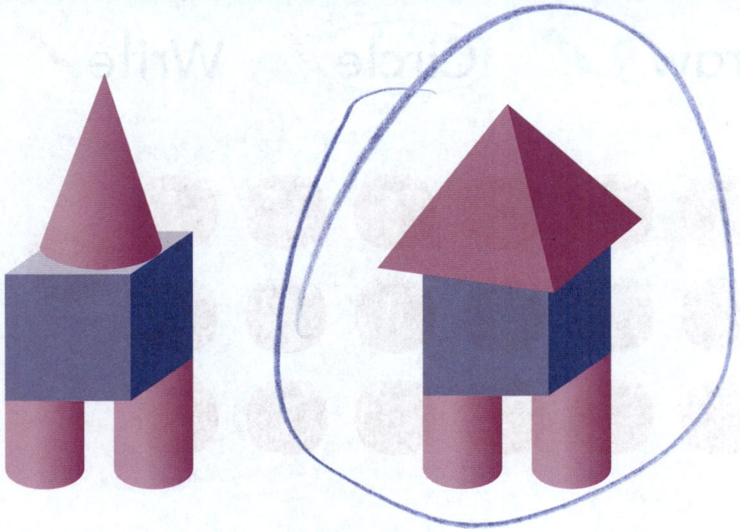

Draw Write

13

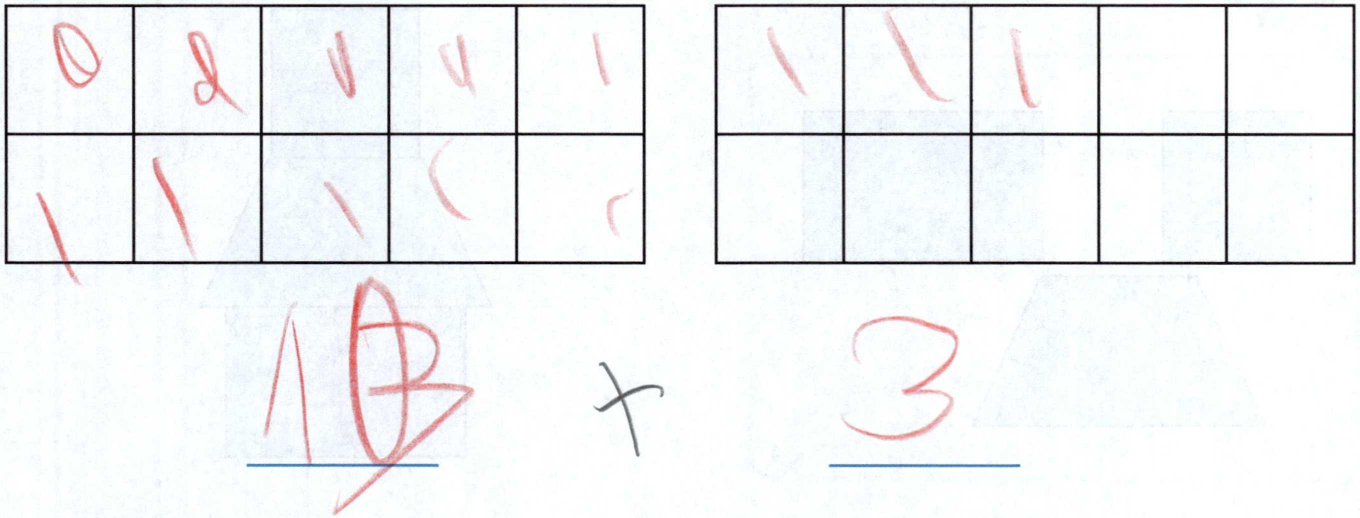

For the first problem, have children circle the object that is made from the given solid objects. For the next problem, have children draw counters in the 10-frames to show the number of counters as 10 and some more, and then write the number of counters in each 10-frame.

NAME:

First have children count and write the number of cereal boxes. Then have them count and write the number of jars. Next have children write the number 2 and circle two of the same item. Finally have children write the number 3 and draw a line under three of the same item.

2 5

3 1

First have children count and write how many pasta boxes and how many cans. Then have them circle the number that is less. Repeat for how many cereal boxes and how many jars. Finally have children compare each pair of numbers and write the number that is greater.

NAME:

UNIT 4

4 + 1 = ____

2 + 2 = ____

Say: *There are 4 cats and 1 soccer ball. How many in all?* Children write the total. Repeat.
Say: *There are 2 drums and 2 guitars. How many in all?*

$3 - 2 =$ ______

$4 - 1 =$ ______

Say: *There are 3 dinosaurs. Take away 2 dinosaurs. How many dinosaurs are left?*
Children may mark or underline the dinosaurs they are subtracting. Repeat.
Say: *There are 4 cats. Take away 1 cat. How many are left?*

NAME:

UNIT 5

Have children count and write the number of flying birds. Then have them write the number that shows one more. Repeat with the number of polka-dot swim rings.

7 4

6 8

First have children count and write how many flowers and how many striped towels. Then have them circle the number that is greater. Repeat for how many small ducks and how many polka-dot swim tubes. Next have children compare each pair of numbers and write the number that is less.

NAME:

First have children count and write the number of duck books. Then have them count and write the number of square cushions. Next have them write the number 8 and circle eight of the same item. Finally have them write the number 9 and draw a line under nine of the same item.

10 ______ and ______

10 ______ and ______

 ______ and ______

 ______ and ______

First have children circle two groups of items that make 10 in all and then write how many in each group. Repeat for another two groups. Next have children count and write the number of square pillows and then write how many more make 10. Repeat for the number of computer chairs.

NAME:

UNIT 6

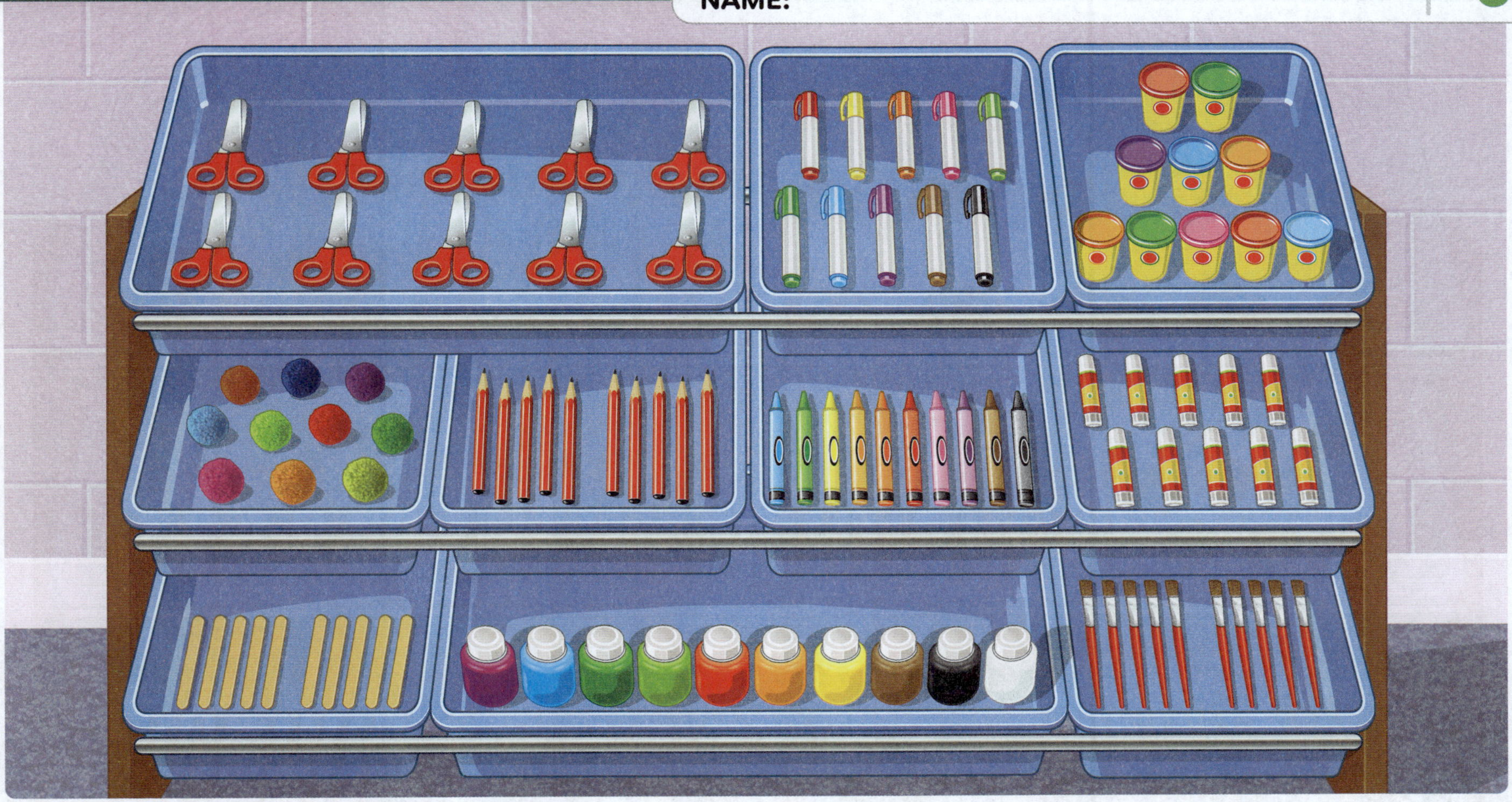

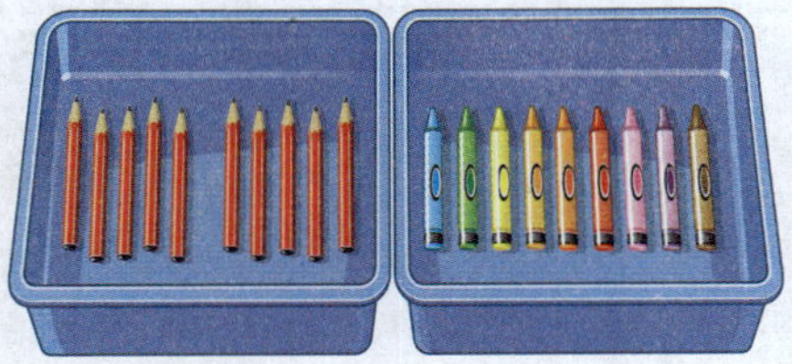

First have children count and write the number of markers and crayons. Then have children write the number 12 and circle twelve items. Finally have children write the number 17 and draw a line under seventeen items.

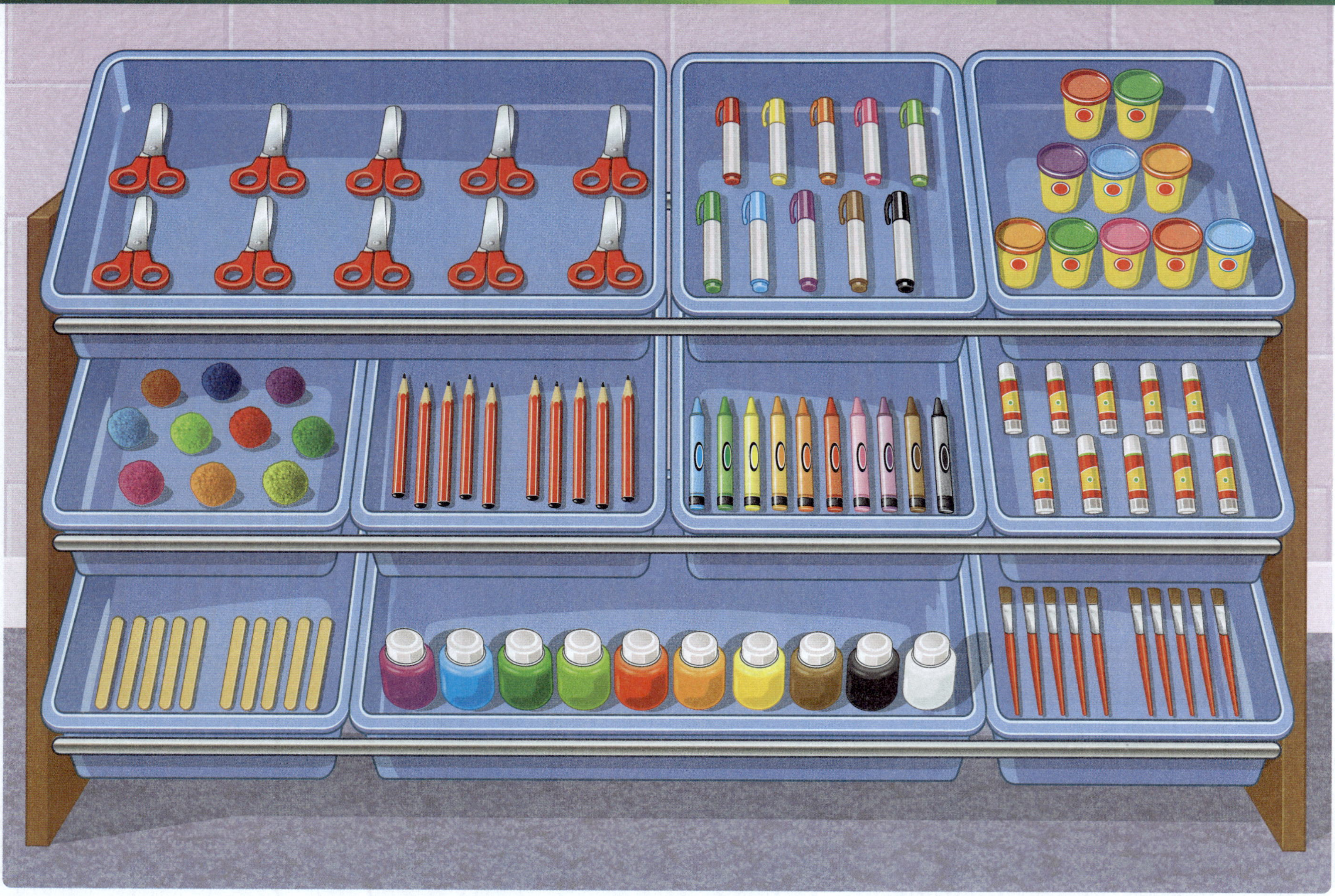

Each bin shows a group of 10. First have children circle 33 items. Then have them draw a line under more items to count to 42. Finally have children count by 10s to 100, crossing out each group of 10 items as they count.

NAME:

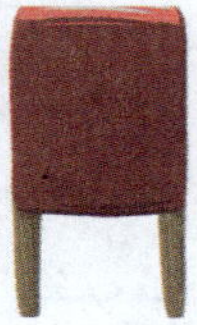 6 = ____ + ____

 7 = ____ + ____

Have children circle two groups of chairs to make number partners for 6 and write the number partners in the equation. Then have children circle two groups of oranges to make number partners for 7 and write the number partners in the equation.

 8 = ______ + ______

 9 = ______ + ______

Have children circle two groups of snowpeople to make number partners for 8 and write the number partners in the equation. Then have children circle two groups of snowballs to make number partners for 9 and write the number partners in the equation.

NAME:

UNIT 7

$5 + 1 =$ ____

$2 + 6 =$ ____

$2 + 5 =$ ____

$7 + 3 =$ ____

Say: *5 kites and 1 more kite. How many kites are there now?*
Say: *2 bikes on the road and 5 more bikes on the grass. How many bikes in all?*
Have children complete each addition equation.

 $10 - 3 =$ ______

$8 - 3 =$ ______

 $7 - 2 =$ ______

$9 - 6 =$ ______

Say: *10 bubbles take away 3 bubbles. How many bubbles are there now?*
Say: *7 bikes take away 2 bikes. How many bikes are there now?*
Have children complete each subtraction equation.

NAME:

 7 ◯ 3 = ______

 5 ◯ 2 = ______

Say: *There are 7 leaves on one branch and 3 leaves on another branch. How many leaves are there in all?*
Say: *There are 5 orange slices on a plate. 2 more slices are put on the plate. How many orange slices are on the plate now?*

 9 ◯ 2 = ____

 7 ◯ 1 = ____

Say: *There are 9 butterflies. 2 butterflies fly away. How many butterflies are there now?*
Say: *There are 7 leaves on a branch. 1 leaf gets eaten. How many leaves are there now?*

Glossary • Glosario

Aa

above • sobre

add, addition • sumar, suma

2 + 1 = 3

Bb

behind • detrás de

below • debajo de

beside • junto a

Cc

circle • círculo

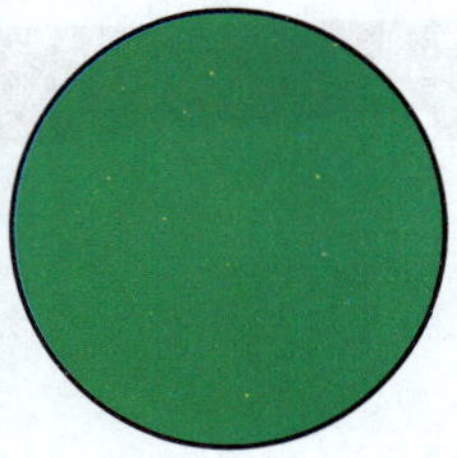

cone • cono

corner • esquina

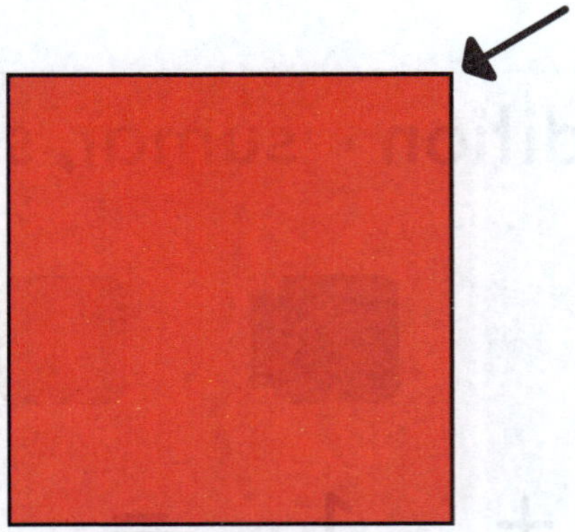

count • **contar**

count on • **contar hacia delante**

cube • **cubo**

cylinder • **cilindro**

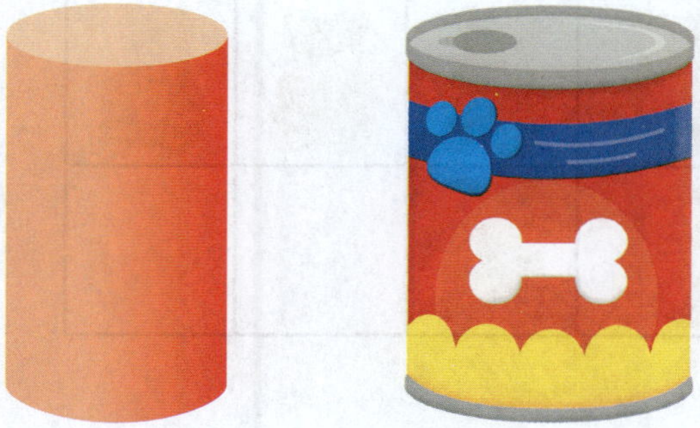

Ee

edge • **arista**

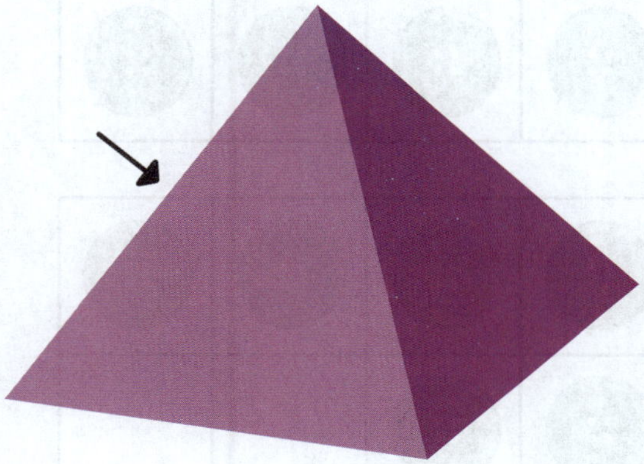

eight • ocho

8

eighteen • dieciocho

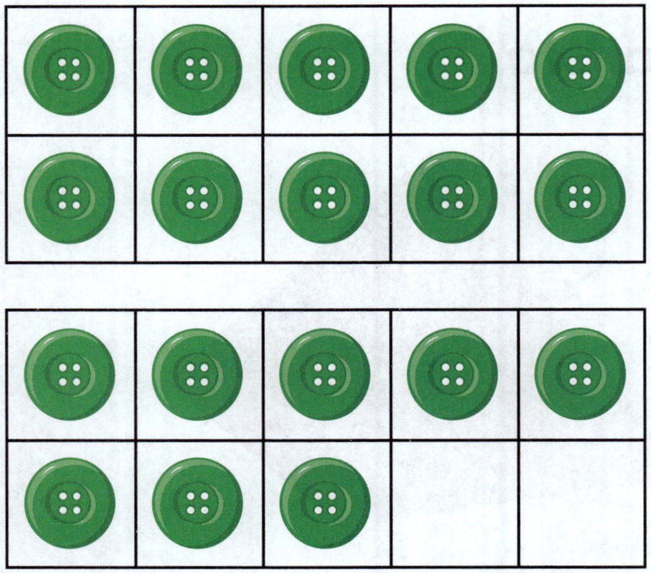

18

eleven • once

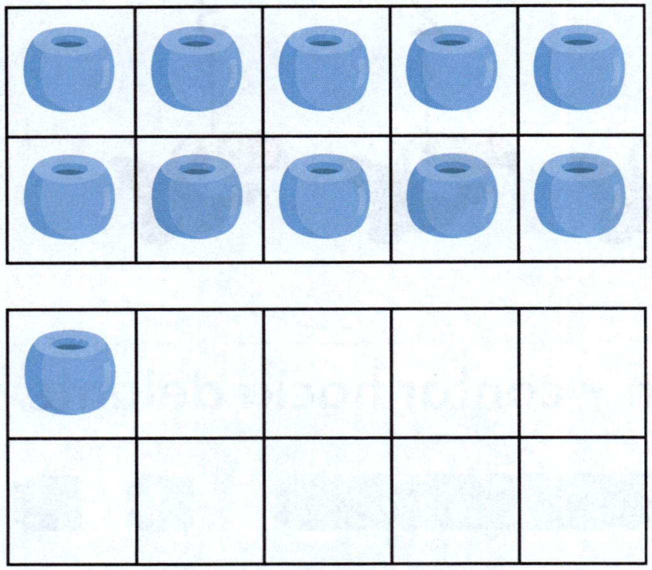

11

equal, equal to • igual, igual a

equal sign (=) • **signo de igual (=)**

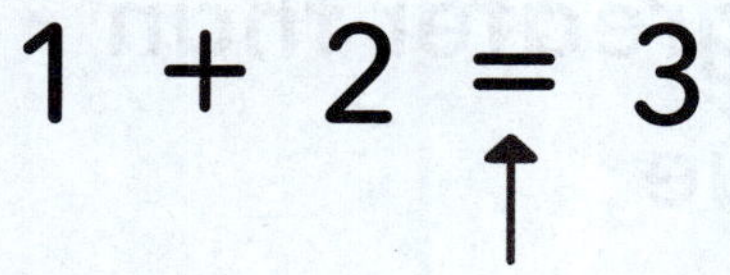

equation • **ecuación**

$6 - 2 = 4$

Ff

face • **cara**

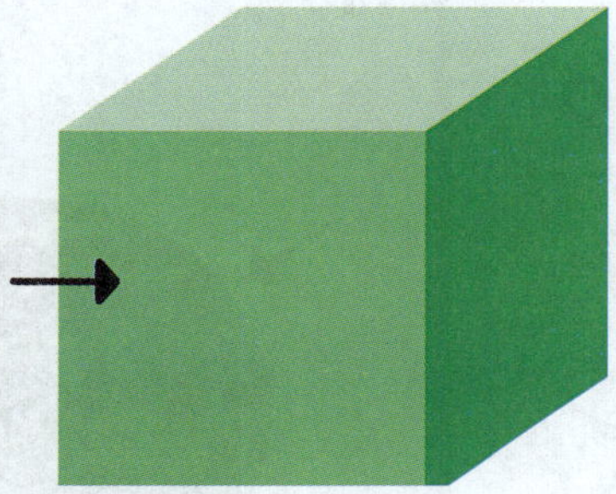

fifteen • **quince**

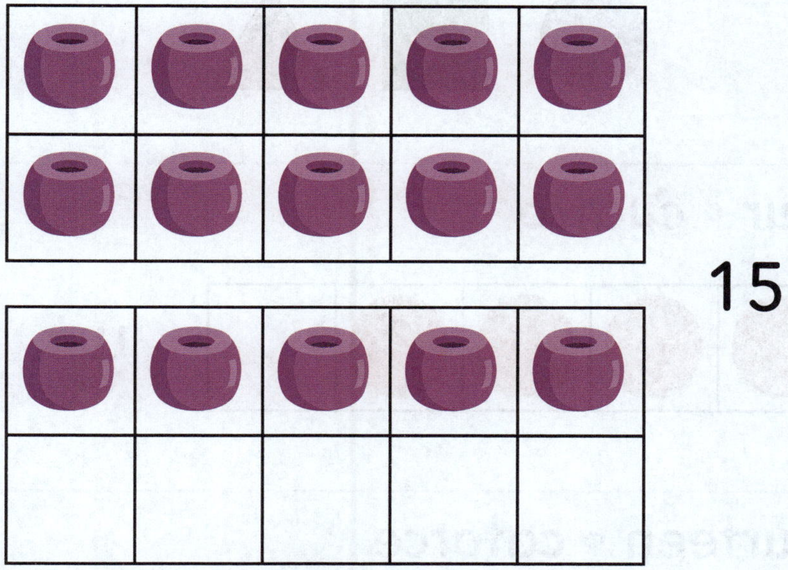

five • **cinco**

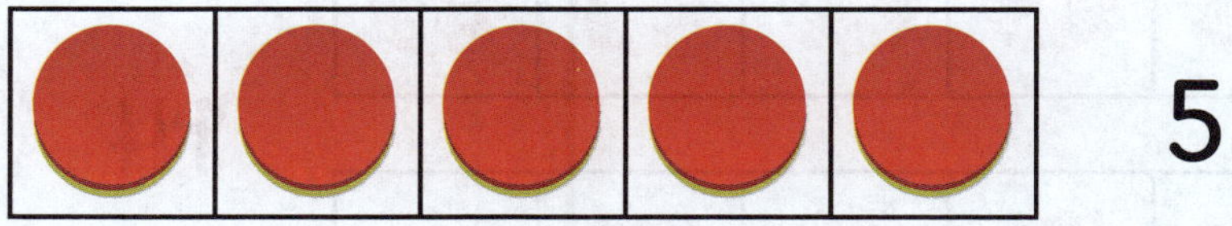

flat • plano

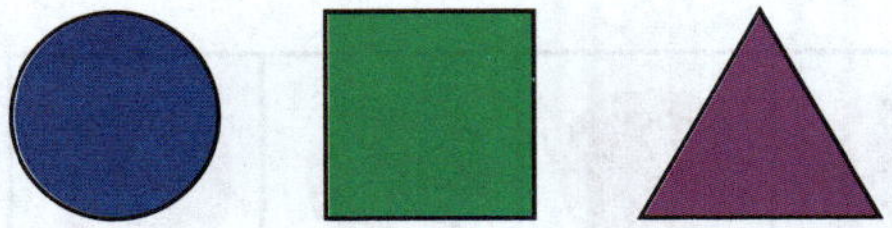

four • cuatro

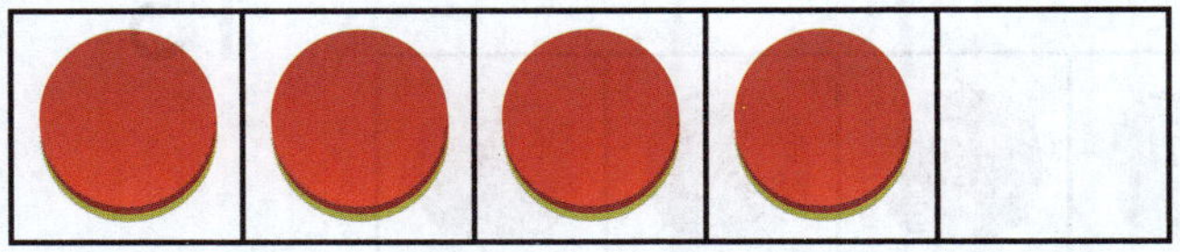

4

fourteen • catorce

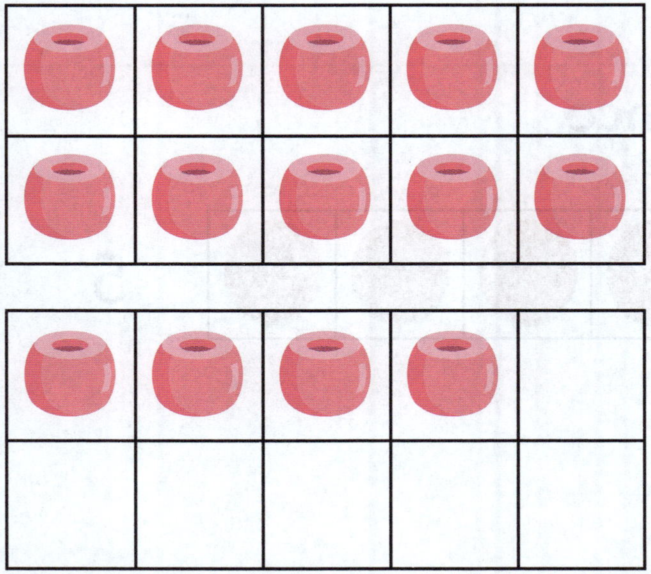

14

Gg

greater, greater than • mayor, mayor que

4

2

Hh

heavy, heavier • pesado, más pesado

height • **altura**

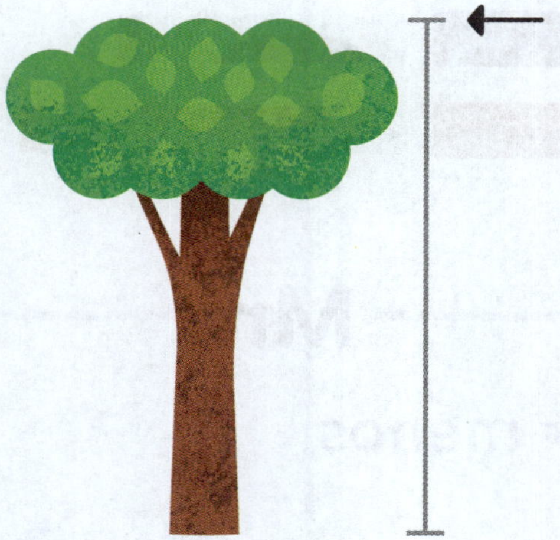

hexagon • **hexágono**

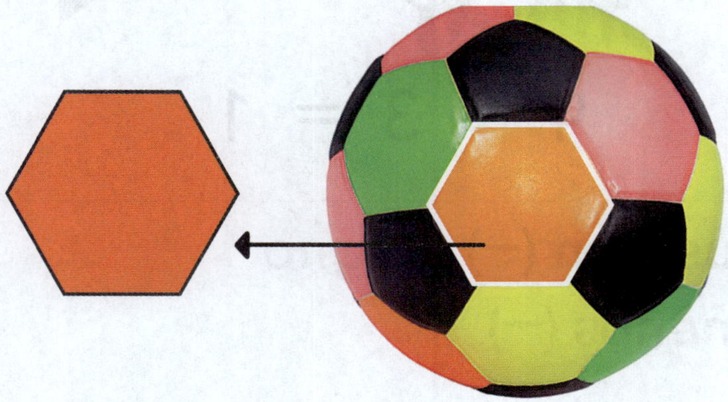

Ii

in front of • **delante de**

Ll

length • **longitud**

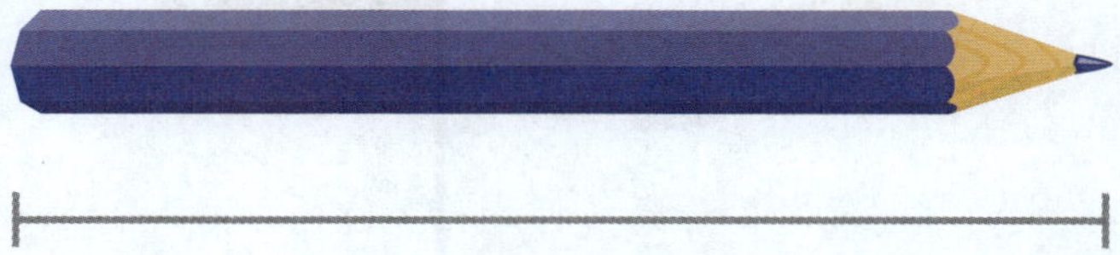

less, less than • menos, menos que

light, lighter • liviano, más liviano

long, longer • largo, más largo

Mm

minus • menos

$$4 - 3 = 1$$

minus sign (–) • signo de menos (–)

$$3 - 1 = 2$$

↑

more, more than • más, más que

Nn

next to • al lado de

nine • nueve

9

nineteen • diecinueve

19

number • **número**

5

↑

Oo

one • **uno**

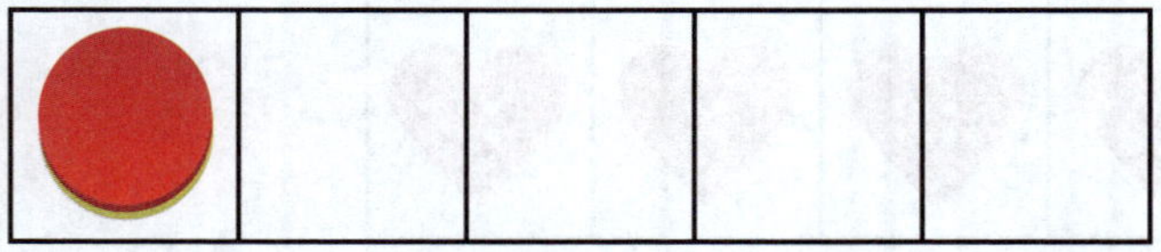

1

Pp

plus • **más**

$$1 + 2 = 3$$

plus sign (+) • **signo de más (+)**

$$1 + 2 = 3$$

↑

prism • **prisma**

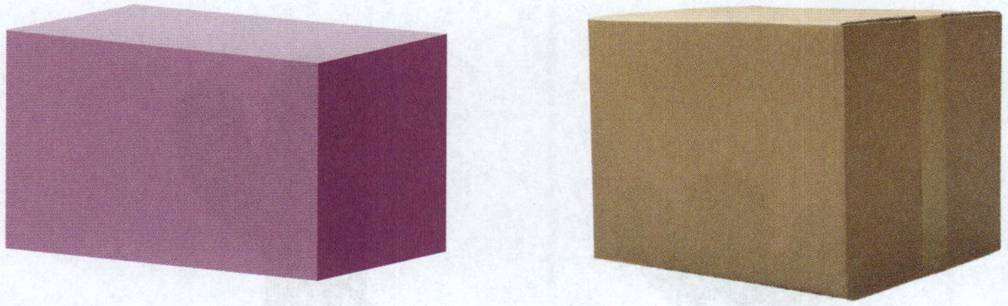

pyramid • **pirámide**

Rr

rectangle • **rectángulo**

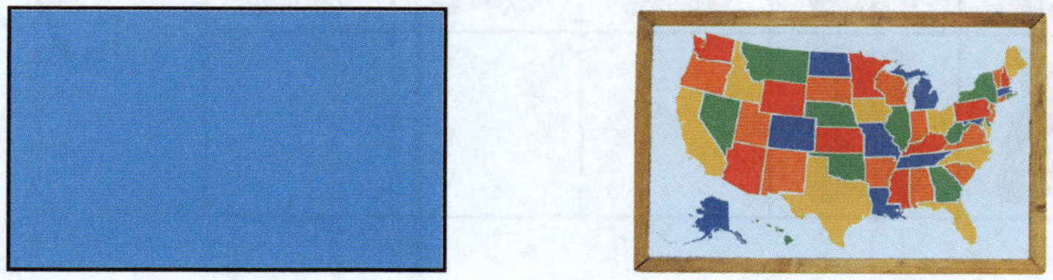

Ss

same, same as • **mismo, mismo que**

seven • siete

7

seventeen • diecisiete

17

short, shorter • bajo, corto, más bajo, más corto

side • lado

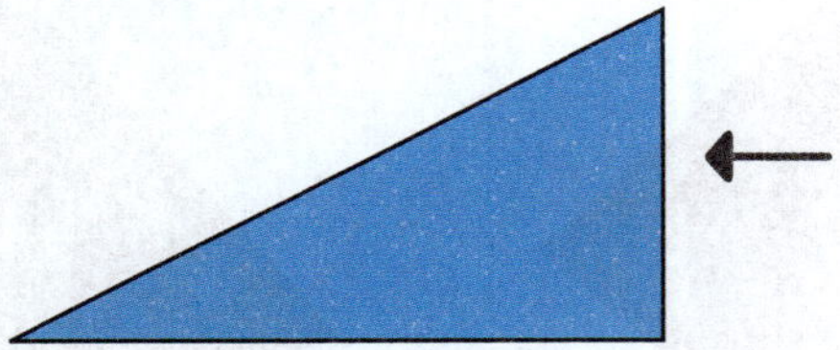

six • seis

6

sixteen • dieciséis

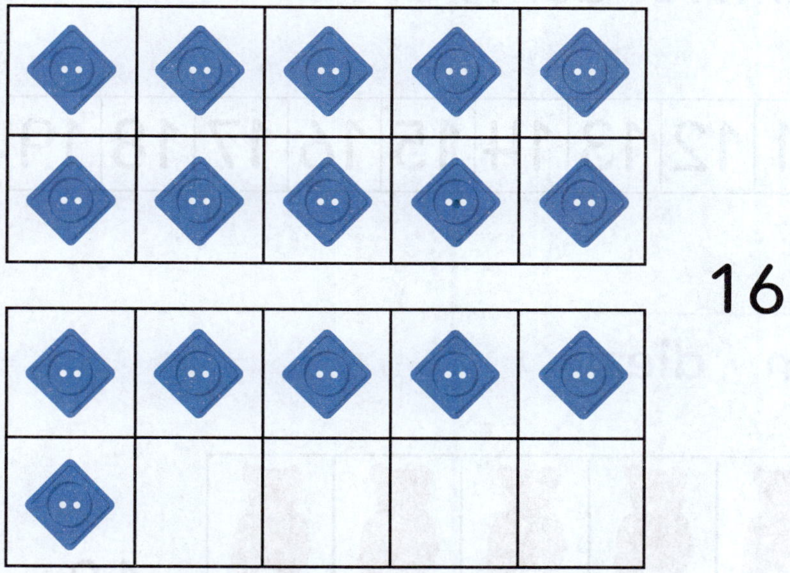

solid • sólido

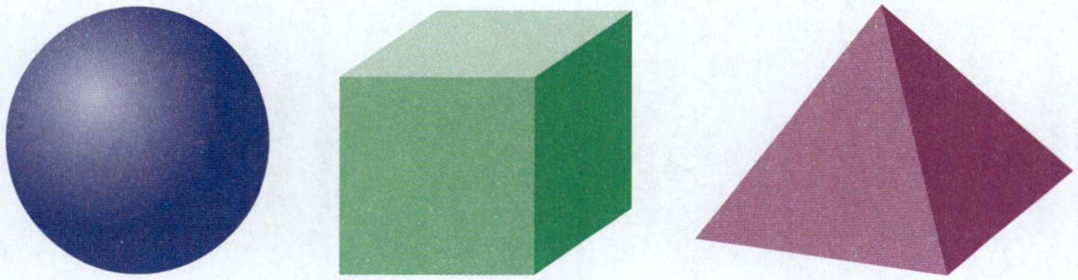

sort • clasificar

sphere • esfera

square • cuadrado

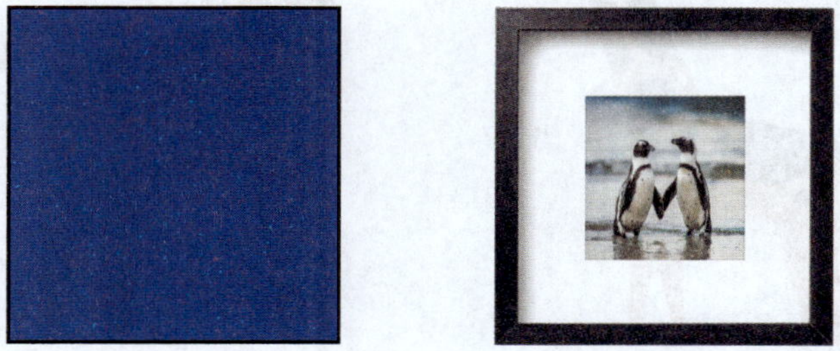

subtract, subtraction • **restar, resta**

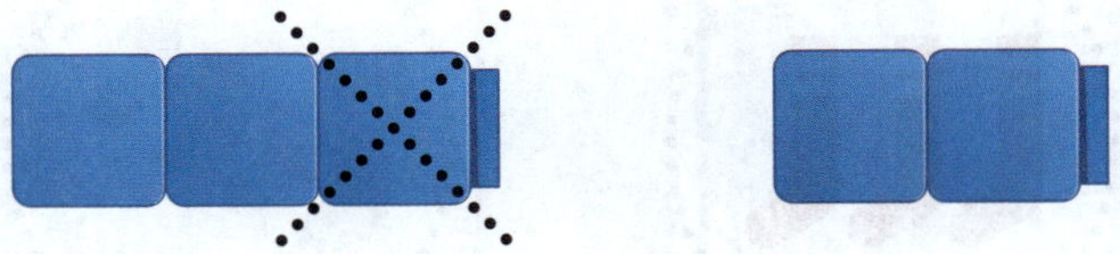

3 − 1 = 2

Tt

tall, taller • **alto, más alto**

teen numbers • **números del 11 al 19**

11	12	13	14	15	16	17	18	19

ten • **diez**

10

thirteen • trece

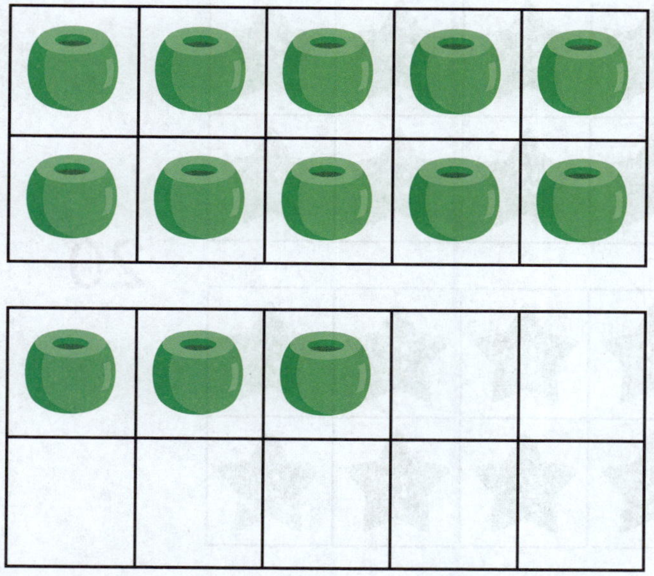

13

three • tres

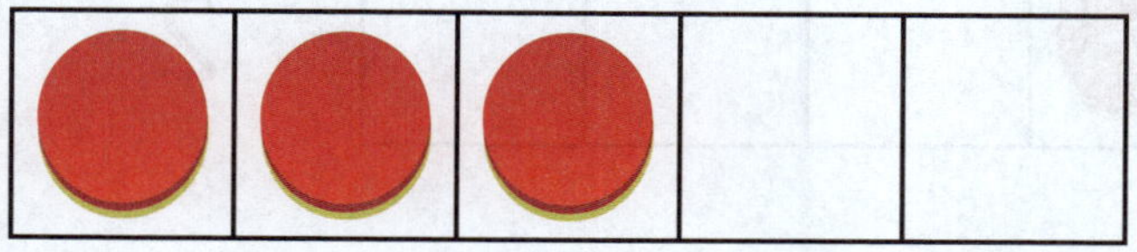

3

total • total

2 + 1 = 3

↑

triangle • triángulo

twelve • doce

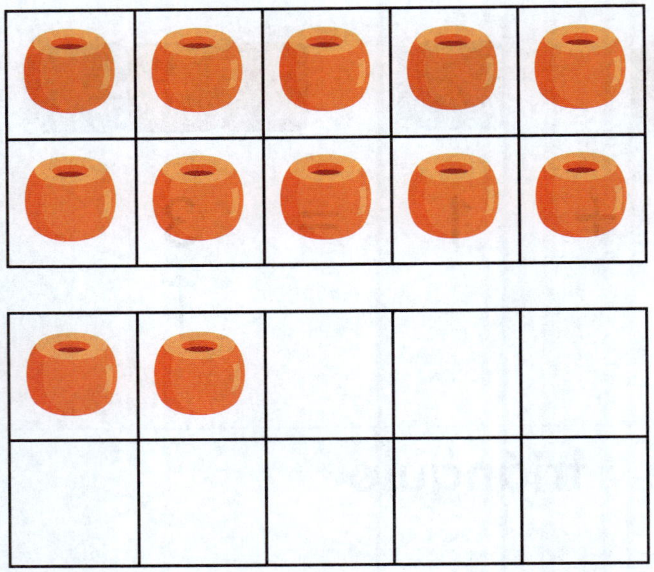

12

twenty • veinte

20

two • dos

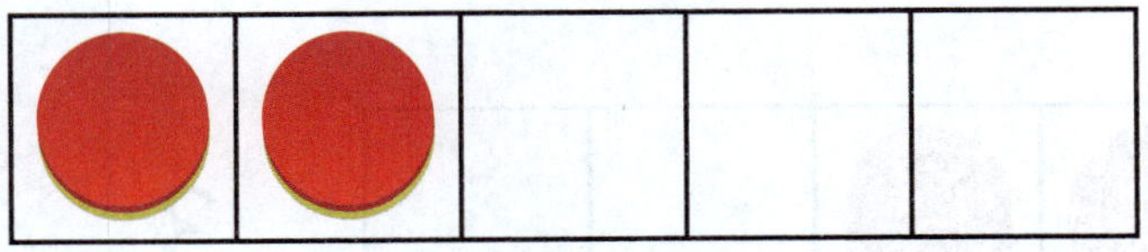

2

Vv

vertex • vértice

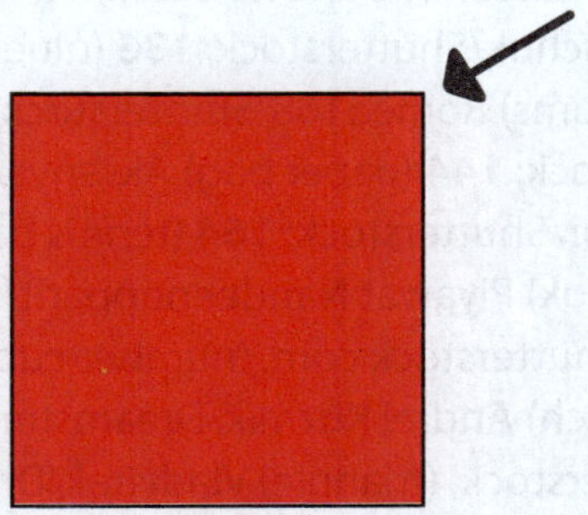

Ww

weight • peso

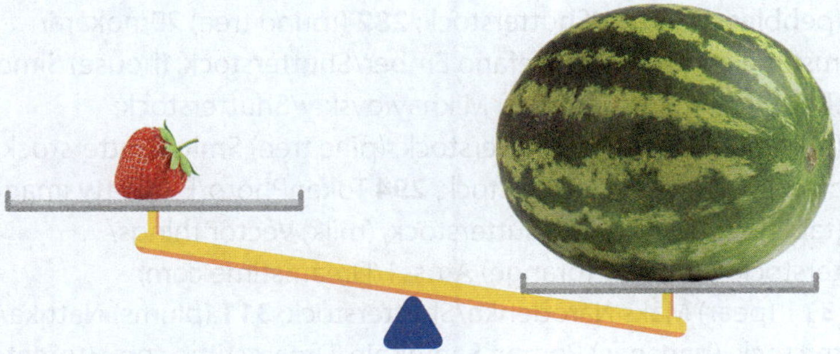

Zz

zero • cero

Acknowledgments

Notice and Wonder is used with permission from The National Council of Teachers of Mathematics (NCTM). The use of this term is not intended to imply any endorsement or affiliation with NCTM.

Illustration Credits

Helen Graper; Maki Koto; Steve Mack; Doug McGredy; Andrew Pagram; Carlos Puentes; Ana Sondesa; Amy Wong

Number Sense: 5, 345, 525 Courtney Dawson; **25** Sr. Sánchez; **45** Rachel Moss; **75, 145, 475, 545** Gisela Bohórquez; **95, 205, 295, 455, 505** Wendy Leach; **115, 165, 185, 275** Susan Szecsi; **235, 315** Gustavo Mazali; **255** Doug McGredy; **365** Andrew Pagram; **385** Vivienne To; **405** Yoss Sánchez; **435** Reggie Brown

Photography Credits

Cover (birds) serkan mutan/Shutterstock, (hats) M.Stasy/Shutterstock, (bird doodle) lena_nikolaeva/Shutterstock, (hat doodle) AyselDesign/Shutterstock; **4** (chair) DJ Srki/Shutterstock, (marble) timquo/Shutterstock; **6** (chair) doomu/Shutterstock, (door) denisik11/Shutterstock, (clock) Hal_P/Shutterstock; **24** (spoon) Valentyn Volkov/Shutterstock, (crayon) Mtsaride/Dreamstime.com; **25** Anton Starikov/Dreamstime.com; **44** (metal utensils) AlenKadr/Shutterstock, (wooden utensils) Volodymyr Krasyuk/Shutterstock; **63–66** (tropical foliage) Chansom Pantip/Shutterstock; **74, 94** TokenPhoto/E+/Getty Images; **113** (orange) Atoss1/Dreamstime.com; **113, 114, 123, 127, 128** (number cube) Sanjmur/Dreamstime.com; **114** (traffic cone) Teamarbeit/Dreamstime.com, (can) sockagphoto/Shutterstock, (box) ESB Professional/Shutterstock, (soccer ball) aimadbro/Shutterstock, (cheese grater) Melica/Shutterstock; **117** (soccer ball) warat42/Shutterstock, (box) restyler/Shutterstock; **123** (crayons) PATIDPATOR/Shutterstock, (box) Sergei Kardashev/Shutterstock, (glue stick) MsMaria/Shutterstock, (marble) Kosmayer/Shutterstock, (book) Elnur/Shutterstock, (paper cone) Piyawat Nandeenopparit/Shutterstock, (juice box) F16-ISO100/Shutterstock, (label) Anna.zabella/Shutterstock, (marker) Wyk/Shutterstock; **127** (mug) Kabardins photo/Shutterstock, (paper plate) Kazitsyn/Shutterstock; **127, 128** (paper clip) Xaki646/Shutterstock; **128** (cereal box) Gts/Shutterstock, (basketball) FocusStocker/Shutterstock, (pencil) Ahmet Misirligul/Shutterstock, (can) sockagphoto/Shutterstock, (reusable bottle) Shyamalamuralinath/Shutterstock, (paper cup) FabricioUZ/Shutterstock; **133** (buttons) Lucie Lang/Shutterstock, (glue stick) Shyamalamuralinath/Shutterstock; **134–136** (table background) Irina Tkachuk/Shutterstock; **136** (glue) Aksenova Natalya/Shutterstock, (pom poms) Romeo168/Shutterstock, (craft sticks) Larcsky789/Shutterstock; **144** (paper bag) Aksenya/Shutterstock, (pennies) Craig Wactor/Shutterstock; **164** (tennis ball can) Pixelrobot/Dreamstime.com, (book) Piyawat Nandeenopparit/Shutterstock, (nut & bolt) Nico Prasetyo/Shutterstock.com, (number cube) exopixel/Shutterstock, (sandwich) Andrei Kuzmik/Dreamstime.com; **169** (sign) FAMILY STOCK/Shutterstock, (triangle) Vladvitek/Dreamstime.com, (clock) Hpphoto/Dreamstime.com, (map) Dewartara/Shutterstock, (frame) schankz/Shutterstock; **170** (remote) Jr images/Shutterstock, (penny) TokenPhoto/E+/Getty Images, (flag) Mileatanasov/Dreamstime.com, (frame) Lesuhova/Dreamstime.com, (penguins) Sergey Uryadnikov/Shutterstock; **184** Irina Rogova/Shutterstock; **204** Xaki646/Shutterstock; **209** (orange & strawberry) Atoss1/Dreamstime.com, (pear & lemon) Maks Narodenko/Shutterstock; **223–226** (tabletop) Sichon/Shutterstock; **223, 224** (craft sticks) Passakorn sakulphan/Shutterstock; **226** (markers) bayualam/Shutterstock; **234** (pennies) Craig Wactor/Shutterstock; **254** (pebbles) DSBfoto/Shutterstock; **282** (round tree) 29mokara/Dreamstime.com, (tower) Stefano Ember/Shutterstock, (house) Simon Annable/Shutterstock, (rocket) Mikhaylovskiy/Shutterstock; **284** (pumpkin) topseller/Shutterstock, (pine tree) Smit/Shutterstock, (toy truck) Beloborod/Shutterstock; **294** TokenPhoto/E+/Getty Images; **297** (table) Who is Danny/Shutterstock, (milk) Vector things/Shutterstock; **303, 311** (orange) Atoss1/Dreamstime.com; **303, 311** (pear) Maks Narodenko/Shutterstock; **311** (plums) Nattika/Shutterstock, (bananas) Roman Samokhin/Dreamstime.com, (tomatoes & apples) Tim UR/Shutterstock, (lemons) Maks Narodenko/Shutterstock, (kiwi) CWIS/Shutterstock, (strawberries) Atoss1/Dreamstime.com, (peaches) Maks Narodenko/Shutterstock; **314** (cup) FabricioUZ/Shutterstock, (pennies) Craig Wactor/Shutterstock;

333–336 (playground mat) Bojani/Shutterstock; **336** (playground) KAMChokE/Shutterstock; **344** (buttons) Nik Merkulov/Shutterstock; **364** (paper bag) Aksenya/Shutterstock; **364, 384, 404** (pennies) Craig Wactor/Shutterstock; **384** (mug) Kabardins photo/Shutterstock; **404** (paper cup) FabricioUZ/Shutterstock; **423–426** (grass) cammep/Shutterstock; **423, 424** (wood frame) domnitsky/Shutterstock; **426** (fence) Pow-Mia/Shutterstock; **474** (buttons) Preto Perola/Shutterstock; **493–496** (stage floor) Markus Pfaff/Shutterstock; **495–496** (chairs) Andrey_Kuzmin/Shutterstock, (curtains) Katrina Brown/Shutterstock; **504** (pennies) Sascha Burkard/Shutterstock; **523** (blocks) Yavdat/Shutterstock; **544** (pebbles) DSBfoto/Shutterstock; **563–566** (grass) irin-k/Shutterstock; **563** (tree branch) Wichai Prasomsri1/Shutterstock; **566** (tree) Krumao/Shutterstock; **GL2, GL9** (puppy & kitten) Utekhina Anna/Shutterstock; **GL2** (clock) Hpphoto/Dreamstime.com, (box) restyler/Shutterstock; **GL6, GL8, GL17** (watermelon) HomeArt/Shutterstock; **GL7** (soccer ball) warat42/Shutterstock; **GL10** (box) ESB Professional/Shutterstock; **GL11** (map) Dewartara/Shutterstock, (frame) schankz/Shutterstock; **GL13** (orange) Atoss1/Dreamstime.com, (penguins) Sergey Uryadnikov/Shutterstock, (frame) Lesuhova/Dreamstime.com; **GL17** (fishbowls) r.classen/Shutterstock